Voyages in English
Writing and Grammar

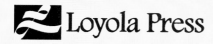 Loyola Press

Carolyn Marie Dimick
General Editor

Marie T. McVey
Revision Editor

Jeanne M. Baker
Carolyn Marie Dimick
Joan I. Rychalsky
Authors

Editorial

Margaret O'Leary Coyle

Catherine Marcic Joyce

Contributors

Beth Duncan

Diane Gonciarz

Elizabeth Cook Fresen

Karen M. Harrington

Cathy Ann Tell

Patricia Walsh

Richard Weisenseel

Production

Mary Bowers

Genevieve Kelley

Ellie Knepler

Anne Marie Mastandrea

Carla Jean Mayer

Julia Mayer

Molly O'Halloran

Jill Smith

Leslie Uriss

Cover Design

Steve Straus, Think Design

Cover Art

Nanette Biers, *Boston Harbor*

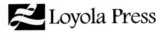 Loyola Press

3441 North Ashland Avenue
Chicago, Illinois 60657
1-800-621-1008

ISBN 0-8294-0992-0

© 1988, 1995, 1999 Loyola Press

Table of Contents

Part I Written and Oral Communication

1

CHAPTER 4 Kinds of Writing

CHAPTER 5 Learning More About Writing

CHAPTER 6 — Writing Letters

CHAPTER 7 — Speaking and Listening Skills

CHAPTER 8 — Library Skills

Table of Contents

Part II Grammar, Usage, and Mechanics

CHAPTER 9

Nouns

CHAPTER 10

Pronouns

Adjectives

Verbs

Table of Contents

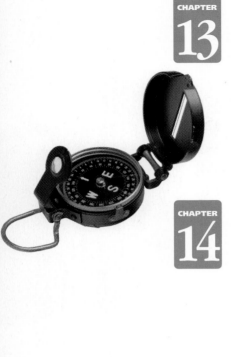

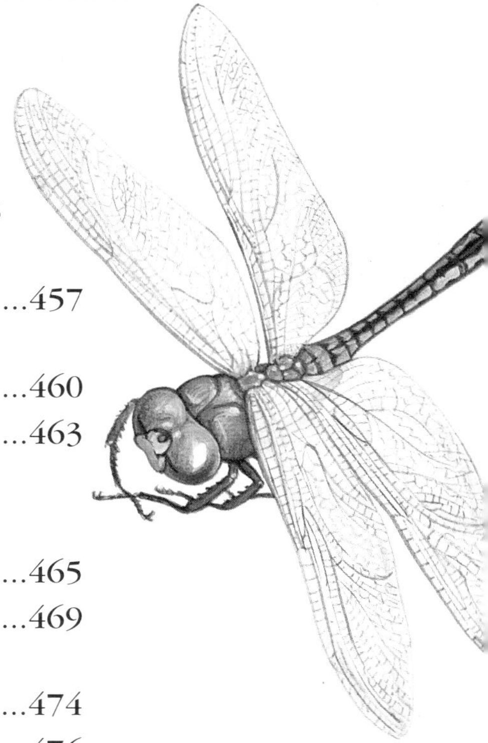

CHAPTER 16

Punctuation and Capitalization

CHAPTER 17

Model Diagrams

PART 1
Written and Oral Communication

9

Writing a Story

The selection beginning on the next page is an excerpt from a well-known book called *The Wind in the Willows.* The book tells about the riverside adventures of four characters, Rat, Mole, Toad, and Badger. You will meet Rat and Mole in this excerpt. The adventures began as bedtime stories and letters from the author, Kenneth Grahame, to his son.

The book has claimed its place in children's literature because the adventures involve sharply drawn characters, familiar and surprising events, and a setting that shows the nooks and crannies usually known only to the river's animal inhabitants.

As you read, pay attention to details of the characters' personalities. Notice how the events form a kind of chain reaction. And, of course, explore the landscape that is home to the Rat and the Mole. Paying attention to these three story elements—character, plot, and setting—and following the steps of the writing process will help you write a story of your own.

Home Sweet Home

Excerpts from The Wind in the Willows

by Kenneth Grahame

Mole and Rat are returning from a day's outing with Otter. They have been hunting and exploring the wide uplands. After plowing their way through the countryside on their long way home, they happen upon a little village. There they take time to peer into windows to observe the humans and their pets who are settled in for a long winter's night. Having satisfied their curiosity, Mole and Rat move on.

Once beyond the village, where the cottages ceased abruptly, on either side of the road they could smell through the darkness the friendly fields again; and they braced themselves for the last long stretch, the home stretch, the stretch that we know is bound to end, some time, in the rattle of the door latch, the sudden firelight, and the sight of familiar things greeting us as long-absent travellers from far oversea. They plodded along steadily and silently, each of them thinking his own thoughts. The Mole's ran a good deal on supper, as it was pitch-dark, and it was all a strange country to him as far as he knew, and he was following obediently in the wake of the Rat, leaving the guidance entirely to him. As for the Rat, he was walking a little way ahead, as his habit was, his shoulders humped, his eyes fixed on the straight grey road in front of him; so he did not notice poor Mole when suddenly the summons reached him, and took him like an electric shock.

We others, who have long lost the more subtle of the physical senses, have not even proper terms to express an animal's intercommunications with his surroundings, living or otherwise, and have only the word "smell," for instance, to include the whole range of delicate thrills which murmur in the nose of the animal night and day, summoning, warning, inciting, repelling. It was one of these mysterious fairy calls from out the void that suddenly reached Mole in the darkness, making him tingle through and through with its very familiar appeal, even while as yet he could not clearly remember what it was. He stopped dead in his tracks, his nose searching hither and thither in its efforts to recapture the fine filament, the telegraphic current, that had so strongly moved him. A moment, and he had caught it again; and with it this time came recollection in fullest flood.

Home! That was what they meant, those caressing appeals, those soft touches wafted through the air, those invisible little hands pulling and tugging, all one way! Why, it must be quite close by him at that moment, his old home that he had hurriedly forsaken and never sought again. Now, with a rush of old memories, how clearly it stood up before him, in the darkness! Shabby indeed, and small and poorly furnished, and yet his, the home he had made for himself. And the home had been happy with him, too, evidently, and was missing him, and wanted him back, and was telling him so, through his nose.

The call was clear, the summons was plain. He must obey it instantly, and go. "Ratty!" pleaded the poor Mole, in anguish of heart. "You don't understand! It's my home, my old home!"

The Rat was by this time very far ahead, too far to hear clearly what the Mole was calling.

"Mole, we mustn't stop now, really!" he called back. "We'll come for it tomorrow, whatever it is you've found. But I daren't stop now—it's late, and the snow's coming on again, and I'm not sure of the way! And I want your nose, Mole, so come on quick, there's a good fellow!" And the Rat pressed forward on his way without waiting for an answer.

Poor Mole stood alone in the road, his heart torn asunder and a big sob gathering, gathering, somewhere low down inside him. But even under such a test as this his loyalty to his friend stood firm. Never for a moment did he dream of abandoning him.

Only after a while of walking does the Rat notice that the Mole is silent, sluggish, and sullen. They stop to rest and Mole eventually tells of finding his old home. The Rat is moved by Mole's terrible sadness, and he decides that the two of them will go back and visit Mole's old home.

They moved on in silence for some little way, when suddenly the Rat was conscious, through his arm that was linked in Mole's, of a faint sort of electric thrill passing down that animal's body.

Mole stood a moment rigid, while his uplifted nose, quivering slightly, felt the air.

Suddenly, without giving warning, he dived; but the Rat was on the alert, and promptly followed him down the tunnel to which his unerring nose had faithfully led him.

It was close and airless, and the earthy smell was strong, and it seemed a long time to Rat ere the passage ended and he could stand erect and stretch and shake himself. The Mole struck a match, and by its light the Rat saw that they were standing in an open space, neatly swept and sanded underfoot, and directly facing them was Mole's little front door, with "Mole End" painted, in Gothic lettering, over the bell-pull at the side.

Mole's face beamed at the sight of all these objects so dear to him, and he hurried Rat through the door, lit a lamp in the hall, and took one glance round his old home. He saw the dust lying thick on everything, saw the cheerless, deserted look of the long-neglected house, and its narrow meagre dimensions, its worn and shabby contents—and collapsed again on a hall chair, his nose in his paws. "O, Ratty!" he cried dismally, "why ever did I do it? Why did I bring you to this poor, cold little place, on a night like this, when you might have been at River Bank by this time, toasting your toes before a blazing fire, with all your own nice things about you!"

The Rat paid no heed to his doleful self-reproaches. He was running here and there, opening doors, inspecting rooms and cupboards, and lighting lamps and candles and sticking them up everywhere. "What a capital little house this is!" he called out cheerily. "So compact! So well planned! Everything here and everything in its place!"

Encouraged by his inspiriting companion, the Mole roused himself and dusted and polished with energy and heartiness, while the Rat, running to and fro with armfuls of fuel, soon had a cheerful blaze roaring up the chimney. He hailed the Mole to come and warm himself; but the Mole promptly had another fit of the blues, dropping down on a couch in dark despair and burying his face in his duster.

"Rat," he moaned, "how about your supper, you poor, cold, hungry, weary animal? I've nothing to give you—nothing—not a crumb!"

"What a fellow you are for giving in!" said the Rat reproachfully. "Why, only just now I saw a sardine opener on the kitchen dresser, quite distinctly; and everybody knows that means there are sardines about somewhere in the neighbourhood. Rouse yourself! pull yourself together, and come with me and forage."

They went and foraged accordingly, hunting through every cupboard and turning out every drawer. The result was not so very depressing after all, though of course it might have been better; a tin of sardines—a box of captain's biscuits, nearly full—and a German sausage encased in silver paper.

"There's a banquet for you!" observed the Rat, as he arranged the table. "I know some animals who would give their ears to be sitting down to supper with us tonight!"

While Rat busies himself getting knives and forks and plates, Mole begins to unwind and to tell how he came to have some of his possessions. Lost in his thoughts, he pays little attention to Rat's beckoning to come and eat. Only the sudden sound of voices just outside the door brings Mole back to present concerns.

"What's up?" inquired the Rat, pausing in his labours.

"I think it must be the field mice," replied the Mole, with a touch of pride in his manner. "They go round carol singing regularly at this time of the year. They're quite an institution in these parts. And they never pass me over—they come to Mole End last of all; and I used to give them hot drinks, and supper too sometimes, when I could afford it. It will be like old times to hear them again."

"Let's have a look at them!" cried the Rat, jumping up and running to the door.

It was a pretty sight, and a seasonable one, that met their eyes when they flung the door open. In the forecourt, lit by the dim rays of a horn lantern, some eight or ten little field mice stood in a semicircle, red worsted comforters round their throats, their forepaws thrust deep into their pockets, their feet jigging for warmth. With bright beady eyes they glanced shyly at each other, sniggering a little, sniffing and applying coat sleeves a good deal. As the door opened, one of the elder ones that carried the lantern was just saying, "Now then, one, two, three!" and forthwith their shrill little voices uprose on the air, singing one of the old-time carols that their forefathers composed.

The voices ceased, the singers, bashful but smiling, exhanged sidelong glances, and silence succeeded—but for a moment only. Then, from up above and far away, down the tunnel they had so lately travelled was borne to their ears in a faint musical hum the sound of distant bells ringing a joyful and clangorous peal.

"Very well sung, boys!" cried the Rat heartily. "And now come along in, all of you, and warm yourselves by the fire, and have something hot!"

"Yes, come along field mice," cried the Mole eagerly. "This is quite like old times! Shut the door after you. Pull up that settle to the fire. Now, you just wait a minute, while we—O, Ratty!" he cried in despair, plumping down on a seat, with tears impending. "Whatever are we doing? We've nothing to give them!"

"You leave all that to me," said the masterful Rat. "Here, you with the lantern! Come over this way. I want to talk to you. Now, tell me, are there any shops open at this hour of the night?"

"Why certainly, sir," replied the field mouse respectfully. "At this time of the year our shops keep open to all sorts of hours."

"Then look here!" said the Rat. "You go off at once, you and your lantern, and you get me—"

The rest of the field mice, perched in a row on the settle, their small legs swinging, gave themselves up to enjoyment of the fire, and toasted their chilblains till they tingled; while the Mole, failing to draw them into easy conversation, plunged into family history and made each of them recite the names of his numerous brothers who were too young, it appeared, to be allowed to go out a-carolling this year, but looked forward very shortly to winning the parental consent.

It wasn't too very much longer before . . .

The latch clicked, the door opened, and the field mouse with the lantern reappeared, staggering under the weight of his basket.

Under the generalship of Rat, everybody was set to do something or to fetch something. In a very few minutes supper was ready, and Mole, as he took the head of the table in a sort of dream, saw a lately barren board set thick with savoury comforts; saw his little friends' faces brighten and beam as they fell to without delay; and then let himself loose—for he was famished indeed. As they ate, they talked of old times, and the field mice gave him the local gossip up to date, and answered as well as they could the hundred questions he had to ask them. The Rat said little or nothing, only taking care that each guest had what he wanted, and plenty of it, and that Mole had no trouble or anxiety about anything.

They clattered off at last, very grateful and showering wishes of the season, with their jacket pockets stuffed with remembrances for the small brothers and sisters at home. When the door had closed on the last of them and the chink of the lanterns had died away, Mole and Rat kicked the fire up, and discussed the events of the long day. At last the Rat, with a tremendous yawn, said, "Mole, old chap, I'm ready to drop. Sleepy is simply not the word. That your own bunk over on that side? Very well, then, I'll take this. What a ripping little house this is! Everything so handy!"

He clambered into his bunk and rolled himself well up in the blankets.

The weary Mole also was glad to turn in without delay, and soon had his head on his pillow, in great joy and contentment. It was good to think he had this to come back to, this place which was all his own.

TALK IT OVER

1. Why were the Rat and the Mole out on such a cold and wintry night?

2. What three adjectives would you choose to describe Rat's character? Mole's character?

3. How would the story be different if the setting (place and time) were changed?

4. Why do you think the author included the "little story" of the carolers coming by? How does it contribute to the story?

WRITER'S CRAFT

Story

What an eventful day for Mole and Rat! It had a little of everything—sadness, excitement, celebration, and satisfaction.

The excerpt you just read from *The Wind in the Willows* was written by a master storyteller, Kenneth Grahame. The book, written in 1908, is a classic and models the expert handling of the main elements of a story.

A story, as you know, tells about an event, or something that happened. You probably tell different stories every day. If you share a joke, for example, or describe a movie you saw, you are telling a kind of story.

A story has three main elements:

- The setting is the time and place of the story.
- The characters are the people or animals in the story.
- The plot is the action or what happens to the characters.

A well-written story also has three main parts:

- The beginning introduces the characters and setting. It also describes a problem that characters face.
- The middle tells how characters try to solve their problem.
- The ending tells how everything turns out.

Storytelling with a British Accent

Although a Scot by nationality, Kenneth Grahame is considered a British writer. Look back over the excerpt to find details that are particularly British. Notice the names for everyday things and the British spellings.

Take a Closer Look

REREAD **Look again at "Home Sweet Home." Answer these questions as you read.**

1. What is the setting at the beginning of the story? How does the setting change as the story continues?
2. Who are the characters in the story?
3. In the beginning of the story, what problem does Mole face?
4. What new problems do Mole and Rat face in the middle of the story?
5. How do Rat and Mole try to solve their problems?
6. What happens at the story's end?

DISCUSS Talk over your answers to the questions on page 18 with a partner or in a small group. Compare your ideas with the following.

Setting	The time is winter at day's end. The place is a country road, and later Mole's old home down a tunnel.
Characters	Mole, Rat, field mice
Problem at beginning	Mole wants to go to his old home, but Rat does not.
Problems in middle	Mole has no food to serve Rat. Later there is no food to serve the field mice.
How characters try to solve their problems	Mole and Rat search for food for their own supper. Later Rat organizes the mice to find more food.
Ending	Mole, Rat, and the mice enjoy a lovely supper. Mole and Rat go to sleep contented.

PRACTICE Read this brief story. Make notes similar to those above. Discuss your notes with a partner.

Cow, Hen, and Bee were walking on a farm one hot afternoon. All three were quite hungry. "I'd like a snack," Cow mooed. "Me, too," Hen clucked. "Me, three," Bee buzzed.

The animals looked all around but could find no food for a snack. They searched for over an hour. Finally Cow had an idea. "I can make milk," she said. "And I can make eggs," said Hen. "And I can make honey," added Bee.

The three animals pooled their talents and mixed their foods together. Before long, they had created a tasty custard treat, which they all enjoyed!

Story

Prewriting
Drafting
Revising
Proofreading
Publishing

Below is a story written by Tanya, a sixth grader. It is the final version of her work. Read it, and then learn how Tanya followed the steps of the writing process to arrive at her finished product.

Lost in the Desert

It was over 100 degrees in the desert. Karen and Mario sat in their hot sedan. Mario turned the key and tried the engine again. Like all the other times, the motor would not start.

Mario looked at Karen and frowned. Their car had broken down seven hours earlier. Mario said, "I can't believe it still won't start."

Karen said, "I can't believe no one is driving by to help us."

"We're too far off the main highway," Mario explained. "When we left it to explore more of the desert, that was a mistake. We should have stayed where others could see us. Planes are flying overhead, but they're too high to see us."

Karen honked the car horn a long time.

"Honking won't do any good," Mario laughed. "No one can hear it."

"How do you know?" Karen asked. "Maybe someone will drive nearby. I'm sure we're not the first people ever to think of exploring this area."

Karen took a pocket mirror from her purse and looked at her face and hair. "I look awful," she sighed.

Mario laughed again. "Who's going to see you here?" he asked. "We're stranded in the desert!"

Suddenly Karen shouted, "Wait! I've got an idea!" She left the car and waited for a plane. When one flew over, Karen flashed her mirror to reflect the sun's rays.

High in the sky, the airplane pilot saw the flashes of light. "Looks like a signal," he said to the copilot. "We'd better radio this to police headquarters."

Less than an hour later, a patrol car showed up to rescue Karen and Mario.

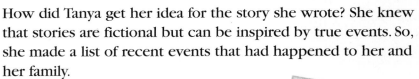

Prewriting
Drafting
Revising
Proofreading
Publishing

STEP 1

Prewriting

How did Tanya get her idea for the story she wrote? She knew that stories are fictional but can be inspired by true events. So, she made a list of recent events that had happened to her and her family.

Tanya looked at her list. She was proud of her reading award, but she wasn't sure it would make a very exciting story. She remembered how her cat had disappeared for a day, but even that didn't seem too exciting now.

> I got a reading award.
> Our cat ran away for one day.
> My aunt and uncle visited the desert.

Tanya thought about her aunt and uncle's visit to the desert. Their trip had gone fine. But Tanya wondered, "What if?" For example, what if they had gotten lost? What if they had run out of gas?

Tanya decided to write a story about a couple's trip to the desert because

- it had an interesting setting.
- she could easily imagine the characters.
- she could imagine a good problem for them to face.

Try It!

▶ Make a list of possible topics for a story. Review your list the same way Tanya did. Ask yourself:

- Would my story have an interesting setting?
- Would it have characters that I can imagine well?
- Would there be a problem for the characters to solve?
- Would the story hold my readers' interest?

▶ Place a star next to your favorite story idea.

Tanya knew that her story would be fictional. She planned many details that were not part of her aunt and uncle's real trip. For one thing, she made up new names for the characters. For another, she planned to describe the desert as she imagined it, not as her aunt and uncle had described it to her. Also, she would invent a problem that never arose during the real trip. Here is an outline that Tanya made to plan her story.

1. Characters: Mario, Karen, airplane pilot, police

2. Setting: hot desert, off main highway

3. Plot: Car breaks down, no one nearby

4. Beginning: Describe Mario, Karen, desert, car problem

5. Middle: Karen honks horn, then uses mirror

6. Ending: Pilot sees light, police arrive

Tanya used a numbered list as an outline. But she didn't have to do it that way. She could have drawn a word map that detailed the main parts of the story.

Try It!

▶ Think more about the story idea you starred for Try It! on page 22.

▶ Decide on the best way to put your ideas and details on paper. You might use a numbered outline, a word map, or a story line.

▶ Share your work with a partner.

Looking at Characters, Setting, and Plot for Prewriting

When you prewrite a story, you plan the ideas and details to use in your work. Ask yourself these questions as you prewrite.

Characters

- Which characters are in my story? Who are the most important ones?

- What do my characters look like? How old are they?

- How do the characters think? Act? Speak? What are their likes and dislikes?

Setting

- In what place does the story begin?

- What is the time of year or day? What is the weather like?

- How does the setting change, if at all, as the story continues?

Plot

- What problem do characters face at the beginning of the story?

- Is the problem caused by another person or an animal? Is it caused by a force of nature, such as a snowstorm or darkness? Is it caused by a feeling within the main character, such as fear or shyness?

- How do characters first try to solve their problem? What happens as a result? Does the problem become worse? If so, how?

- Do characters finally manage to solve the problem, or does the problem defeat them? What happens at the end of the story?

PRACTICE Below are lists of possible characters, settings, and plots to use in a story. Add five more ideas of your own to each list.

Characters

- sixth-grade students and their substitute teacher
- space aliens and the president of the United States
- opposing ballplayers in a championship game
- a strange sea creature and a boatful of sailors
- a doctor and a patient with a mysterious disease

Settings

- a deserted warehouse at midnight
- an earthquake across several states
- a mad scientist's laboratory
- a blimp above the Super Bowl game
- the ocean floor in the year 2020

Plots

- dog tries to save its drowning master
- computers around the world plot against humans
- child becomes lost during a citywide blackout
- teen refuses to apologize to his or her best friend
- woman struggles to survive on a desert island

PRACTICE Choose the one idea that you like most from each list above. On a sheet of paper, write an outline for a story that uses the ideas you chose for characters, setting, and plot.

Prewriting
Drafting
Revising
Proofreading
Publishing

STEP 2

Drafting

Tanya used her outline to write the first draft of her story. She called the draft her "sloppy copy." That's because she wrote very quickly to get her ideas down on paper. Later she could go back to change the content and correct any spelling or punctuation errors. As Tanya wrote, she kept in mind that her audience would be her classmates. Her purpose would be to entertain them.

In the Desert

It was very hot in the desert. Karen and Mario sat in their hot car. Mario turned the key and tried the engine again. Like all the other times, the moter would not turn over.

Mario looked at Karen and frowned. Their car had broken down earlier. Mario couldn't believe it still wouldn't start. Karen couldn't believe noone was driving by to help them.

Mario explaned that they were too far off the main highway. They had left it to explore more of the desert. Now he felt it had been a misteak he knew they should have stayed where others could see them. Planes were flying overhead, but they were to high up to see Karen and Mario

Take a Closer Look

DISCUSS Talk about Tanya's first draft with a partner. Then share your ideas with the whole group.

- Does Tanya's first draft have all the things that belong in the beginning of a story? Explain.

- How interesting is Tanya's beginning? How would you change it?

- Is Tanya's story clear to you? What details would you suggest that she add?

◐ Student-Teacher Conference

After finishing her first draft, Tanya showed it to her teacher. The teacher read it and then spoke with Tanya about it. During their conference, he told Tanya what he liked about her story. He also suggested some changes. The teacher explained why each change might improve the story. He encouraged Tanya to express her feelings about each suggestion. He was careful not to make Tanya feel bad about her work.

Tanya found the teacher's remarks helpful. It was good to know that her story

- had an interesting setting.

- described a problem that made readers want to read on.

It was also helpful to know that

- adding details would make it easier for readers to understand and imagine the setting.

- adding dialogue would make the characters seem livelier and more interesting.

DISCUSS What would you say to Tanya? Talk about it with a partner.

Story
- introduces characters and setting.
- describes problem that characters face.
- tells how characters try to solve problem.
- tells how everything turns out in end.

Uses of Dialogue
Dialogue is a handy way to reveal characters' personalities and to help advance the plot of a story.

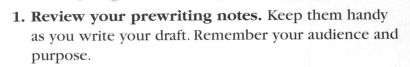

Prewriting
Drafting
Revising
Proofreading
Publishing

How to Write a First Draft

Here's a checklist for writing any kind of first draft.

1. **Review your prewriting notes.** Keep them handy as you write your draft. Remember your audience and purpose.

2. **Keep writing.** Don't stop to correct mistakes or make things neat. Get all your ideas down on paper before making corrections.

3. **Start drafting anywhere.** Feel free to write the ending first. You can always write the beginning and middle later.

4. **Jump around.** You might get a great idea for the ending as you're working on the beginning. Jot this idea down before you forget it, and return to it later.

5. **Do more prewriting.** If you get stuck, brainstorm with a friend for new ideas. Add new ideas and details. You might even narrow or broaden your topic.

6. **Write on every other line.** By skipping lines, you give yourself room to add ideas and details later.

7. **Have a peer conference.** When you have finished your draft, read it aloud to a partner and ask for comments.

STEP 3

Revising

After talking with her teacher, Tanya revised her story beginning. Revise means to make changes to improve your work. Tanya added details to make the setting clearer. She also changed one phrase that she wasn't sure her audience would understand. She added dialogue to make the characters more interesting. She even revised her story title.

READ Look at how Tanya revised her first paragraph. Notice the editor's marks she used to show her changes.

> Lost
> ∧ In the Desert
> over 100 degrees
> It was ~~very hot~~ in the desert. Karen and
> sedan
> Mario sat in their hot ~~car.~~ Mario turned the key
> and tried the engine again. Like all the other
> start
> times, the motor would not ~~turn over.~~

DISCUSS How did Tanya revise her first paragraph? Do you think it is improved? Talk about it with a partner.

Keep a Copy!

Before you start to revise, make a copy of your first draft. That way you can refer to it even after you've begun to change it.

Editor's Marks

⁋ New paragraph

∧ Add

⌐ Take out

↶ Move

Prewriting

Drafting

Revising

Proofreading

Publishing

Take a Closer Look

Look at how Tanya revised the rest of her story beginning.

Mario looked at Karen and frowned. Their
car had broken down, ~~earlier.~~ *seven hours* Mario ~~couldn't~~ *said, "I can't*
believe it still ~~wouldn't~~ *won't* start. Karen ~~couldn't~~ *said, "I can't*
believe noone ~~was~~ *is* driving by to help ~~them.~~ *us."*
~~Mario explaned~~ that they were too far off *"We're*
the main highway. ~~They had~~ left it to explore *"When we*
more of the desert. ~~Now he felt it had been~~ a *that was*
misteak ~~he knew they~~ should have stayed *we*
where others could see ~~them.~~ *us.* Planes ~~were~~ flying *are*
overhead, but they ~~were~~ to high up to see ~~Karen~~ *us."* *'re*
~~and Mario~~

PRACTICE Work with a partner to list all the changes that Tanya made in her story beginning. Then talk about the reason that she made each change. Make notes on how the changes improved her story.

Writing Good Dialogue

Good dialogue helps readers get to know the characters in a story. As you read the following dialogue, notice what the dialogue tells you about the two characters, Ellen and Fred. Notice the sort of things each of them likes to do.

Ellen turned the car off the main highway onto the little winding road to the campground.

"I can't wait to get out, breathe a big breath of fresh air, and put up our tent," she said.

"I can wait," Fred said, "—forever."

"You'll love camping in the woods. Birds sing, fresh breezes blow."

"Bugs biting, rain falling." Fred glanced at his watch. "This place has a TV, doesn't it? I don't want to miss my favorite program."

"No, Fred, no TV's out here. Well, this is it. Pretty, don't you think?"

"If you like looking at nothing but trees and water."

"Let's get to work."

"Is that a mosquito out there? I need a nap. Wake me when the tent's up and dinner's ready."

This dialogue shows that Fred and Ellen are two very different people who have very different ways of reacting to things. How would you characterize these two people?

Try It!

▶ Now, you continue the dialogue between Fred and Ellen. What will happen next? Who will unpack the car? Who will put up the tent? Try to show the action through dialogue. As you write, remember that your characters are very different from each other. Try to make everything they say and do reflect these differences.

Check It Out!

As you revise the first draft of your work, use the following checklist.

Checklist for Revising

☑ Have I achieved my original purpose for writing? If not, what can I now change, add, or remove in order to reach my goal?

☑ Have I kept my audience in mind? Is there any part of my work that readers may not be interested in or will not understand?

☑ Are all my ideas clear? If not, how can I rewrite sentences to make the ideas clearer?

☑ Have I included enough details to make my ideas clear and understandable? What new details might I add to improve my writing?

☑ Is my organization of details the best that it can be? How might I rearrange sentences or paragraphs to make my ideas easier to understand?

☑ Have I used the best words that I can, especially to name actions and to describe things? Where might more colorful or exact words be helpful?

☑ Are my sentences the right length? If some are too short and choppy, how can I combine them to read better? If some are too long, how can I break the ideas into smaller sentences?

☑ Does my work have an interesting beginning? Is there another way I can start out that will grab my readers' attention even more?

☑ Is the middle of my writing clear? Are there any details I should remove because they make my writing confusing or boring?

☑ Does my work have a powerful ending? Is there another way I could write the ending to make it more effective?

STEP 4

Proofreading

Prewriting

Drafting

Revising

Proofreading

Publishing

After revising her draft, Tanya proofread her story. Proofread means to check for mistakes in spelling, capitalization, punctuation, and grammar. She kept her *Voyages in English* text and a dictionary nearby as she worked. Of course, Tanya proofread her entire revised draft. Here is how Tanya corrected mistakes in the middle of her story.

> Karen honked the car horn a long time.
>
> "Honking won't do any good." Mario
> laughed. "No one ~~Noone~~ can hear it."
>
> "How do you know?" Karen asked.
> "maybe someone will drive nearby ~~nearbye~~. I'm sure
> we're not the first people ever to think of
> exploring this area."

Editor's Marks

¶ New paragraph

∧ Add

⏦ Take out

↶ Move

≡ Capitalize

Take a Closer Look

DISCUSS **Look carefully at Tanya's proofreading. Notice the changes she made.**

1. She changed one lowercase letter to a capital letter. Tell why.
2. She corrected two spelling mistakes. What are they? How do you think she checked her spelling?
3. She changed one period to a comma. Do you know why? If you're not sure, check page 470.
4. She added quotation marks. Do you see where? Why did she add them? Check page 480 to be sure.

PRACTICE Below is the last part of Tanya's story. On a sheet of paper, show the corrections that are needed.

Editor's Marks

¶ New paragraph
∧ Add
Take out
Move
≡ Capitalize

Karen took a pockit mirror from her purse and looked at her face and hair. "I look awful" she sighed.

Mario laughed again. "Who's going to see you here? he asked. We're stranded in the dessert!"

Suddenly Karen shouted, "wait! I've got an idea!" She left the car and waited for a plane, when one flew over, Karen flashed her mirror to reflect the suns rays.

High in the sky, the airplane pilut saw the flashes of light. "Looks like a signal" he said to the Copilot. We'd better radio this to police headquarters.

Less than an hour later, a patrol car showed up to reskue Karen and Mario.

Try It!

▶ Make your own proofreading checklist, similar to the revising checklist on page 32. Write down questions to ask yourself when you proofread.

STEP 5

Publishing

The final step for Tanya was to publish her story.

Here is what Tanya did:

- She used a computer to type a final copy of her story.

- She checked that all her revising and proofreading changes were made in the final copy.

- She read the story once again to be sure there were no errors.

- She recorded her story on tape.

One Publishing Plan

The students in Tanya's class each wrote a story. They decided to create a Literary Lounge, a relaxing place to read or listen to stories, in their classroom. They followed these steps:

- Students each recorded their stories on an audiotape. They read with feeling and expression.

- Students each labeled their tapes with the title of the story and their name.

- They placed all the tapes on a shelf in a classroom corner. During free time, students could visit the Literary Lounge, pick out a tape, and listen with headphones.

DISCUSS **Talk about these questions with your class.**

1. Do you think Tanya's class had a good publishing plan? Why?

2. Would you want to listen to stories on tape? Why?

3. How is it different to hear a taped story than to read it on paper?

| Prewriting |
| Drafting |
| Revising |
| Proofreading |
| **Publishing** |

Speaking Expressively
For helpful tips on speaking expressively, see page 37.

Expanding the Publishing Plan

Tanya's class enjoyed listening to all the stories on tape. One student said, "It's too bad other classes can't hear these stories. They're really good!" That gave Tanya an idea. Why not start "Stories a la Cart"? Once a week at a preplanned time, a cart carrying the tapes could be wheeled to different classrooms. Students could select story tapes for listening. In the weeks following, students could request that the authors of their favorite tapes visit their classrooms and talk about their stories. The teacher thought it was a great idea.

Tanya's class followed these steps:

- After school, students talked with other teachers about their publishing plan.

- The other teachers made a schedule of the best times for "Stories a la Cart" visits.

- Students in the other classes notified their teachers about whom to invite as storyteller speakers.

- The speakers would visit at preplanned times to talk about their story-writing process and to answer questions.

WRITE Audience members asked these questions of the authors in Tanya's class. List some questions you would ask.

- How did you get the ideas for your story?

- What was the hardest thing about writing your story?

- What do you like most about your story?

- What changes did you make while writing it?

DISCUSS Think of other creative ways to share stories with an audience. Meet with a small group of classmates to discuss your ideas. Then share your ideas with other groups.

Speaking Expressively

When you read a story to others, you want your audience to listen. If you speak with feeling and expression, listeners will pay attention. But if you do not, listeners may begin to lose interest and tune out. Here are tips on how to speak expressively to a group.

Rehearse your words. Before reading a story to others, read it aloud several times to yourself. Speak loudly and clearly, even though you are alone. If any words are hard to pronounce, say them over several times.

Speak with feeling. Find the places in your story where you will pause as you read aloud. Find the words that you wish to emphasize. Do not mumble your words or say them too quickly.

Keep good eye contact. When you practice alone, read in front of a mirror. Become familiar enough with your story that you do not have to look at it every second that you read. Try to look from time to time at the audience. Make them feel that you know they are there.

Practice body gestures. As you read, you may wish to include gestures or other body motions. Practice your movements in front of a mirror until they look and feel natural.

Be creative. When you read a story, there may be dialogue for several different characters. As you read the characters' words, try to give each person a distinct tone of voice. However, do not "ham it up" so much that it distracts from the story.

Try It!

▶ Look again at Tanya's story on pages 20 and 21. Read it aloud to yourself, following the above tips for speaking expressively. Later, read the story to a partner, a small group, or the whole class.

Listening to Predict

Sometimes while listening to a story, you may think to yourself, "I'll bet I know what's going to happen next." If you're listening carefully, your prediction may be correct.

For example, in "Home Sweet Home," Rat and Mole eagerly invite ten field mice inside for a meal. At that moment, you might guess that the hosts will have a problem serving their guests. Why? Earlier, Mole had told Rat there was no food for even the two of them. If it is hard to serve just two individuals, you might guess that it will be even harder to serve ten more!

Tips for Predicting

When you listen to a story, consider these questions in order to predict future events:

● What do I know about each character so far? How does that individual behave? What is his or her personality like? The way people act is a clue to how they will act in the future.

● How important is the setting in the story? Could the same story events happen anywhere, at any time? Or could they only happen here and now? The time and place of a story are often clues to what will occur next.

● What does my own common sense tell me? Have I ever witnessed a similar situation in real life? What happened in that case? Could it happen again here? Your personal experiences may help you predict a story event.

Try It!

▶ Look again at Tanya's story on pages 20 and 21. Have a partner read it aloud to you. Stop your partner along the way to identify clues that would help you to predict what happens next in the story.

Putting It All Together

By looking at the way Tanya used the steps in the writing process to create her story, you can see that writing is another way of communicating your ideas using your thinking and speaking skills.

STEP 1 Prewriting
- Select a subject.
- Decide on your audience.
- Collect details.

STEP 2 Drafting
- Get all your ideas on paper.
- Don't worry about mistakes.

STEP 3 Revising
- Read and review your draft.
- Share your draft with someone.
- Make changes to improve your writing.

STEP 4 Proofreading
- Check your spelling, capital letters, punctuation, and grammar.
- Write a neat final copy.
- Check one last time for errors.

STEP 5 Publishing
- Share your writing.

Writer's Corner

▶ It's your turn! Write a story. Use the topic you chose and starred on page 22 or feel free to begin fresh. Maybe, like *Wind in the Willows* author Kenneth Grahame, you would like to try creating memorable animal characters to be the stars of your story.

Building the Paragraph

Selecting and Narrowing a Topic

A topic is the idea about which a paragraph or a composition is written.

The first step in writing is to decide on a topic. Do you think choosing a topic is difficult? Actually, it is easier than you might imagine. Professional writers usually find topics from their experiences and interests, and you can choose your own topics the same way. You probably will be surprised at how many topics there are for you to write about!

The best way to find a topic is to brainstorm for ideas. Think about some of your interests and about experiences you have had. Then take out a sheet of paper and write down as many topics that come to mind. For example, some of your topics might be "trips," "movies," "sports," or "friends."

As you look over your list, you will see that some of the items are things that are familiar to you. Others are things you like, but about which you need to learn more. Write the headings "Things I Know About" and "Things I Like (But Need to Learn About)" on a sheet of paper, and put each topic you listed under the appropriate heading.

About the Photograph

The boy in this photograph looks like he might enjoy writing a paragraph about the topic of soccer. He could then narrow his topic by writing about the first goal he ever scored in a soccer game.

For now, concentrate on choosing things familiar to you as paragraph topics. Suppose one of the topics you listed was "trips." That is such a big topic it would be difficult to know where to begin. So before you start to write, you must narrow the topic "trips" to one specific idea. That specific idea will become the topic of your paragraph.

Look at the two examples below. What happens to each topic?

Topic: Trips
Narrowed topic: A class trip
Narrower topic: Our class trip to the planetarium
Specific idea: How I got lost in the planetarium

Topic: My neighborhood
Narrowed topic: My block
Narrower topic: People on my block
Specific idea: My best friends on my block

Activity A

In each list below, a topic is narrowed down to a specific idea. However, the items in the list are out of order. Rewrite each list in the correct order.

Topic:
Narrowed topic:
Narrower topic:
Specific idea:

1. Movies
   My favorite movie of the year
   Movies I like
   Movies I liked this year

2. Soccer
   My soccer team
   Sports
   How my soccer team almost won the championship

3. Houses of the Algonquians
   Native Americans
   The Algonquians
   Native Americans of our area

4. Why I liked *The Left Hand of Darkness*
   The Left Hand of Darkness
   Science fiction books
   Books

5. How I learned to do a cartwheel
   Stunts I learned in gymnastics class
   Gymnastics
   My gymnastics class

6. Some good advice from my older sister
   My family
   Families
   My older sister

7. American history
   Zebulon Pike
   Exploration by Zebulon Pike
   Famous explorers in American history

8. Piano
   Music
   My first piano recital
   Learning to play the piano

Zebulon Pike

Activity B

**Narrow each of the topics below to one specific idea.
Write each specific idea as a statement.**

1. Computers
2. Clothes
3. Food
4. Parties
5. Games

Writer's Corner

▶ Think of three topics about which you would like to write. Narrow each topic down to a specific idea. Then discuss with another student what you might include in a paragraph about that specific idea.

Writing Topic and Beginning Sentences

Topic Sentences

A topic sentence states the specific idea of a paragraph. It is often the beginning sentence.

Has anyone ever asked you, "What was that movie about?" If you answered that it was about alien beings coming to Earth or about how Egyptians built pyramids, then you have given the specific idea of the movie. When you write a paragraph, it is important to tell the reader your specific idea. The specific idea is expressed in a topic sentence.

Here are three topic sentences. What information do you think would be included in each paragraph?

- Stickball is becoming a popular sport in our neighborhood.
- My bedroom looks like a miniature zoo.
- A shower of popcorn signaled my first real cooking disaster.

Now find the topic sentence in the following paragraph.

> Lively monkeys chattered nonstop as they swung about in their roomy cages. Puppies whimpered and made little barks when anyone approached them. Melodious songs came from sleek canaries, and chirps were produced by baby chicks. From their perches overhead, brightly colored parrots squawked to be heard above the din. The pet shop we visited last week was an orchestra of competing sounds.

In the paragraph above, the topic sentence is the last sentence. The specific idea is "the noises in a pet shop." The topic sentence states the specific idea. All the other sentences in the paragraph give details about that idea.

The topic sentence is often—but not always—the first sentence in a paragraph. In the paragraph you have just read, the writer put the topic sentence last. All the sentences in the paragraph lead up to the topic sentence. The writer might also have put the topic sentence first to let the reader know the location of the noises immediately. If you had written this paragraph, where would you have put the topic sentence? Why?

Activity A

Find the topic sentence in each of the following paragraphs.

1   Making quilts is a traditional American art. It dates back to the days of the American colonies. A quilt results when two layers of cloth are stitched together with a soft stuffing between them. American pioneers often stitched many pieces of colorful cloth together in their quilts. Because all the sewing was done by hand, making a quilt took a long time. To speed the process, pioneers would join in quilting bees. Families would sew quilts in the afternoon, and they would eat and dance in the evening. Quilts were valued by pioneers as warm bedcovers and as shields from cold drafts. Their quilts are still valued by Americans today—mostly for the beauty of the quilts as colorful, original works of art.

2 I felt unsure, but I decided to try anyway. I took a firm grip on the sticks. My first attempt ended with a "plop" and splatter. I looked around to see if anyone in the restaurant had noticed, but no one had. I practiced moving the sticks until I felt more comfortable with them. Gathering my courage and determination, I tried again and managed to get a piece of vegetable into my mouth. My first experience at using chopsticks in a Chinese restaurant started out shakily but ended in success.

3 Why is a porcupine a porcupine? Why is a hippopotamus called by such a strange, hard-to-spell name? The variety in the origin of animal names is almost as varied as the animals themselves. Some animals are named after places. Shetland ponies are named for islands near Scotland. Some animals are named after people. The Doberman pinscher, a large, smooth-coated dog, is named for Ludwig Dobermann, the German who first bred the dog. Some names describe the animal. Often, however, these names are in foreign languages. For example, *porcupine* comes from Latin words meaning "pig with thorns." The Greek word for "river horse" makes the word *hippopotamus*. Check your dictionary or other word-origin books to learn more about how different animals got their names.

Beginning Sentences

A good beginning sentence introduces the topic and tries to interest the reader in the paragraph.

Whenever you write, you are writing to someone. You may be writing a composition for your teacher, a note to your parents, or a letter to a friend. You want to make sure that your audience will be interested in what you write. To create interest, you should write a good beginning sentence. A good beginning sentence will introduce the topic of the paragraph, arouse the reader's curiosity, and encourage him or her to read on.

- Sometimes a beginning sentence may be written as a simple topic sentence, which tells the specific idea of the paragraph.

    The day finally arrived for our trip to the wax museum.

- Sometimes a beginning sentence may be written in a more interesting and creative way. Such a sentence may still give the specific idea of the paragraph.

    How many famous people would greet me on my journey through the halls of the wax museum?

The first example tells the reader that the paragraph will be about a trip to the wax museum. The second example gives the same information, but it does so in a more creative style. The writer questions with an interrogative sentence and uses colorful language so that the reader will want to continue reading to discover more about the famous people in the wax museum.

Below is an example of each kind of beginning sentence. Either one could be used at the beginning of a paragraph about fossils. What is the difference between the two sentences?

Topic sentence: Fossils are records of the distant past.
Creative sentence: Fossils are a kind of ancient photography that captures life as it was millions of years ago.

Here are two beginning sentences. Think about how they are different and what each one tells you about the topic.

Topic sentence: Autumn is my favorite season.
Creative sentence: When leaves turn to red and yellow and a cool wind blows, I anticipate some of my favorite things—apple picking, the World Series, and pumpkin pie.

Activity B

Tell whether the beginning sentences below are simple topic sentences or creative sentences.

1. The family gathered together for Thanksgiving.

2. Will a typical lunch of the future be a "hamburger" tablet?

3. Wow! I never thought all this could possibly happen to me in one day.

4. The Fourth of July is always a great deal of fun.

5. I watched the rain making patterns on my window and wondered if the waif would find shelter out there.

6. Len's face beamed as he surveyed the delicious dinner spread before him.

7. An astronaut's training is very difficult.

8. Zoom! Our spaceship sped like lightning through the vast empty space of the galaxy.

9. "Oh, no!" Anita cried. "I forgot to study for the math test."

10. Caring for tropical fish can be a fascinating hobby.

Activity C

Below are five simple topic sentences. Each expresses the specific idea, or topic, of a paragraph. Try writing a creative beginning sentence to go along with each topic sentence. If you do not know enough about a topic, use your imagination.

1. Last year my family took a trip to New York City.

2. Cars of the future will be longer and sleeker.

3. Life was an adventure for King Arthur's knights.

4. My friend Sally had a huge insect collection.

5. Buildings shook as an earthquake rumbled through the city.

Activity D

Supply a beginning sentence for each of the paragraphs that follow. Be sure to write one that is interesting and gives a hint of what the paragraph is about. Decide whether you want to write a simple topic sentence or a more creative sentence. You may write two sentences to begin a paragraph if you need to.

1 _____ .

My uncle and I sat at either end of the canoe and paddled, and my little brother Jimmy sat in the middle. Jimmy was content to sit still and watch the world go by until he spied a frog resting on a floating log. I saw what he was going to do and shouted, "Jimmy—no!" It was too late. Jimmy reached out to grab the frog, the canoe tipped over, and we all tumbled into the lake. Although it was a frightening moment, luck was with us. We fell onto a sandbar where the water was shallow, and we were safe. I didn't see the frog again, but I'm sure that wherever it went, it was laughing all the way.

2 _____ .

The typical cowboy of the mid-1800s was a short, rather ordinary-looking man. He rarely, if ever, shot his gun, got into fights, or chased desperadoes. Much of his time was spent on long and hazardous cattle drives, where blankets and some extra clothing were all he could bring along. Often, there was not even a tent in which to sleep. If he was injured on the drive, he was likely to be left behind. It was a hard life, and very different from the way we picture it today.

3 _____ .

Each day I feed him, clean his cage, and let him fly around the house. If he lands on my arm, I say "Hello" in the hope that he will learn to say the same thing to me. Taking care of Petey is not much trouble, but yesterday I was careless and left a window open. I saw a flash of brightly colored feathers, and Petey was gone. It was such a shock that at first I stood perfectly still. Then I raced to the window and peered anxiously in every direction. There was no sign of Petey anywhere. I turned sadly away and started to walk across the room when suddenly I heard "Hello." Spinning around, I saw Petey perched on the windowsill. He had come back on his own— and announced his arrival!

Writer's Corner

▶ Write a simple topic sentence for each of the topics below. Then write a more creative beginning sentence for each topic. If you do not know enough about one topic, use an informational resource or your imagination.

1. The flight of monarch butterflies south for the winter
2. My favorite ride at the amusement park
3. Food that astronauts eat on spaceflights
4. Winning a contest
5. The day I disappeared

LESSON 3

Writing Supporting Sentences

Supporting sentences give details that explain the topic.

You have already learned how to choose a topic, narrow it, and write an interesting beginning sentence. After you write your beginning sentence, you will want to tell more about your topic. Supporting sentences, or middle sentences, tell the important details. Each supporting sentence adds information and carries the idea of the paragraph forward.

Read the paragraph below. Notice how the supporting details develop the idea expressed in the topic sentence.

A Useful Plant

The whole life of Egypt seemed to depend on the papyrus plant. The young shoots were eaten, and the juice was made into a drink. Weavers learned how to twist its fibers into a kind of cloth, and shoemakers made shoes of its bark. Boat makers tied bundles of it together to make small canoes and even larger boats. Out of its stems were made utensils for the house. Last, but not least, paper was made from it! Is it any wonder that the Egyptians valued papyrus so highly?

The topic of the paragraph is "the usefulness of the papyrus plant." The beginning sentence explains that life in Egypt depended on this plant, and the supporting sentences proved the details that show this. The supporting sentences do not tell what the plant looked like or how it was grown. Instead, they keep to the topic and explain how the plant supplied things needed for life.

The diagram below is a word map that describes the paragraph about papyrus. At the center of the word map is the topic of the paragraph. Around the center are the supporting details. You may want to draw a word map during the prewriting stage of the writing process, before you write a paragraph. A word map is a useful tool to help you organize your ideas and decide what details to include.

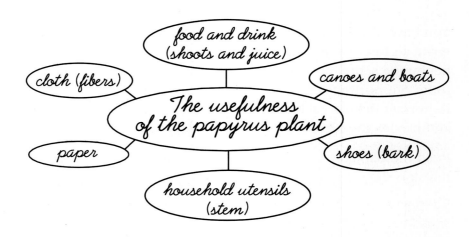

Activity A

Read the specific idea in each oval below. Then complete the word maps by giving four supporting details for each topic.

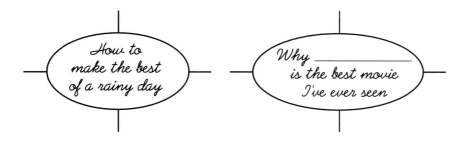

Activity B

Write a beginning sentence for each topic in Activity A. Then complete the paragraph, putting your supporting details in order and adding any additional information you think the reader might need to know. Remember to keep to your topic! Read your paragraph and decide if it makes sense and reads smoothly. If not, move sentences and words around to improve it. Reread your paragraph one more time.

Writer's Corner

▶ Choose any two of the five topics below. Make a word map with four to six details for each topic. Then choose the word map that has the most ideas and write a paragraph using the word map as a guide. Write a good beginning sentence and supporting sentences that give the details. Put the sentences in the order that seems most logical to you.

A. How to skate

B. Why _____ is my favorite _____

C. An afternoon in the year 2050

D. A punishment I really deserved

E. The best adventure of my life

Writing Ending Sentences

An ending sentence draws the paragraph to a close.

In Lesson 3, you wrote paragraphs with beginning sentences and supporting details. Perhaps you added a sentence at the end to express your opinion or to sum up the ideas in the paragraph. You might have done this simply to bring your paragraph to a smoother conclusion. If you did, you were writing an ending sentence.

An ending sentence, besides just bringing the paragraph to a close, may do several things.

● An ending sentence may give a last fact or detail.

> An old red cloth thrown over the cage soon silenced the bird.

> Suddenly, the diver emerged from the glistening blue-green water with a handful of gold coins.

● An ending sentence may tell what the writer thinks or feels.

> After that experience, I'll never hike in shorts and gym shoes again.

> Now I know that joining the neighborhood swim team was a good idea.

● An ending sentence may also draw together everything in the paragraph.

> With all these uses, it is no wonder that microwave ovens are part of the modern kitchen.

> The magician's fast-paced tricks left Jonathan wide-eyed with amazement.

Activity A

Choose the ending sentence that would best complete each of the paragraphs described below. Explain the reason for your choice.

1. Gary is writing about how he sold the most candy in the candy drive at school and won a prize for his efforts. Which of the following sentences would be an ending sentence that expresses Gary's feelings about the contest?

    a. When the teacher announced a candy drive, I just groaned.

    b. This is the most exciting thing that ever happened to me!

    c. Finally, I sold twenty boxes to my favorite aunt.

2. Tina has just finished writing about a collection of stories by Ray Bradbury. She is ready to draw the ideas in her paragraph together. Which of the following sentences would be an ending sentence that would do this?

    a. Everyone interested in science fiction should sample a Ray Bradbury story.

    b. I can't believe I read the whole book in one sitting!

    c. Are you hooked on stories about strange happenings?

3. Hannah is writing a paragraph about her first experience waterskiing. Which sentence could end the paragraph and give a detail?

    a. Waterskiing will be part of my summer activities from now on.

    b. If my little brother could waterski, so could I.

    c. I let go of the ropes and collapsed into the water, ready to take up the challenge once again.

Activity B

Supply a good ending sentence for each of the following paragraphs. Think of one that is interesting and will really wrap up the story.

1 "I'll never make any friends in this new neighborhood," I thought, as I bounced a ball against the brick wall. The block seemed deserted, and I missed my old friends. As the ball thumped against the wall, I noticed someone standing near me. A dark-haired, freckle-faced girl was watching me. She seemed to be wondering who I was. I didn't know what to say, but suddenly I had an idea and flipped the ball over to her. "Nice catch," I said. _____

_____ .

2 The sound of people clapping attracted my attention, so I gazed across the park. What a surprise to see a bearded man in blue jeans and an old sweatshirt juggling different-colored balls. Before long, I learned about this unusual young man. He had spent the winter at clown school in Florida where he studied such skills as magic, juggling, gymnastics, and mime. He had not yet found a job as a professional clown, but each evening he went to the park to practice his new craft. Day by day, more people gathered to watch. _____

_____ .

3 Shortly after the Civil War, American theatergoers watched a young actress named Belle Boyd give dramatic readings about the adventures of a Confederate spy. It was more than just an act, however, since Boyd had really led the life of a Civil War spy. By the age of seventeen, she was watching the Northern army move through her native South and sending coded messages to Southern leaders. Northern soldiers captured her twice, but each time she was released. _____ _____ .

Writer's Corner

▶ Here are five topics for paragraphs. Write an ending sentence for each paragraph, and explain what purpose or purposes the ending sentence serves.

1. My worst injury

2. A troublesome neighbor

3. A surprise birthday party

4. An unexpected friend

5. If I could explore outer space . . .

Paragraph Unity

Paragraph unity means that all the sentences in a paragraph are related to the specific idea.

In the previous lessons, you wrote some paragraphs. Then you reread your paragraphs to see if they made sense. What does it really mean for a paragraph to make sense? For one thing, it means that all the sentences are related to the topic.

Sometimes when you reread a paragraph you have written, one or two sentences just do not seem to belong. These misfit sentences, which are not related to the topic, must be taken out. Read the following paragraph and note how one sentence interrupts the thought. Which sentence does not belong? Why is it a misfit?

"Can this thing really play music?" I thought as Willie handed me his electric guitar. It wasn't hollow like other guitars, and when I plucked a string, there was no noise. Willie said that he would explain to me how an electric guitar worked. Willie's group is called the "Soul Rockers." He plugged the guitar in, and when I plucked the string again, there was a rich, loud sound. "The strings don't really make the music," he explained. "When you play a string, it gives an electric signal to the amplifier and to the loud-speaker. That's where the music comes from!"

Activity A

Each topic below has four supporting details. For each topic, one detail does not fit. Find the misfit details.

1. Hurricane safety tips

    a. Board up your windows.

    b. Keep a supply of food in the house.

    c. Make sure you have candles.

    d. Tornadoes are also dangerous.

2. Why sixteen-year-olds should be allowed to drive

    a. They can run family errands.

    b. They will vote in two years.

    c. They should be responsible by that age.

    d. They may need a car for dates and parties.

3. Why every family will want to own a robot

    a. It can do household chores.

    b. The word *robot* means "work."

    c. It can be a companion.

    d. It can help with homework.

4. My costume for the party

    a. Jessica dressed as a scarecrow.

    b. I dressed as an astronaut.

    c. I was supposed to be astronaut Sally Ride.

    d. My costume was shiny and silver-colored.

Activity B

Read the following paragraphs and find the misfit sentence in each paragraph. Explain why each misfit is not related to the topic of the paragraph.

1 "Help me," yelled the frightened man from the pool. A large man, weighing maybe two hundred pounds, was in the deep water and could not stay afloat. The lifeguard ran to the side of the pool. She was a girl of about fifteen and weighed no more than one hundred pounds. She wore a red-and-white swimsuit and a striped bathing cap. I didn't think she could save such a big man, but she worked quickly. She threw him the nearest kickboard and said, "Calm down. Relax. Just hold the board and kick to the nearest side of the pool." Her method worked, and the man kicked safely to the side. She had learned her lifesaving lessons well.

2 I saw quite an unusual sight last week. A wrecking crew was scheduled to remove a large old building. I had previously seen many buildings being torn down. For those buildings, a wrecking ball was used to knock down the building piece by piece. Wrecking equipment can be quite expensive. The process was slow but fascinating. The event last week was quite different. People like me were allowed to watch—but from a safe distance. The crew placed explosives throughout the building. These were then set off, and the building collapsed straight down. It was all over in less than a minute. The process was fast—and fascinating.

3 The first known valentine dates back to 1415. Then a French noble who was imprisoned in England sent one to his wife in France. By 1750, it had become a custom in England and America to tuck valentines into doors. These early valentines were made by hand and were not signed. By 1850, valentines were made by machine, and over three million were sold in the United States. Although valentines of this time were machine-made, decorations were often added to them by hand, and these valentines are considered among the most beautiful ever produced. They often had frilly lace borders, flowers, and colorful pictures added to them. Valentines were just one example of the beautiful arts of the 1800s. By the mid-1800s, postcard valentines with humorous messages were popular. These are not unlike some of the valentines we send today.

Writer's Corner

▶ Choose one of the topics from Activity A and write a short paragraph. You may add new supporting sentences and make changes in the ones that are already written. Create an interesting beginning sentence, keep the middle sentences unified, and write an effective ending.

Creating a Title

A title is the name that is given to any piece of writing.

The title is the first part of your paragraph, composition, or story that the reader will see. Sometimes the title helps a reader decide whether to read on or not. Do you think a story called "Building a Boat" would interest you? Would you want to read an article called "Whales"? Perhaps you would, but wouldn't titles like "Modern-Day Vikings" and "Underwater Giants" spark your interest a bit more?

Titles are fun to create. There are several different approaches you can take to writing titles. Sometimes titles tell the specific idea of the paragraph, such as "Danger: Sharks!" What do you think that paragraph is about?

Other titles give just a hint of what is in the paragraph. The title "A Narrow Escape" sounds exciting. It makes you ask yourself these questions: From what situation must the main character escape? How will he or she accomplish this?

Still other titles are more creative, such as the titles of C. S. Lewis's novels *That Hideous Strength* and *The Lion, the Witch, and the Wardrobe* or of Mary Stewart's novel *Crystal Cave.*

Notice that most titles are short and that each important word begins with a capital letter. The words *a, an, the,* and *and* are capitalized only when they are the first word of the title.

Activity A

Each of these five topics has two possible titles. Which title do you think is better for each topic? Give the reason for your choice.

1. Getting lost on a camping trip
   a. Lost in the Woods
   b. A Quick Lesson in Survival
2. Your first experience at cooking
   a. Pancakes—I Think!
   b. An Unsuccessful Meal
3. Hitting your first home run
   a. The Crack of the Bat
   b. I Hit a Home Run
4. Using a pen with evaporating ink
   a. A Disappearing Note
   b. For Your Eyes Only
5. Moving to a new city
   a. Destination: Atlanta
   b. My Family Moves to Atlanta

Activity B

Reread the paragraphs in the activities on pages 45 and 46 or pages 49 and 50. Create an interesting title for each.

Writer's Corner

▶ Here are five topics. Create an interesting title for each.

1. Learning to dance
2. A woman who becomes a police officer
3. Watching a big fire
4. The first day of spring
5. Watching a new music video on TV

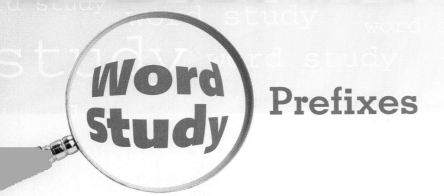

Prefixes

A prefix is a syllable (or syllables) added to the beginning of a word that changes the meaning of that word.

You already know many prefixes. If your teacher tells you to rewrite a paragraph or reread a story, you know that the prefix *re-* tells you to do something again. If a task is impossible, the prefix *im-* tells you the task is not possible. Notice that a prefix is always followed by a root. The prefix will give the root a new meaning.

Here is a list of prefixes. Study them carefully.

PREFIX	MEANING	EXAMPLE
bi-	two	bicycle
co-	together	copilot
dis-	not	disapprove
micro-	small	microcomputer
mini-	small	miniskirt
non-	not, without	nonstop
over-	above, too much	overcook
re-	again	reunite
tri-	three	triangle
uni-	one	unicycle

Activity A

Copy the chart below, and fill in the missing parts.

PREFIX	ROOT	NEW WORD	MEANING
1. re-	_____	retrace	_____
2. _____	load	_____	to load too much
3. _____	_____	microfilm	small film
4. non-	returnable	_____	_____
5. mini–	van	_____	_____
6. _____	lateral	_____	two-sided
7. _____	satisfied	dissatisfied	_____
8. tri-	color	_____	_____
9. co-	_____	cowinner	_____
10. _____	_____	unisyllabic	with one syllable

Activity B

Complete each sentence with the correct word by adding a prefix from the list on page 64 to the word at the left.

grown   **1.** The field was _____ with bushes and weeds.

set   **2.** Because of the electrical failure, we had to _____ the clocks.

bike   **3.** If I had a _____ , I could ride to school every day.

sense   **4.** Humorous poems are often called _____ poems.

cycle   **5.** I remember riding a _____ when I was very small.

operate   **6.** If this project is to succeed, everyone must _____ .

corn   **7.** There was a picture of a _____ in the mythology book.

scope   **8.** In science class, I spent fifteen minutes looking through a _____ at different kinds of leaves.

agreed   **9.** "Strike three," yelled the umpire, but the batter _____ .

weekly   **10.** Jamie receives the magazine every two weeks. It must be a _____ subscription.

Putting Your Journal to Work

What do you do when your teacher says, "Write about anything"? Do you sit and stare at a blank sheet of paper? Or, do you turn to your journal, choose an idea, and start writing? Add writing ideas to your journal. Write about one of your ideas. Then publish your "before and after" writing.

 Prewriting

Start a writing ideas section in your journal. To begin, list several ideas you would like to write about. From now on, whenever you think of a new writing idea, jot it in your journal.

Questions like these will help you think of writing ideas.

- How do different seasons or kinds of weather make me feel?

- What is my idea of the perfect friend?

- How would I spend my time if TV didn't exist?

- If I could spend the day with my favorite person, what would we do together?

- What career do I want when I grow up?

Choose a topic idea from your journal. Make a word map of ideas that your topic brings to mind.

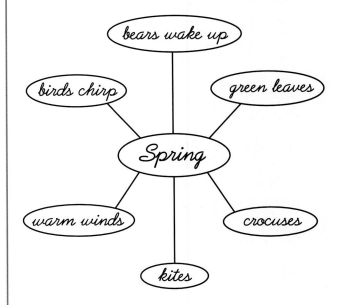

Drafting

Think about the different forms of writing you know. Decide what the words on your word map make you feel like writing. If you're not sure, try out a few different ways to write. Maybe you'd like to write a paragraph.

During the long winter, I felt as if I were hibernating. Maybe bears like to hibernate, but I don't! So I'm glad there's a new feeling in the air today. Birds are chirping, and trees are showing a little green fuzz. Crocuses are blooming, and warm breezes have chased away the cold winter wind. I think I'll go fly a kite!

Or maybe the ideas in your word map make you feel like writing a poem.

*It's time for bears to yawn
    and stretch
To open their eyes, look outside,
    and watch
Birds chirp and chatter
Trees and bushes look fuzzy
    and green
Crocuses and snowdrops bloom
Winds warm and play
Kites bob and float
Because it's finally SPRING!*

WRITER'S WORKSHOP

Guidelines for Writing Your Draft

1. Write quickly.
2. Write your draft while all your prewriting ideas are fresh in your mind.
3. Don't worry about spelling or punctuation right now.
4. Keep your prewriting notes in front of you.
5. Don't be afraid to add things to your draft that are not in your notes. You can always take them out later.
6. Remember, your draft may not be perfect. The purpose of a draft is to get all your ideas down on paper quickly.
7. After writing your draft, have a peer conference to get feedback from another writer. (See page 29 for conferencing tips.)

EDITOR'S WORKSHOP

Revising, Proofreading, and Publishing

 Revising

Time to Take Another Look

All writers, young or old, professional authors or people who are writing a letter to a friend, revise their drafts to improve their writing. Use the questions below to help you examine your writing.

❏ Does my writing include enough interesting details?

❏ Do I want to add details from my word map that I left out?

❏ Do I need to rearrange any lines or sentences?

❏ Do I need to rewrite lines or sentences so my ideas will be clear to my reader?

❏ Do I need to replace weak and boring verbs and adjectives with more vivid words?

❏ Do I need to cut out any unnecessary words, phrases, or sentences to make my writing flow better?

Reread your writing to answer each question. Make your revisions with a colored pencil so they will be easy to see when you make your final copy.

Use a Thesaurus

A thesaurus is a book of words and their synonyms. Writers use this important tool to turn a good piece of writing into a great one. Use the thesaurus to find just the right word to paint a vivid word picture for your reader.

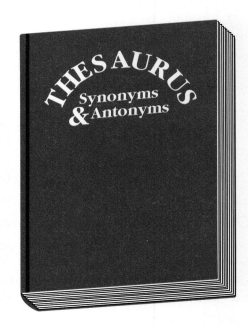

 **Proofreading**

Time to Look at Capitalization, Punctuation, and Spelling

After you have revised your writing so it says just what you want it to say, it's time to check your capitalization, punctuation, spelling, and grammar. Correct little mistakes that would distract your reader.

Use the checklist below to edit and proofread your paragraph.

❏ Did I begin each sentence and proper noun with a capital letter?

❏ Did I use the correct mark of punctuation at the end of each sentence or line?

❏ Did I indent the first word if I wrote a paragraph?

❏ Did I spell each word correctly?

One Line at a Time

Place a blank sheet of paper under the line you are proofreading. This will help you focus all your attention on proofreading instead of on your ideas. Proofread the line you see, and then move down to the next one.

 Publishing

Time to Share

Publish your journal page along with your final copy to show how an idea grows to become a final, polished piece of writing.

To publish, follow these steps:

1. Copy your revised draft in your neatest handwriting.

2. Reread your final copy against your draft to make sure you did not leave anything out.

3. Proofread your final copy once more.

Make a class before and after bulletin board.

1. Fold a large sheet of paper in half to create a sheet with two sections.

2. Write *Before* at the top of the left section and *After* at the top of the right one.

3. Glue your journal page on the left and your final copy on the right.

4. Sign your name.

5. Display your writing on the bulletin board.

CHAPTER 3

Refining Your Writing Skills

Expanding Sentences

You can expand a sentence by adding adjectives, adverbs, and prepositional phrases that help to give the reader a clearer picture.

Adding Adjectives and Adverbs

Sometimes you may decide that a paragraph you have written is dull and uninteresting because it fails to give the reader a clear picture. Sentences in such a paragraph can come to life if you add colorful and expressive adjectives and adverbs.

If you write *The lanterns swayed,* for example, your sentence is not very specific. You could add adjectives and an adverb to make the sentence read, *The colorful Chinese lanterns swayed rhythmically.* Now the reader gets a clearer picture!

Study this example. Note the words that are added to the second sentence.

> The tightrope walker balanced herself.

> The daring, graceful tightrope walker balanced herself effortlessly.

The writer has added

- the adjectives *daring* and *graceful.*

- the adverb *effortlessly.*

About the Photograph

As you get more practice in writing, you will refine your writing skills. Not only will you make fewer mistakes, but you will also learn to make your writing richer and more interesting.

Activity A

These ten sentences could use improvement. Whenever you see this symbol, ^ (called a caret), put in one or more adjectives or adverbs.

1. The ^ rain fell ^ .
2. The ^ hikers ^ walked through the ^ forest.
3. The ^ pirates ^ boarded the ^ ship.
4. ^ bees swarmed ^ over the rose garden.
5. The puck flew ^ past the ^ goalie.
6. The ^ campfire blazed ^ .
7. The artist did a(n) ^ painting.
8. I bought a(n) ^ frozen yogurt.
9. Two ^ shadows ^ emerged from the ^ spaceship.
10. The ^ frog leaped ^ from the log.

Adding Prepositional Phrases

You have seen how adjectives and adverbs can make your sentences come to life. Prepositional phrases are another helpful tool that you can use.

Look at this sentence again.

> The colorful Chinese lanterns swayed rhythmically.

You could also add a prepositional phrase to make the sentence read:

> The colorful Chinese lanterns swayed rhythmically in the light breeze.

With the addition of a prepositional phrase, the picture becomes even clearer.

Study the example below. Note the prepositional phrases that are added to the second sentence.

> The graceful, daring tightrope walker balanced herself effortlessly.

> The graceful, daring tightrope walker in a blue leotard balanced herself effortlessly on the wire above the crowd.

The writer has added

- the prepositional phrase *in a blue leotard* after a noun.
- the prepositional phrases *on the wire* and *above the crowd* after the verb.

Activity B

The sentences below are not very specific. Add a prepositional phrase or phrases to each sentence to give a clearer picture.

1. The hot-air balloon landed.
2. Doug dribbled the ball.
3. The river overflowed.
4. The drums boomed.
5. The snow drifted.
6. Cactus grew.
7. The scuba diver floated.
8. Crowds of people stood.
9. The lion crouched.
10. The rocket rose.

Activity C

Expand the following sentences. Add colorful adjectives, adverbs, and prepositional phrases. Try doing this activity in two steps:
- **First add adjectives and adverbs.**
- **Then go back and add prepositional phrases.**

1. David was a keyboard player.

2. He wanted to start a rock group.

3. He knew that John and Eddie were guitar players.

4. They agreed to join the group.

5. The next member was Josh, a drummer.

6. David heard a singer named Maggie.

7. He asked Maggie to join, and she agreed.

8. The group got together and practiced.

Writer's Corner

▶ **Make this dull paragraph come alive by adding interesting adjectives, adverbs, and prepositional phrases. If you need to, you may also change other words in the paragraph.**

The canoe moved along the Amazon River. The three explorers and their guide gazed at the rain forest. The forest looked like a green wall. Monkeys and other animals made noises. Above, birds flew. Fish and crocodiles swam nearby. The explorers saw snakes on the shore. The explorers wanted to reach their destination.

LESSON 2   Combining Independent Clauses

> **You can add variety and length to a paragraph by combining independent clauses.**

In Lesson 1 of this chapter, you learned to expand and enliven sentences by adding adjectives, adverbs, and prepositional phrases. You can also expand sentences and add variety to paragraphs by connecting independent clauses (which are really simple sentences) with coordinate conjunctions. Below are the most common coordinate conjunctions and the special purpose that each serves. As you read the sample sentences, notice what kind of punctuation you must use to connect two independent clauses.

COORDINATE CONJUNCTION	SPECIAL PURPOSE
and	*And* connects two ideas that are similar or that happen together.
	Bernie and David went to the movie theater, and they saw an exciting western.
but, yet	*But* and *yet* connect clauses that have opposite or contrasting ideas.
	Bernie had a lot of homework, but he went to the movie anyway.
or	*Or* suggests that there is a choice.
	David could stay home to watch his favorite TV program, or he could go to see the movie.

Activity A

Choose the best coordinate conjunction to combine the following pairs of sentences. Explain each of your choices.

1. Marti must practice each day.
   She won't make the field hockey team.

2. I rode over to the bike repair shop.
   It was closed.

3. Enrique reads many detective stories.
   Sometimes he even writes a mystery of his own.

4. Ballets tell a story.
   The dancers do not speak any words.

5. After high school, you can go to college.
   You can find a full-time job.

6. The test seemed very easy.
   I got a low grade.

7. Tony is an excellent shortstop.
   He is a good hitter.

8. Delia wants to be a nurse.
   Sheila wants to be one, too.

9. Sugar can give you energy quickly.
   It can also cause your teeth to decay.

10. Liza likes to play the clarinet.
    The orchestra leader wants her to try the saxophone.

Activity B

Here is a paragraph of short sentences for you to revise. Combine at least two pairs of sentences by using coordinate conjunctions. Expand as many sentences as you can with adjectives, adverbs, and prepositional phrases. If you need to, you may change other words in the paragraph.

> One of the most famous cowboys was an African-American man. His real name was Nat Love. People called him Deadwood Dick. Love was born a slave in Tennessee in 1854. He was freed when he was fifteen years old. Then Love had a choice. He could work on his father's farm. He could go west and become a cowboy. Love decided to become a cowboy. He worked on cattle drives for twenty years. His riding ability was exceptional. His roping was unmatched. He even won a contest among cowboys in Deadwood, South Dakota. There he got his nickname. As Love grew older, he wanted to tell his story. He wrote his autobiography. He called it *The Adventures of Nat Love, Better Known in Cattle Country as Deadwood Dick.*

Writer's Corner

▶ Write three sentences for each coordinate conjunction: *and, but* or *yet,* and *or.* Then, to prove that you have connected independent clauses, take the coordinate conjunction out of each sentence and write the two simple sentences for each sentence you wrote.

Revising Rambling and Run-On Sentences

Sentences that contain too many ideas to be clearly understood must be divided.

Rambling Sentences

In the previous two lessons, you have learned to lengthen sentences in two ways: by adding adjectives, adverbs, and prepositional phrases, as well as by connecting independent clauses. However, do not let "longer is better" become your motto for writing. A well-written paragraph usually has sentences of varying lengths. Some of the sentences in a paragraph may become too long and complicated. Often the reader cannot tell where one idea ends and another begins. To improve a rambling sentence, divide it into two or more sentences. Notice how the following rambling sentence can be broken down to form a few clearer sentences.

Rambling Sentence

Rebecca was watching her favorite TV program, which is a show about a group of young scientists, and today's story was especially interesting because it was about scientists who discovered a "caveman" who had never had contact with modern society and who was found walking across the Golden Gate Bridge, and he was as confused about how he got there as the scientists were about finding him.

Improved Sentences

Rebecca was watching her favorite TV program, a show about a group of young scientists. Today's story was especially interesting. It was about scientists who discovered a "caveman" who had never had contact with modern society. The "caveman" was found walking across the Golden Gate Bridge. He was as confused about how he got there as the scientists were about finding him.

Activity A

Improve these rambling sentences. You may add or change words to make your improved sentences read smoothly.

1. In 1985, a massive earthquake jolted Mexico City, killing people and destroying property, and groups across the United States immediately began sending medical aid and money to the battered city because they hoped to save lives and help the homeless.

2. This was my best summer ever because my family spent the entire month of August in Wisconsin where we rented a cabin that was on a lake and we could swim, row our boat, windsurf, dive off a raft, or just lie in the sun on the sandy shore.

3. The forests of the world are one of our most valuable resources but they are disappearing and we should do what we can to protect them because it would take many years to replace them when they are gone.

4. My neighborhood is near the airport and when planes fly directly overhead, the noise is deafening and we can hardly hear each other speak, so last week a group of neighbors went to visit the mayor to see if she could arrange to have the takeoff and landing patterns changed.

5. Copper is a strong, tough metal and it carries heat and electricity well and it has many important uses and among them is its use in wires of all kinds, including telephone, telegraph, and power lines.

Activity B

Here is a paragraph for you to revise. Shorten the rambling sentences so the reader can understand the paragraph more easily.

Florence Nightingale was a British nurse who became famous for her work during the Crimean War in which Britain and France fought Russia, and she was the leader of a small group of nurses who had to care for hundreds of wounded soldiers but there were not enough medical supplies or hospital cots. Florence worked hard to organize the army hospital and get it cleaned up, and she demanded medical supplies from British leaders and every night walked the hospital halls to check on the patients. She even visited the battlefield where she caught a serious illness called Crimean-Congo fever but she did not let her illness stop her work and said, "I can stand out this war with any man." Florence Nightingale's tireless, unselfish efforts saved many lives and set an example of organization, cleanliness, and hard work that are the basis of the nursing profession today, and all modern nurses should be thankful to her.

Run-On Sentences

Sometimes when you write, one sentence will run into the next. It is difficult to tell where one idea ends and the next idea begins. Often there is no punctuation between two thoughts or an incorrect mark of punctuation is used. This is called a run-on sentence. Look carefully at the following sentences.

A. Some people in the Sahara build their houses below ground they dig twenty-five feet into the earth.

B. Underground, the people of the Sahara find water and shelter from sandstorms, it is also cooler there on hot days.

Each of the above sentences is a run-on sentence because there are two separate thoughts, but they are written as one sentence. In sentence A, there is no mark of punctuation. In sentence B, there is an incorrect mark of punctuation.

Can you tell where the first thought ends in sentence A? It ends after the word *ground;* therefore, a period should be inserted and a new sentence begun. Can you tell where the first idea ends in sentence B? It ends after the word *sandstorms;* therefore, a period should be inserted and a new sentence begun. When they are corrected, the sentences would read and look like this:

A. Some people in the Sahara build their houses below ground. They dig twenty-five feet into the earth.

B. Underground, the people of the Sahara find water and shelter from sandstorms. It is also cooler there on hot days.

Activity C

Correct the following run-on sentences. Make sure the proper mark of punctuation is inserted between the different ideas.

1. A camel is a large desert animal it can travel long distances.

2. The camel's hump is a "storage tank" it stores fat.

3. Camels can survive with little food or water they draw on the reserve in their "storage tank" for energy.

4. Some camels have one hump and some have two it depends on what type of camel they are.

5. Some Middle Eastern camels, called dromedaries, are used for riding and racing they can travel about ten miles an hour and about one hundred miles a day.

6. The dromedary camel has one hump the Bactrian camel has two humps.

7. Camels are well adapted for desert life their feet are padded for walking on sand.

8. Camel's milk is used for drinking and for making cheese it is so thick that it forms lumps in liquids.

9. The hair of the Bactrian camel can be woven blankets, tents, and clothing are made from this hair.

10. Camels are useful animals they are a source of milk, meat, wool, and hides.

Writer's Corner

▶ Look at sentence 2 in Activity A on page 79. Pretend that last summer was *your* best summer ever. Write four or five sentences about what you did. Write some shorter sentences and some longer (but not run-on) sentences.

Choosing the Best Word

You can liven up a paragraph by using picture words or precise words to replace lifeless words.

To become a skilled writer, you need to develop a strong vocabulary. If you reread a paragraph you have written and find some dull, lifeless words, you must search for more vivid picture words. Often a good picture word will be a synonym for the word it replaces. Compare the sentences in the left-hand column with those in the right-hand column. Do you see pictures in these sentences on the right that you did not see in the ones on the left? Do you find more precise words on the right? What are they?

A light appeared before me.	A light *flashed* before me.
The fire burned in the distance.	The fire *blazed* in the distance.
The water ran down the rocks.	The water *trickled* down the rocks.
Red leaves covered the ground.	*Crimson* leaves covered the ground.
I was awakened by a loud noise.	I was awakened by a *shrill scream.*
The dog ran into the field.	The dog *loped* into the field.

As you reread your writing, look for words that are dull and overused. To help you in thinking of new words to replace the dull ones, you might use a dictionary or a thesaurus. Some dictionaries give lists of synonyms after an entry. A thesaurus is a book of synonyms.

Activity A

"Polish" some words yourself. For each italicized word below, think of two other words that are more vivid or that express the idea more precisely. Use a dictionary or thesaurus for help.

1. A *bad* storm
2. A *pretty* painting
3. My *aim* in life
4. A *brave* knight
5. To *hold* a life preserver
6. A *big* glacier
7. A *fast* antelope
8. A *trip* down the Mississippi
9. An *interesting* dream
10. The *increasing* popularity of soccer

Activity B

1. Think of a vivid picture word to replace *moved* in each example below. Then complete each sentence.

   a. The space shuttle moved . . .
   b. An old car moved . . .
   c. The supersonic jet moved . . .
   d. The lame dog moved . . .
   e. The lion moved . . .
   f. The last person to finish the marathon moved . . .

2. **Describe each noise with a colorful verb.**

   a. A crying baby
   b. A snake hissing
   c. Two cats fighting
   d. The splash of a waterfall
   e. The crowd at a basketball game
   f. The people in a library

3. **What adjective could be used in place of *old* if you were writing about the following?**

   a. A grandfather clock
   b. A style of clothing
   c. A book
   d. A friend
   e. An Egyptian pyramid
   f. A running shoe

Writer's Corner

▶ The following paragraph has a number of dull, lifeless words. Liven up the paragraph by substituting either a picture word or a more precise word for each word in italics. Use a dictionary or thesaurus if you need help.

As I *walked* through the park Saturday afternoon, I *saw* a big totem pole. The pole itself was painted brown, but the faces *made* on it were *bright* reds and yellows. They were faces of people and of *odd* animals, both *funny* and *scary* at the same time. What an interesting thing to see in the middle of a *big* city!

Using Similes and Metaphors

Similes and metaphors are comparisons of unlike things. Both can help you write more expressively.

You have learned how to enliven your sentences with colorful picture words. Another way to make writing vivid is with comparisons. Read these comparisons.

> The spiderweb, wet with dew, was like a piece of fine lace.

> The hang gliders were enormous, colorful birds against the sky.

Notice how each comparison creates a clearer image. The first example is a simile, a comparison that uses the words *like* or *as*. Since lace is delicate and exquisite, the sentence gives a picture of a spiderweb as a delicate, airy work of art.

The second example does not use the words *like* or *as*. It states directly that the hang gliders were birds. Such a comparison is called a metaphor. In this metaphor, the comparison with birds gives the reader a picture of a sky filled with brilliant flying objects. Vivid similes and metaphors help writers paint pictures in their sentences.

Sometimes a simile or a metaphor is overused. For example, have you ever heard the expression "as cold as ice" or "as happy as a lark"? Such overused similes and metaphors are clichés. In using similes and metaphors, be creative and avoid clichés.

Below is a list of comparisons describing fireworks, a stream, and white clouds. Can you tell which are similes and which are metaphors?

Fireworks
bouquets of light
as bright as a million lightning bugs
popping popcorn in the sky

A Stream
a silver serpent
bubbling like soda pop
a shiny ribbon unrolling through the forest

White Clouds
like scoops of vanilla ice cream
white elephants, whales, hippopotamuses in the sky
floating like parachutes

Activity A

Read these sentences and tell whether the comparison is written as a simile or a metaphor. Then name the two objects that are being compared, and explain how they are different and what they have in common.

1. The giant redwoods are the skyscrapers of the forest.

2. The opposing fullback was as wide as a garage door.

3. To the astronaut, Earth was a huge, blue-green ball.

4. The sun was a player in a game of hide-and-seek.

5. The corridors of the building are like a maze.

6. Dina's arrival brightened the room like a lightbulb.

7. The last day of school crawled as slowly as a turtle.

8. When the skunk came out from behind the tree, Teddy ran like an Olympic gold medal sprinter.

9. The entire class was chattering like a bunch of monkeys.

10. Aunt Lou's face is an accordion of wrinkles.

Activity B

Complete the following sentences on a sheet of paper. If the phrase uses *like* or *as,* create a simile. If it does not, create a metaphor. Remember to use things that are unlike in your comparisons.

1. During rush hour, the cars move like _____ .

2. When it is full, the moon is _____ .

3. The water lilies cover the pond like _____ .

4. The room on the cold winter morning was _____ .

5. The creatures who emerged from the spaceship seemed like _____ .

6. The hose lying on the grass was _____ .

Writer's Corner

▶ Practice writing some of your own similes and metaphors. The paragraph below has none. Revise it by adding at least two similes and one metaphor. You may change or add sentences if you want.

Ben loves to ride his bicycle on the path by Lake Michigan. It is always an interesting adventure, full of wonderful sights. The lake is so wide that Ben cannot see across it. He likes the clear, sunny days when the water is bright blue. On windy days, the lake is choppy, and water splashes on the concrete path. Then Ben gets soaked, and his bike hisses as he rides over the wet concrete. Whenever he rides, he notices everything around him—joggers, skaters, swimmers, trees, bushes, and even the city skyline. When Ben is on the bicycle path, he feels happy and free.

Suffixes

> A suffix is a syllable (or syllables) added to the end of a root to create a new word. A suffix may change the part of speech of a word.

You use many words that have suffixes. On a lovely summer morning, you might exclaim, "What a *beautiful* day!" On a very hot day, you might think, "I don't feel very *energetic*."

For each italicized word above, a suffix is added to the end of a root to change a noun to an adjective. The suffix *-ful* meaning "full of" is added to the root *beauty* to form *beautiful*. *Beautiful* is an adjective that means "full of beauty." The suffix *-ic* meaning "relating to" is added to the root *energy* to form *energetic*. *Energetic* is an adjective that means "relating to energy."

Sometimes there is a spelling change when you add a suffix. In the word *beauty,* the *y* becomes an *i* before the suffix is added. In the word *energy,* the *y* is dropped, and an *e* and *t* come before the suffix. Study the list of suffixes below.

SUFFIX	MEANING	EXAMPLE
-ette	little	dinette
-ful	full of	skillful
-ic	relating to	athletic
-ish	somewhat, like a	childish
-like	resembling	catlike
-some	the quality of	troublesome
-th, -eth	in the order of a certain number	sixth, fiftieth
-y	full of	cloudy

Activity A

Copy the chart below, and fill in the missing parts.

	ROOT	SUFFIX	NEW WORD	MEANING
1.	sorrow	-ful	_____	_____
2.	_____	-ish	_____	like a fool
3.	majesty	_____	_____	relating to majesty
4.	mud	-y	_____	_____
5.	_____	_____	sixtieth	number sixty in order
6.	child	_____	childlike	_____
7.	_____	_____	lonesome	the quality of being alone
8.	_____	-ette	kitchenette	_____

Activity B

Complete each sentence with the correct word by adding a suffix from the list on page 90 to the word at the left. Use the dictionary to check spelling.

tickle **1.** I never knew Pat was so _____ .

winter **2.** It was a cold _____ day with the snow a foot deep.

grace **3.** The _____ ballerina seemed to float on the stage.

five **4.** Reading mystery stories is _____ on my list of favorite things.

life **5.** The figures in the wax museum were very _____ .

base **6.** The book *How Things Work* gives a very _____ explanation of how astronauts communicate with each other in space.

adventure **7.** Do you think that Huckleberry Finn was _____ ?

athlete **8.** Even though Paulette was not _____ , she proved to be an excellent football player.

Poetry into Prose

You probably have several favorite poems, so you already know what poetry is. You know what prose is, too, even if you don't recognize the name. Prose is the kind of writing you do when you write a paragraph. Poetry and prose can express the same thoughts in different ways.

Write the ideas from a poem in prose. Make a classroom display to share your prose.

Prewriting

Read the two poems in the box on the next page. Choose one of the poems to write about. Use the questions below to help you analyze the ideas in the poem you chose.

- What is the main idea of the whole poem?

- What is the main idea of each part of the poem?

- What special words and images did the author use to express ideas?

- What ideas of my own do I have about the poem's subject?

Use your answers to the questions to make a list of words, ideas, and images you can use as you turn the poem into prose.

Stanzas and Paragraphs
Notice that both poems are divided into two parts, with extra space between each part. The parts of a poem are called stanzas, or verses. A poem's stanzas are like paragraphs. Each stanza has its own main idea.

Drafting

Before you begin your draft, think about the differences between poetry and prose.

- Poetry uses fewer words, but the words paint vivid images. Many of the words in a poem are descriptive words. Some poems rhyme.

- Prose gives the reader more complete information. Prose paragraphs are written in complete sentences, while poems may not be.

To write your draft, circle the ideas on your prewriting list that you want to use in your prose. Number them to show the order in which you will use them.

Write a beginning sentence to capture your reader's attention and state the main idea of your paragraph. Then expand your notes into complete sentences. You may use words and images from the poem if you wish.

Write a title for your prose. Your title may be the same as the title of the poem.

Poems to Write About

Read both poems. Think about the ideas in each. Turn one of the poems into prose.

Stop-Go

Automobiles
In
  a
    row
Wait to go
While the signal says:
        STOP

Bells ring
Tingaling
Red light's gone!
Green light's on!
Horns blow!
And the row
Starts
  to
       GO

Dorothy Baruch

Autumn Woods

I like the woods
    In autumn
When dry leaves hide the ground,
When the trees are bare
And the wind sweeps by
With a lonesome rushing sound.

I can rustle the leaves
    In autumn
And I can make a bed
In the thick dry leaves
That have fallen
From the bare trees
Overhead.

James S. Tippett

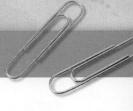

Revising, Proofreading, and Publishing

Revising

Time to Take Another Look

Think of revising as an opportunity to rethink your ideas and make your good writing even better.

❑ Does my prose have the same main idea as the poem?

❑ Do I capture my reader's attention with my beginning sentence?

❑ Do I need to add details from the poem or from my own list of ideas?

❑ Do I need to rewrite lines or sentences so my ideas will be clear?

❑ Do I need to rewrite to replace overused words?

❑ Do I need to cut out unnecessary words, phrases, or sentences to make my writing flow better?

❑ Do I need to rearrange my details into a more logical order?

Like poetry, prose can have poetic language that paints a vivid picture. Revise to give your prose striking words and images. Make your revisions with a colored pencil so they will stand out.

Using Similes and Metaphors

Similes and metaphors are comparisons that help you write more expressively. Similes use the comparison words *like* or *as*.

The traffic light glares at slow-to-stop cars like a big red eye.

Add life to your prose by finding a place to use a simile or metaphor.

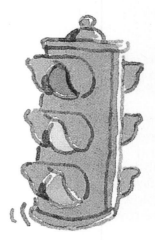

 **Proofreading**

Time to Look at Capitalization, Punctuation, and Spelling

When you're satisfied with the ideas in your prose, check your capitalization, punctuation, spelling, and grammar.

Use the checklist below to edit and proofread your writing.

- ❏ Did I begin the important words in my title with capital letters?

- ❏ Did I use the correct mark of punctuation at the end of each sentence?

- ❏ Did I indent the first word of each paragraph?

- ❏ Did I spell each word correctly?

Get Help from a Computer

If you typed your final copy on a computer, the computer can help out by checking your spelling. Run the spell-checking program before you do your own proofreading. Remember, a computer can't find words that are spelled right but used incorrectly, such as *to*, *too*, and *two*.

 Publishing

Time to Share

Publish your prose along with your classmates' to see many different ways to express the same idea.

To publish, follow these steps:

1. Copy your revised draft in your neatest handwriting or type it on a computer.

2. Reread your final copy against your draft to make sure you did not leave anything out.

3. Proofread your final copy once more.

Make the class poetry and prose display.

1. Have one student neatly copy the poems from the lesson.

2. Mount the poems at opposite ends of the bulletin board.

3. Pin your prose on the bulletin board near the poem you wrote about.

Kinds of Writing

Using Transition Words

Transition words help to make smooth connections between sentences and paragraphs.

A good writer knows how to take the reader through a series of connected ideas or events skillfully. The reader never has to wonder how two ideas or two sentences fit together. A good paragraph flows smoothly, and it has no gaps. One of the best tools for creating a smooth paragraph is the use of transition words, which show the relationship between two sentences or ideas.

Many transition words create a time relationship. When you write a paragraph or story, you often arrange events and ideas according to the time sequence in which they occur. Here are some connecting words that indicate time. They can help make your paragraphs read more smoothly.

afterward	later
at first	meanwhile
at last	next
at the same time	now
earlier	second
finally	soon
first	then
last	third

About the Photograph

In a race you need to get from the start to the finish smoothly. In writing you need to get from the beginning to the end, and transition words will help you do this smoothly.

Read the sentences below. On the left are five unconnected sentences. On the right, transition words have been added at the beginnings of sentences 2, 3, and 5. The transition words are *First, Then,* and *Finally*. Adding transition words makes the paragraph flow more smoothly.

1. David didn't know which sport he wanted to try out for—basketball or baseball.

2. He thought he should play basketball, because his dad really wanted him to play.

3. He thought he really wanted to play baseball because all his friends were on the team.

4. David practiced very hard at both sports throughout the summer.

5. He decided to try out for both teams, and he remained happily busy throughout the school year.

David didn't know which sport he wanted to try out for—basketball or baseball. *First,* he thought he should play basketball, because his dad really wanted him to play. *Then,* he thought he really wanted to play baseball because all his friends were on the team. David practiced very hard at both sports throughout the summer. *Finally,* he decided to try out for both teams, and he remained happily busy throughout the year.

Activity A

Below are five sets of sentences. Rewrite the sentences in each set so they fit together smoothly. Use at least one transition word. Refer to the list of transition words on page 97 and the example on page 98 for help.

1. a. Using a computer is not so difficult.
   b. You put in a diskette.
   c. You type in your information, or data.

2. a. There was a flash of light.
   b. There was a loud noise.
   c. The little shack was just a pile of rubble on the ground.

3. a. Ms. O'Malley asked for Timothy's homework.
   b. Timothy looked through his English folder and his desk.
   c. He found his homework in his science folder.

4. a. Tiffany was listening to her CDs.
   b. She was trying to do homework.
   c. She realized that she had to choose one or the other.

5. a. Firefighters circled the blazing forest in small planes.
   b. Smoke jumpers parachuted into safe areas with their equipment.
   c. The fire was under control.

Activity B

Complete this paragraph on a sheet of paper by filling in information. You might imagine that you recently had a day that was filled with good or bad surprises. Notice how the transition words express a time relationship. When you are finished, read your paragraph aloud to hear how the transition words help make connections.

It all started when _____ .
Next, _____ . Later, _____
_____ . Meanwhile, _____
_____ . Then, _____ . Finally, _____ .

Writer's Corner

▶ **The paragraph below needs some transition words. Decide on the best ones to use, and then revise the paragraph. Add at least three transition words. The list on page 97 will help you.**

When Sam invited Joe to go to the roller rink, Joe could not bring himself to admit that he had never skated. At the rink, Sam put on his skates and began swiftly gliding along in time to the music. Joe rented a pair of skates. He thought it would be simple to teach himself to skate. He realized that he could move only a few feet before tumbling to his hands and knees. He swallowed his pride and called to Sam for help. Sam laughed at how stubborn Joe had been and gave him a quick lesson. Joe was able to skate slowly and cautiously around the rink.

LESSON 2

Writing a Narrative Paragraph

A narrative paragraph tells a story. The paragraph usually tells about the events in the order in which they happened.

Narrative paragraphs should be familiar to you. You have probably heard narratives all your life, beginning with the stories that were read to you as a child. Many of the short stories and novels you read now are also narratives. You even create narratives yourself in everyday conversations. If someone asks you, "What happened?" for instance, your answer is probably in the form of a narrative. You would tell the events in the order in which they happened.

Study the following example of a narrative paragraph from Walter Farley's novel *The Black Stallion*. In the paragraph, young Alec Ramsey and the stallion are trapped on a deserted island after a shipwreck.

> One night Alec sat beside his campfire and stared into the flames that reached hungrily into the air; his knees were crossed and his elbows rested heavily upon them; his chin was cupped in his two hands. He was deep in thought. The *Drake* had left Bombay on a Saturday, the fifteenth of August. The shipwreck had happened a little over two weeks later, perhaps on the second of September. He had been on the island exactly nineteen . . . days. That would make it approximately the twenty-first of September. By now his family must think him dead! He doubled his fists. He had to find a way out; a ship just had to pass the island sometime. Daily he had stood up on top of the hill peering out to sea, frantically hoping to sight a boat.

In the paragraph, Alec is thinking back on events that occurred since he arrived on the island. Notice the words that show time: *one night, by now,* and *daily.* How do they help to make the order of events clear?

Your own story might have a more simple time sequence, such as from morning to evening of one day. You could use the transition words that show time that you learned in Lesson 1, or you could use other words or phrases that show time, such as *at noon, by one o'clock,* and *by the end of the day.* Like the time words in the paragraph from *The Black Stallion,* these words help show the order of events.

There is another decision to make when you plan a narrative paragraph besides choosing appropriate connecting words. You must decide whether the narrator (the one who is telling the story) is a character in the story or an observer. Read the two sentences below and see if you can tell whether the narrator is inside the story as a character or outside the story as an observer.

- When lightning struck the tree, we all headed for cover.
- When lightning struck the tree, the boys headed for cover.

Now reread the paragraph from *The Black Stallion* and answer the same question.

In a good narrative paragraph, the narrator is either a character in the story or an observer, but not both. The time sequence is clear by the use of transition words and time words. Most important, the events that the narrator tells must be interesting.

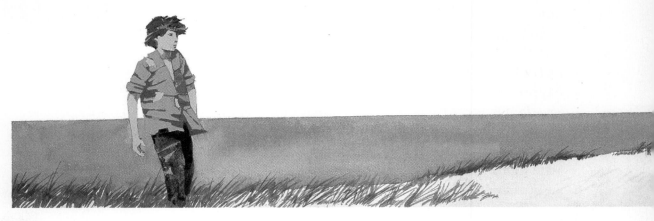

Activity A

Here are some events that could make up a narrative paragraph. On a sheet of paper, write the events in the correct order.

1. "Calm down; we'll work this out," said Jason's father.
2. Jason's parents decided to take the family to New Orleans during the summer vacation.
3. "That's not fair—my friends and I are planning a bike trip then!" Jason exclaimed.
4. Jason's father suggested that Jason call his friends to see if they could make their trip at a later date.
5. "Let's all think of solutions," said Jason's mother.
6. He offered to help the boys choose a place to ride and take them there.
7. "And next time," said Jason's mother, "we'll include you when we make our plans."
8. They told Jason about it one evening at supper.
9. "Wow," said Jason, "that's a pretty good offer! I'm sure my friends will change their plans."
10. Jason and his parents talked over the problem for the next half hour.

Activity B

Here are some more events that are out of order. Put them in order in paragraph form, and add at least four transition words. Then review the paragraph to make sure it reads smoothly.

1. Her family was pleased to see such a delicious meal awaiting them at home.
2. With two overflowing pails in the basket of her bike, she took the ferry back to shore.
3. Last summer Jeanne and her family were spending the month of August at a seaside cottage in Maine.
4. Clever Jeanne had $11.25 to show for her skill at cooking on a budget.
5. For seventy-five cents, she bought a round-trip ticket to an island called Islesboro.
6. Jeanne had an idea, and she quickly rode her bike to the ferry landing.
7. "We'll be back from the beach at 6:30," she added as they left.
8. Once she was home, she cleaned and steamed the clams and mussels, made some butter sauce, and chopped up vegetables for a salad.
9. One afternoon Jeanne's mother said to her, "Dinner is up to you tonight."
10. She rode to a little beach on the island where she knew she could collect plenty of clams and mussels.
11. She gave Jeanne $12.00 and said, "Whatever is left over, you can keep."
12. She dug for shellfish—clams and mussels.

Writer's Corner

▶ Now write your own narrative paragraph. First, brainstorm for an idea. Then list the events as they happened. Finally, write them out as one paragraph. Make sure you use transition words to keep the paragraph flowing smoothly. Reread your paragraph and continue to revise it until you are satisfied with your work.

LESSON 3

Using Your Senses in Writing

> **Writing can come alive when you use your senses—seeing, hearing, touching, smelling, and tasting.**

To become a skilled writer, you must create pictures in the minds of your readers. You need to show them what you mean, not just tell them. One way to help create a picture is to describe things in terms of the senses: seeing, hearing, touching, smelling, and tasting.

Read these two sentences and notice the difference between them. Which sentence just tells and which one shows? What do you see, hear, smell, taste, or touch? What words appeal directly to the senses?

The campfire blazed.	The huge, crackling campfire blazed bright red in the dark forest clearing.

Study the following sentences. Notice how each appeals to a different sense.

Sight
The snow-white horses wore shining silver harnesses and were hitched to a brightly painted circus carriage.

Sound
The foghorn's deep muffled sound rolled through the harbor.

Touch
The youngster ran her hand over the sleek skin of the dolphin. Near its snout, she felt a few smooth hairs and wiry whiskers.

Smell

A mixture of aromas flooded the outdoor market as vendors sold fresh fish, strong cheese, and exotic spices.

Taste

As I heaped the juicy hot dog with mounds of succulent onions, hot green chilies, spicy mustard, tangy ketchup, and a slice of sour dill pickle, my mouth watered in anticipation.

Activity A

Make a chart like the one below. Brainstorm for different words that appeal to the senses. Write them in the appropriate columns.

SIGHT	SOUND	TOUCH	SMELL	TASTE
glistening	shrill	scaly	woodsy	spicy
blinding	thumping	silky	rancid	salty

Activity B

Write a one-sentence description of each item below. Include as many sensory impressions as you can.

1. a flag flying in the wind
2. the feel of a snake
3. a bowl of granola
4. a ride in a helicopter
5. the coldest day of the year
6. the skyline of a big city
7. an ice-cream cone
8. a snowstorm
9. sitting next to a person who is smoking a cigar
10. an oil painting at an art museum
11. a runner finishing a 100-meter sprint
12. a building under construction

Writer's Corner

▶ Choose one of the topics below, and write five descriptive sentences about it. Use as many sensory details as you can. Try to create a clear picture in the reader's mind.

A. a walk through the zoo
B. an exciting amusement park ride
C. the cafeteria at school
D. a bicycle accident
E. a robot that directs traffic

Writing a Descriptive Paragraph

A descriptive paragraph paints a picture with words.

A descriptive paragraph can be challenging to write. It is interesting to try to make the reader see things as you do, and it even frees you to observe more closely. Ideas for descriptive paragraphs can come from just about anywhere—from your own experiences or from your imagination. Read the descriptive paragraphs below from the novel *Sounder* by William H. Armstrong about a boy and his dog, Sounder. These paragraphs occur soon after Sounder was wounded by a sheriff's deputy.

Suddenly a sharp yelp came from the road. Just like when a bee stung Sounder under the porch or a brier caught in his ear in the bramble, the boy thought. In an instant the boy was on his feet. Bruised foot and fingers, throbbing head were forgotten. He raced into the dark. Sounder tried to rise but fell again. There was another yelp, this one constrained and plaintive. The boy, trained in night-sight when the lantern was dimmed so as not to alert the wood's creatures, picked out a blurred shape in the dark.

Sounder staggers home and crawls under the porch to nurse his injury. The boy can only go inside and wait.

Inside the cabin the younger children sat huddled together near the stove. The boy rubbed his hands together near the stovepipe to warm them. His bruised fingers began to throb again. His foot and his head hurt, and he felt a lump rising on the side of his head. If Sounder would whimper or yelp, I would know, the boy thought. But there was no sound, no thump, thump, thump of a paw scratching fleas and hitting the floor underneath.

To what senses do these paragraphs appeal? Give the words or phrases from the paragraphs that appeal to each of the senses you can identify. Describe one picture that either paragraph paints in your mind.

Activity A

From the list below, choose one person, one place, and one thing to describe. Then list as many sense impressions as you can for each one.

Example: A BULL

          Sight: glossy, black, muscular
          Sound: snorting, grunting, bellowing
          Smell: earthy, sweaty
          Touch: solid

1. People: an Olympic swimmer, a circus animal trainer, a salesperson in a fast-food restaurant, a rock singer, a flower vendor, a magician, a chimney sweep

2. Places: a forest, a cave, an empty movie theater, a crowded football stadium, a deserted house

3. Things: a turkey, a space suit, a campfire, a new car, a scarecrow

Activity B

Choose one of the three subjects you described in Activity A, and write a descriptive paragraph of about six sentences. Use the sensory impressions you listed and any others that come to mind. Make sure that what you write follows the rules for writing a good paragraph.

Writer's Corner

▶ Using as many sensory impressions as you can, write a descriptive paragraph about this picture. What would you see, hear, taste, smell, and touch if you were actually in this scene?

LESSON 5

Fact and Opinion

Facts can be proven. Opinions cannot be proven either true or false.

Read the following statements about a political campaign.

A. Yolanda Jones is the best candidate for mayor.
B. Yolanda Jones has lived in the city all her life, and she has supported many community projects in her five years on the city council.

Statement A is a statement of opinion. Other people may have a different opinion about the best candidate for mayor. Statement B expresses facts. It can be shown how long Yolanda Jones has lived in the city, and her voting record on community projects can be checked.

Statement A, the opinion, can be "supported" by statement B. Statement B gives a fact to show why Yolanda Jones might be the best candidate. One good way of supporting opinions is by using facts.

Now read the following two statements from a debate over the best candidate for mayor.

> **RON:** Clyde Baker is the best person for mayor. He has lowered city taxes, attracted new industries to boost employment, and built new hotels to accommodate tourists. Mayor Baker is one of the friendliest political leaders. He is always willing to talk to people about their problems. He's definitely the mayor our city needs.

> **RICK:** Clyde Baker is the best person for mayor. He is one of the nicest, most pleasant persons you would ever want to meet. He is always trying to do what is best for the people. Mayor Baker is fifty-five years old, and both he and his wife are natives of this city. People seem happy and satisfied with Clyde Baker.

Notice how Ron uses both fact and opinion to support his view that Clyde Baker should be reelected mayor. What are the facts? Can they be proven? What are his opinions?

Notice how Rick also uses fact and opinion to support his view about Clyde Baker. What are his facts? Can they be proven? What are his opinions?

When you are trying to persuade someone to think as you do, it is important that the statements supporting your opinions be convincing. For example:

- This is an excellent novel. *It cost $14.95.*
- This is an excellent novel. *It recently won the Newbery Medal.*

The supporting statement *It cost $14.95* is a fact, but the price of the novel does not make it excellent. The supporting statement *It recently won the Newbery Medal* is also a fact. Winning a major book award, however, is more convincing evidence that the novel is excellent.

Reread the statements about Clyde Baker. Both Ron and Rick support Mayor Baker for reelection. Who provides more facts about the mayor's achievements? Why are Ron's statements more convincing than Rick's?

Activity **A**

Here are two students' views on whether to open the school gym during the summer. Identify which statements are facts and which are opinions. Which of the five statements that support each student's view do you think is the most convincing?

1. Jill feels that the school gym should be open during the day in summer.

   a. Over fifty percent of the mothers in this area work. Some mothers need a safe place for their children to go during the day.

   b. Children should be out of the sun during the afternoon.

   c. The gym is the best place to play basketball games.

   d. The gym is in walking distance of many children's houses.

   e. It is one of the best places to spend an afternoon with friends.

2. Bill feels that the school gym should not be open during the day in summer.

   a. Children should be outside during the summer.

   b. Each summer the number of adult volunteers to supervise recreational activities decreases.

   c. The gym is equipped for only one game—basketball.

   d. The younger children and older ones will not play together.

   e. It would require extra personnel and tax money to maintain the gym.

Activity B

The first sentence in each pair is a statement of opinion. Tell whether the supporting sentence, the second sentence, is convincing or not convincing.

1. Speedy Airlines is the best airline.
   Its friendly service, on-time departures, and safety record cannot be beat.

2. For a class party, it is better to serve cupcakes than a sheet cake.
   Cupcakes bake faster than a sheet cake.

3. The town needs to build public swimming pools.
   This would provide a supervised recreational area for children.

4. Our class is the best in the school.
   We have some of the most popular students.

5. Ho-Bo's has the best food in town.
   The meals there are really cheap.

Writer's Corner

▶ **Each sentence below is an opinion. Choose two sentences, and write three strong supporting sentences for each one.**

   A. I should have a party for my friends.
   B. Everyone should take a computer course.
   C. Day-care centers are necessary in our society.
   D. The Right Wardrobe clothing store sells the best clothes.
   E. Our soccer team is the best in the league.

Writing a Persuasive Paragraph

A persuasive paragraph tries to influence the reader's opinion.

Writing a persuasive paragraph is like being in a debate—you want to prove that your opinion is correct. In writing a persuasive paragraph, you state your opinion in the topic sentence and provide supporting facts in the middle sentences. Save your best and most convincing facts for last. Conclude with a strong ending sentence that restates your opinion and explains how you have shown that it is a reasonable one.

Read this example of a persuasive paragraph.

<u>I think our teacher should assign science fiction books as part of reading class</u>. Science fiction is good literature, often more suspenseful and imaginative than other types of books. In science fiction, anything can happen. The fate of the universe might be at stake, a town might be caught in a time warp, or the human race might become invisible. Much that has been written in the past as science fiction has come true today, and much that is written today will probably be true in the twenty-first century. Is there a better way to learn about the future of the world? Most of all, students will never forget what they read, and they will want to read more. Science fiction plots are so clever that they will long be remembered and enjoyed. <u>If teachers want their students to read, they should treat them to the best books of all—science fiction</u>.	Topic sentence states an opinion. Middle sentences provide supporting details. Ending sentence restates the opinion.

Notice the clear, precise writing in the persuasive paragraph on the previous page. Each sentence states exactly why the writer thinks that science fiction is good writing and should be used in school assignments. The writer points out that science fiction is imaginative and teaches about the future. All the sentences flow in a smooth and logical manner. An effective persuasive paragraph should cause the reader to think, "That's true. I never thought of it in that way before."

Activity A

A good way to plan a persuasive paragraph is to state the opinion and then list a series of "becauses," which become the supporting arguments. For each topic following the example, give four details that favor the idea and four that oppose it. Model your answers on the example.

Example:

I. Recess should be longer
   A. because we would have more of a break from our studies
   B. because it would give us more time to relax or exercise
   C. because it would help us come back to our schoolwork feeling more refreshed
   D. because it would make the school day more enjoyable
II. Recess should not be longer
   A. because a longer recess might make it harder for us to get back to concentrating on schoolwork
   B. because we have enough time after school to relax and exercise
   C. because there is hardly enough time in the school day to get in all the subjects
   D. because school is a place for learning, not for relaxing or running around

1. Everyone should study a foreign language in grammar school.
2. Children under twelve should be able to enter all museums, movie theaters, and sports events free of charge.
3. A law should be passed that all bicyclists must wear helmets.

Activity B

The topic is "Schools should arrange more field trips." Do you favor the idea, or do you oppose it? List the details that support your opinion. Then, write a persuasive paragraph using the paragraph on page 115 as a model.

Writer's Corner

▶ **Write a persuasive paragraph on one of the topics listed below.**

A. There is a neighborhood festival near your house that lasts until ten o'clock at night. Persuade your parents to let you stay out later than usual.

B. Persuade other students that you should be the class president.

C. Persuade your teacher that radio headsets should be allowed in class.

D. You have heard both rock music and jazz. Write a paragraph explaining why one is better than the other.

Roots

> **A root (base) is the main part of a word.**
> **Other words can be built from the root.**

You have already learned to use prefixes and suffixes. Prefixes and suffixes are syllables that are added to a root. The root is the most important part of the meaning of a word.

For example, in the word *reopen*, the root is *open*. The word *reopen* means "open again."

Roots come from a number of different languages, but a great many come from either Latin or Greek. For example, *scope* is a root. It comes from a Greek word that means "watch." The prefix *micro* can be added to it to form the word *microscope*, a device for watching or viewing small things. Also, *scope* is a root in the word *telescope*, a device for viewing things that are far away.

Here are some common Latin and Greek roots and their meanings.

ROOT	MEANING
annu	year
geo	earth, surface
mis, mit	to send
phono	sound
sol	alone
vid, vis	to see

Activity A

Copy the chart below, and fill in the missing parts.

PREFIX/SUFFIX	ROOT	NEW WORD	MEANING
1. trans (across)	mis, mit	_____	to send across
2. tele (far)	_____	telephone	a device to send sound far away
3. logy (the study of)	_____	geology	_____
4. ion (the act of)	vid, vis	_____	_____
5. itude (quality of)	sol	_____	quality of being alone
6. al (relating to)	_____	annual	relating to one year

Activity B

Look at the words in column A. Try to determine the meaning of each word from the root. Match each word in column A with the correct meaning in column B. Once you have finished, use the dictionary to check your answers.

COLUMN A

1. solo _____
2. mission _____
3. geometry _____
4. homophones _____
5. invisible _____
6. phonograph _____
7. missile _____
8. semiannually _____
9. solitary _____
10. videotape _____

COLUMN B

a. the measurement of surfaces
b. unable to be seen
c. task one is sent to do
d. a machine that reproduces sounds
e. an object sent or thrown
f. a performance by one person
g. a magnetic tape that reproduces both sounds and pictures
h. words that sound alike but that have different meanings and spellings
i. occurring every half year
j. pertaining to being alone

WRITER'S WORKSHOP

A Story from Art

You can tell a story with a picture. Of course, you can tell a story with words, too. Imagine what a good story you can tell with both pictures and words! Write a narrative about the painting on the following page. Display the picture or a copy of it, along with your narrative, on a class bulletin board.

 Prewriting

Examine the painting on the next page. Make a list of all your ideas about the painting.

The questions below will help you find a story in the painting.

- What details from the background show where the action in the painting takes place?

- How would you describe the people in the painting?

- About when in history do you think the people in the painting lived? Why do you think so?

- What are the boys in the painting doing?

- Does the painting remind you of anything you've ever done?

- How do you think each person in the painting feels about what is happening?

Imagine that you could rewind or fast forward the scene in the picture. What do you think happened just before the scene? What do you think will happen next? Add your new ideas to your list.

Choose a Point of View
The narrator, or person who tells the story, may be a character in the painting or a person who is observing the scene. If you write your narrative from the point of view of one of the characters, use pronouns like *I, me,* and *we.* If you write your narrative from an observer's point of view, use words such as *the boys* and *they.*

Drafting

In a narrative, the writer usually relates the events in the order in which they occur. Before you begin your draft, circle the events from your list of prewriting notes that you will use in your story. Number the events to show their order.

As soon as you've chosen a point of view, you're ready to start writing. Begin with a sentence that sets the stage and captures your reader's attention.

Use your prewriting notes to write the events in the body of the narrative. Expand your notes into sentences to tell your story. You can make the sequence of events clear by using transition words such as *first, then,* and *finally.*

End with a sentence that sums up your narrator's feelings about the events in the narrative.

Revising, Proofreading, and Publishing

 Revising

Time to Take Another Look

Now revise your narrative. Make sure there are no gaps or holes in your story. Make your narrative sound as exciting as the picture looks.

Reread your narrative carefully, and ask yourself the following questions.

❏ Does my narrative sound as if the whole story was written from the same point of view?

❏ Does the body of my narrative tell the events clearly?

❏ Do I need to add words like *first, then,* and *finally* to make the order of events clear to the reader?

❏ Do I need to add sensory details to make my reader feel a part of my narrative?

❏ Do I need to cut out unnecessary words, phrases, or sentences to make my narrative flow better?

❏ Do I need to substitute more interesting words?

❏ Does my conclusion sum up my narrator's feelings about the events in the story?

Use a colored pencil to revise your narrative so your revisions will stand out.

Vary Your Sentence Order

Look at individual sentences in your narrative. Do all the sentences begin with the subject? Even the most exciting story can sound dull if all the sentences begin the same way. As you revise, begin some sentences with adverbs or prepositional phrases. Try turning a few sentences around.

Gary's draft looked like this:

The line started moving before I was ready. I flew through the air. I rolled over the bumpy ground.

He revised it this way:

Before I was ready, the line started moving. Suddenly I flew through the air. Over the bumpy ground I rolled.

 **Proofreading**

Time to Look at Capitalization, Punctuation, and Spelling

Before you write your final copy, proofread your draft to check your capitalization, punctuation, spelling, and grammar.

Use the checklist below to proofread and edit your narrative.

❏ Did I indent the first word of each paragraph?

❏ Did I begin each sentence and proper noun with a capital letter?

❏ Did I use marks of punctuation correctly?

❏ Did I spell each word correctly?

Start Backwards
To avoid being distracted by the story as you proofread, begin with the last word of your story and read backwards, word by word.

 Publishing

Time to Share

Share your narrative about the painting by publishing it.

To publish, follow these steps:

1. Copy your revised draft in your neatest handwriting or type it on a computer.

2. After you finish, proofread your final copy one more time.

3. Check to be sure you did not leave anything out as you copied.

Make the class bulletin board display.

1. Ask a good artist in the class to draw a copy of the painting for the center of the bulletin board, or prop up the book open to the picture underneath the board.

2. Make a title for the display.

3. Mount your narrative on construction paper and attach it to the bulletin board.

4. Read all the narratives to see how many different ideas can spring from the same painting.

Learning More About Writing

LESSON 1

Taking Notes and Preparing an Outline

Taking notes and making an outline help you organize your ideas before you begin to write.

Taking notes and outlining are especially helpful when you are writing a factual composition, or report. Suppose you choose earthquakes as the topic of your report. You first need to read some books and articles about your topic. You also need to think of at least three questions you would like answered about the topic. Write each question at the top of a separate index card.

For a report on earthquakes, here are three possible questions:

1. What causes earthquakes?
2. Where do earthquakes occur?
3. What damage can earthquakes cause?

As you find answers to your questions, jot the answers down on the appropriate card. At the bottom of each card, write the source of your information. A source is a book, article, or anything you may have read in order to gather information about your topic.

About the Photograph

Choosing a topic is just the beginning when writing a report. What do you do next?

Chapter 5 **127**

Your index cards might look like this:

What causes earthquakes?

Earthquakes are sudden shocks to the surface of the earth. They occur when great pressure is put on rock. The rock begins to bend and fold. The pressure becomes so great that the rock splits and the earth moves. These splits are called faults.

All About Earthquakes, p. 11

Where do earthquakes occur?

Many earthquakes occur along fault lines. The lines usually are in areas where new mountains or trenches have formed, rather than on older, flat parts of the earth. Most earthquakes occur under the sea. Many occur along the circum-Pacific belt, along the edge of the Pacific Ocean.

Young Adult Encyclopedia, Vol. 3, p. 75

What damage can earthquakes cause?

Buildings collapse, tidal waves form, and fires often break out. Thousands of people can lose their lives.

Earthquakes, p. 123

Your questions will become the main topics of your outline. Each main topic begins with a Roman numeral followed by a period. The topics of the outline on earthquakes would be:

I. What causes earthquakes?

II. Where do earthquakes occur?

III. What damage can earthquakes cause?

Next you need to fill in two or more subtopics under each main topic. Each subtopic begins with a capital letter that is followed by a period. The subtopics should come from the material in your notes. Subtopics are the answers to the questions (main topics). The subtopics may be phrases or complete sentences.

I. What causes earthquakes? (main topic)

   A. An earthquake is a shock to the earth's surface. (subtopic)

   B. Great pressure is put on rock. (subtopic)

   C. Rock splits and folds. (subtopic)

   D. The earth moves. (subtopic)

II. Where do earthquakes occur? (main topic)

Once the outline is complete, you are ready to begin writing. Each main topic with its subtopics will be one paragraph in your report.

Activity A

Below is an outline about air traffic controllers. The outline is not numbered or lettered correctly. On a sheet of paper, rewrite the outline as it should be. Use the outline on earthquakes as a model.

A. Requirements for an air traffic controller
   1. College education
   2. Physical and mental tests
   3. Extensive training program

B. Job responsibilities
   1. Give directions to pilots
   2. Ensure on-ground safety
   3. Ensure in-flight safety

C. Working conditions
   1. Irregular working hours
   2. Constant pressure
   3. Feeling of accomplishment

Activity B

Below is a mixed-up outline for a report on dinosaurs. The main topics are labeled correctly, but the subtopics on the right are out of order. Write the outline correctly.

I. What is a dinosaur?
   A.
   B.
   C.

II. How did dinosaurs live?
   A.
   B.
   C.

III. Why did dinosaurs disappear?
   A.
   B.
   C.

Asteroid crash
When they lived
Definition
Change in plant life
Kinds of dinosaurs
Diet
Reproduction
Cooling of climate
Group life

Writer's Corner

▶ The main topics of an outline about caves are given below.
Put them in logical order, and then use an encyclopedia or
other source of information to complete the outline.
Compare your outline with that of another student.

What famous caves are in the United States?
What are caves?
What animals live in caves?

Writing a Report

The composition you write from a factual outline is called a report.

Once you have organized your information in outline form, your report is nearly written. Each main topic with its subtopics will be one paragraph in your report. Each subtopic provides a starting point for the supporting sentences of your paragraph. You can return to your notes to obtain facts to help develop your supporting sentences. In this way, you can put together a rough draft of your report.

Look at the following part of an outline on the topic Technology Changes Our Lives, and then read the first paragraph of the report. Notice how the paragraph tells about main topic I.

Technology Changes Our Lives
I. How did technology change everyday life in the 1950s?
   A. Appliances saved time.
   B. New electronic devices entertained.
   C. Frozen dinners changed eating habits.

The 1950s in America was a time of change. New products changed the way people lived their everyday lives. New appliances, such as electric ranges and frost-free refrigerators, saved working time. New electronic devices, such as color televisions and transistor radios, made for fun entertainment. People's eating habits changed, too. You simply pulled a frozen TV dinner from your frost-free refrigerator, heated it up in your electric range, and ate it while watching your favorite show on your new color TV.

Activity A

The second part of the outline for the report Technology Changes Our Lives is given below. Complete this outline on a sheet of paper using your own knowledge or by looking up facts in an encyclopedia or another information source. Then write a paragraph from your outline. The topic sentence for the second paragraph has been written for you.

II. How has technology changed everyday life today?
    A. Personal computers . . .
    B. Internet . . .
    C. Cable TV . . .
    D. Cellular phones . . .

Topic sentence: Recent technology has made it possible for people to get information and entertainment more quickly and easily.

Activity B

Use the main topic provided below and create your own subtopics to form the third part of the outline. This will help you write the third paragraph of the report. This time, write a topic sentence on your own, and include a sentence for each subtopic you write. You may include other facts that are related to the main topic. In your last sentence, or concluding sentence, sum up everything you have written and bring the report to a close.

III. How might technology change life in the future?

    A. _____
    B. _____
    C. _____

Writer's Corner

▶ Choose a topic from either your social studies or your science class. Take notes from your textbook, an encyclopedia, or another source of information. Write an outline for a three-paragraph report on the topic. After you have finished the outline, write a report based on it. Be sure to develop your paragraphs carefully.

Writing a Story: Setting and Characters

The setting describes when and where a story occurs. Characters are the people and animals in a story.

Writing a story can be very enjoyable. The writer tries to entertain a reader by recounting an interesting set of events. The events do not have to be true. They can come partly, or completely, from the writer's own imagination.

The greatest challenge in writing a story is to capture and keep the reader's interest. A good way of doing this is to make the story seem real. You have already learned many skills that can bring a story to life. You have learned to use colorful words, similes, metaphors, and sensory impressions to create pictures in the reader's mind. You have also learned to write smooth narrative paragraphs with effective transition words. Now you will have a chance to use your skills of description and narration by writing a story.

One of the first steps in writing a story is to create a believable setting. A good writer tries to put the reader into the setting. Read the following paragraph from Irene Hunt's novel *Across Five Aprils,* the story of a woman and her son during the Civil War years. How does the author's description make the setting seem to come to life?

Ellen Creighton and her nine-year-old son, Jethro, were planting potatoes in the half-acre just south of their cabin that morning in mid-April, 1861; they were out in the field as soon as breakfast was over, and southern Illinois at that hour was pink with sunrise and swelling redbud and clusters of bloom over the apple orchard across the road. Jethro walked on the warm clods of plowed earth and felt them crumble beneath his feet as he helped his mother carry the tub of potato cuttings they had prepared the night before.

Once the story's time and place have been established, the author will try to describe the characters in a way that will arouse the reader's interest. In the following paragraph, the author introduces the character of Ellen Creighton. After reading the paragraph, tell what you feel about Ellen. What does she look like? What kind of life has she had?

She was a small, spare woman with large dark eyes and skin as brown and dry as leather. She had been a pretty girl back in the 1830s when she married Matthew Creighton, but prettiness was short-lived among country women of her time; she didn't think much about it anymore except now and then when Jenny's fourteen-year-old radiance was especially compelling. . . . She had borne twelve children, four of whom were dead—perhaps five, for the oldest son had not been heard from since he left for the goldfields of California twelve years before; she had lived through sickness, poverty, and danger for over thirty years; the sight of a pretty face might bring a smile to her lips, but it was a thing of little value in Ellen's world.

Notice how the writer has included information about how Ellen looked, as well as facts about her life. A skilled writer can use descriptions of setting and character to make a story come alive and to capture the reader's interest.

Activity A

Create an interesting setting for any two of the items below. Write at least one paragraph for each. Remember to use the skills you have learned to try to "paint a picture" in your reader's mind.

A. Swimming races at the local pool

B. Your living room decorated for a party

C. A landing of creatures from another planet

D. A busy city street

E. A safari in Africa

F. Any event of your choice

Activity B

Now think of one character for each of the two settings you have just created. Use colorful words to tell what the character looks like. For example, instead of "The guide had an interesting face," you could say, "The guide's tanned, weather-beaten face gave witness to his years of experience in the African bush." Next, tell something more about the character. How does the character fit into the setting or scene? What are his or her thoughts or feelings?

Writer's Corner

▶ Think of another character for a story, and then create a setting into which to put the character. Write at least two paragraphs. Remember to make the character and setting interesting, colorful, and believable.

Writing a Story: Plot

The plot of a story is the series of events it describes.

Although setting and character are important, much of the pleasure of reading a story comes from following an intriguing plot as it unravels. As a reader, you want to know what happens. You may be surprised to learn, however, that the plot of most stories—a novel, a play, or a short story—will follow the same four steps outlined below.

1. *Introduction:* The setting and some of the important characters are presented. Setting and characters by themselves, however, do not make a story. In order for the action to begin, the main character must have a problem. There must be a situation in which something needs to be done. For example, think of a simple detective story. Something may be stolen or missing and the detective must find it. In a series of books by Donald Sobol, Encyclopedia Brown is a young detective who is often called upon to find missing objects.

2. *Development:* The problem or situation moves along and gets more complex. The main character may seek solutions or simply avoid the problem and suffer the consequences. Whatever happens, the problem is always central. In the detective story, for example, Encyclopedia Brown interviews the owner of a stolen giant watermelon, gathers information, and looks for clues.

3. *Climax:* This is the high point of the story—the most interesting and exciting part. All the action up to now has led to this point. The reader finally discovers what really happened. In the climax of a detective story, the detective finds out who the thief is and often goes through an exciting and dangerous chase to catch the person.

4. *Conclusion:* In the conclusion, the problem is solved, but not always happily. There may be a sad or a surprise ending. In the conclusion of the Encyclopedia Brown story, he explains what clues led him to the thief. The reader discovers why the crime was committed—and the fate of the giant watermelon.

Activity A

Your library contains many good stories. Read a story or review one that you have already read. When you have finished, summarize the parts of the plot by completing a chart that looks like this:

Title _____ Author _____

Introduction (setting, characters, and problem) _____

_____

_____

_____

Development (series of events) _____

_____

_____

_____

Climax (high point) _____

_____

_____

_____

Conclusion (problem solved) _____

_____

_____

_____

Activity B

In the activities on page 136, you created two settings with a character for each setting. Choose your favorite and develop a plot by briefly answering the following questions. (Add more characters if necessary.)

1. What will the problem or conflict be?

2. How will the story develop? (List a series of events that involve the character and the problem.)

3. How will the story reach a climax?

4. How will the story end?

Writer's Corner

▶ Use your setting, characters, and plot outline from Activity B to write the first draft of a short story. Remember to use the skills you have learned to make the story interesting, lifelike, and believable.

LESSON 5

Making Characters Talk

Dialogue, or conversation, makes characters come alive.

Stories become more lifelike when characters speak to one another. Dialogue reveals the thoughts and emotions of the characters while also revealing important events in the story.

Read the following dialogue from a short story about a girl's clever attempts to get the autograph of her favorite rock musician. What does the dialogue reveal about the characters? What do you think will happen? (Wendy's friend is the narrator, the *I*. The *she* is Wendy.)

I follow her to one of those telephones that connect the caller to hotel rooms. She dials a number. She waits. Then she says, "Craig the Cat, please." She looks at me. "I found him! Listen!" She tilts the receiver so that I, too, can hear what's being said. It's a strain, but I can hear.

A woman is on the other end. "How did you find out where Craig the Cat is staying?" she asks. "The leak. I need to know where the leak is."

"There isn't any. I'm the only one with the information. Please be nice. I want his autograph."

"Who doesn't!"

"Help me get it, please. What are my chances?"

"Poor to nonexistent."

"Oh."

"I'm his manager and, my dear, I'm his mother. I protect Craig from two vantage points. I keep a low profile. Now, how many other fans know where he's staying?"

140

> "None that I know of."
>
> "You mean you didn't peddle the information to the highest bidder?"
>
> "I wouldn't do that."
>
> "Maybe not, dear, but I'm tired of his fans. They tug at Craig's whiskers. They pull his tail. Leave him alone! I'm hanging up." Click.

To find out what happens with Wendy and the musician who dresses as a cat, read Marjorie Sharmat's "May I Have Your Autograph?"

Here are some points to keep in mind when writing dialogue.

- Indent and begin a new paragraph each time a different character speaks.
- Enclose the speaker's words in quotation marks.
- Use commas to separate the name of the speaker from his or her exact words. For example: "Now that I think about it," said Billy, "maybe I will have some ice cream."
- Remember to put the quotation marks after the punctuation that ends or interrupts the quote.

Activity A

Review the four points above for writing dialogue, and rewrite this dialogue with the correct punctuation and indentation.

> Oooh, groaned Eric, as his father nudged him to wake up Wednesday morning, I feel terrible today. What's the problem? asked his father. My head is throbbing with pain, Eric complained, my stomach is upset, and all my muscles feel weak. Is that all? his father asked. I think I have a fever, too, Eric added. It's probably from playing football out in the snow yesterday. I got all wet and tired. That must be what did it. Well, said his father I guess you'll have to stay home from school today. Will you miss anything important? Oh, not much he replied just a small science test, and I think there might be a math test, too.

Activity B

Make the situations below come alive by creating dialogue. Have each person speak only once.

Example: A lifeguard speaking to a swimmer
        "Please don't run around the sides of the pool," cautioned the lifeguard.
        "Sorry," said Mark, "I was playing a game and I forgot."

1. Two people caught in an elevator during a power failure
2. A person calling the janitor of the apartment building
3. A boy and girl talking about taking part in a fund-raising drive
4. A husband and wife as they see a baseball crashing through their window
5. A student talking with a teacher about a homework assignment

Writer's Corner

▶ Make up two situations like those listed in Activity B, and write each situation on a separate piece of paper. Put your pieces of paper in a jar or box along with the papers of the other students. Pick out one piece of paper and write six interesting lines of dialogue for the particular situation.

LESSON 6
Writing About Characters from Books

Writing a description of a character from a book is one way of reporting on a book you have read.

In each new book and short story you read, you meet new people. Many are colorful and exciting individuals to whom you may become quite attached. These new friends sometimes have a great influence on your life. In fact, you might even want to share your book friends with your real-life friends. Your writing skills can help you do this when you create an interesting paragraph about a favorite book character. Read the following description of a famous detective you might meet in your own book adventures.

My name is Sherlock Holmes, and I reside at Number 221B Baker Street in nineteenth-century London, England. It is there that my clients come to see me, for I am a detective—a *master* detective, one might say. Many consider me the world's greatest sleuth. Perhaps you have seen me at work. I am quite tall and thin with a checked, two-peaked cap and an ever-present pipe that hangs over my chin. With my companion Dr. Watson at my side, I have solved numerous baffling mysteries, such as one eerie case involving the devilish "hound of the Baskervilles." On every case, I look closely at the clues and try to understand what they tell me. Next, I often set a trap to snare the evildoer. Invariably, Dr. Watson is amazed and perplexed at my solutions. "Elementary, my dear Watson," I always exclaim, as I describe my logical deductions from the available clues. Watson may remain confused, but he is always happy that the case has been solved and all is well—at least until the next crime is committed.

Notice how the writer "became" the character by using the pronoun *I*. Writing in the first person is one good way of sharing a character with others. Find the answers to these questions in the paragraph you just read.

1. Who is the main character?

2. When and where does this character live?

3. How does this character look?

4. What makes this character special?

Activity A

List interesting characters you have met in novels or short stories. Write a two- or three-sentence description of three of these characters.

Activity B

Copy the form below on a sheet of paper, and write a first-person descriptive paragraph about one of the characters you listed in Activity A. Use the sample description of Sherlock Holmes on page 143 as a model.

Title _____

Author _____

Type of Book or Story _____

Paragraph About Character _____

_____

_____

_____

_____

Writer's Corner

▶ Choose two more characters from the list you made for Activity A. Use your imagination to describe a meeting between the two characters. The characters do not have to be from the same time or place. Use picture words and dialogue to make the conversation come alive.

Writing a Book Report

A book report is a formal way of writing about a book you have read. The report includes a summary and a personal reaction.

In this chapter, you have learned to write a factual report by first taking notes, then putting together an outline, and, finally, turning your outline into a series of paragraphs. You have also learned to write a story by using colorful language to create an intriguing setting and characters and by constructing a plot that will hold a reader's interest. When you write a book report, you use all of these skills: you are writing a report that tells about a story.

A book report contains the following information:
- the book's title
- the author
- the kind of book it is
- the names of the characters
- a summary of the story
- your own personal reaction to the book

Read the model report beginning on the next page about the novel *Johnny Tremain*.

Book reports like the model are useful for a number of reasons. A book report will help you remember the story and how you felt about it. Others who read the report can decide if they would like to read the book. Most important, writing a book report teaches you to analyze a book and to put your reaction to it into words.

Model: A Book Report

TITLE: *Johnny Tremain*

AUTHOR: Esther Forbes

KIND OF BOOK: Historical fiction

CHARACTERS: Johnny Tremain, Mr. and Mrs. Lapham, Dusty, Dove, Rab, Doctor Warren, Paul Revere, and other patriots of the Revolutionary period

SUMMARY: *Johnny Tremain* is a story about a young boy living in Boston at the time of the American Revolution. The novel begins about 1773 when we meet Johnny living with the Lapham family. Mr. Lapham, at this time, was a silversmith who was teaching Johnny and two other apprentices, Dusty and Dove, the trade. Johnny was bright, gifted, and very capable of performing his duties, but sometimes he seemed to lord it over the other two boys. However, all this changed with a tragic accident. A container of molten silver broke and spilled over Johnny's right hand, making it useless.

Johnny was then forced to look for a new home and new work. During this period of his life, he became very discouraged and depressed.

Johnny met a young boy named Rab, who secured for him a home and work as a dispatch rider for the Committee of Public Safety. The work introduced him to Paul Revere, James Otis, John Hancock, John and Samuel Adams, and other important Boston patriots. These men found Johnny trustworthy and courageous, and permitted him to share in the events leading to the Boston Tea Party and the Battle of Lexington.

On the battlefield, Johnny learned from Doctor Warren that with treatment he would be able to use his hand again. His goal of becoming a great silversmith seemed possible, and the future looked bright.

REACTION: The novel *Johnny Tremain* held my interest from beginning to end. Reading about the exciting adventures of those early days in Boston, I saw a picture of the struggle for American liberty through the eyes of a clever, courageous, and patriotic boy of fourteen.

Activity A

Review the model book report and answer these questions.

1. Who is the author of *Johnny Tremain?*

2. Who is Johnny Tremain?

3. What is the problem, or conflict, in *Johnny Tremain?*

4. How is the problem resolved?

5. Why does the writer of the book report like *Johnny Tremain?*

6. Would you like to read *Johnny Tremain?* Why, or why not?

Activity B

Think of a book or short story that you particularly enjoyed and answer these questions about it.

1. What is the title?

2. Who is the author?

3. What kind of book or story is it?

4. Who are the important characters?

5. What is the problem or conflict?

6. What does the main character do to solve the problem?

7. What is the conclusion?

8. Why did you like this book or story?

Writer's Corner

▶ The information you provided for Activity B gives you the basic outline for a report on the book or story. Complete a report on that book or story in book report form. Remember to make the summary and reaction colorful and interesting. Draw a picture of one scene from the story and include it in your report.

Homophones

> **Homophones are words that sound alike but that have different spellings and meanings.**

Many writers are confused by words that sound alike but that have different spellings and meanings. These words are called homophones.

> Into the pitch black *night*, the *knight* rode on his white charger.

In the sentence above, *night* and *knight* are homophones.

Be careful to use the correct spelling of words that are homophones. Always check the dictionary if you are unsure of a spelling.

Activity A

Give the definitions for each pair of homophones below. Use a dictionary if necessary.

1. bough—bow
2. coarse—course
3. knot—not
4. patience—patients
5. peace—piece
6. root—route
7. stationary—stationery
8. some—sum
9. threw—through
10. weather—whether

Activity B

Complete each sentence with the correct homophone. Use the words listed in Activity A. Each word on the list should be used once.

1. A multicolored bird sat on the _____ of the tree and sang.
2. Vegetables, such as turnips, that grow underground are called _____ vegetables.
3. The submarine was far off _____ .
4. Radar is an instrument used in _____ forecasting.
5. _____ seabirds travel more than 20,000 miles in their migrations.
6. Tricia fielded the ground ball and _____ it to first base.
7. The nomads wear loose garments made out of a _____ material that they weave themselves.
8. Gabriel could _____ decide _____ to study arithmetic or to play volleyball.
9. After one week on the exhausting paper _____ , Araceli added up the _____ of her earnings.
10. Making a tiny model plane requires _____ .
11. We drove _____ a long tunnel on our way into New York.
12. Afraid his arm was broken, Alex sat in the emergency room among the other _____ .
13. Violet writes letters on her new _____ .
14. The sailor fastened the rowboat to the pier with an expertly tied _____ .
15. The magician took a _____ and disappeared from the stage amid smoke and applause.
16. The important telephone number was on a tiny _____ of paper.
17. Now, desks in schools are movable; in the past, they were often _____ .
18. The dove is a symbol of _____ .

WRITER'S WORKSHOP

How and Why Tales

Do you ever wonder how things came to be? Why does the sun rise every day? Why do skunks have white stripes? Long ago, people wondered the same things, and they did not have science to explain. So they told imaginative stories to help them understand. The tales they told are now called how and why tales. Write a how and why tale. Publish it in a class How and Why book.

 Prewriting

Make a list of amazing things that happen in nature. Imagine what you would think if you couldn't go to an encyclopedia to find out what causes these things to happen.

Use the following questions to help you think about nature.

- What animals move in unusual ways?

- What are some strange or unusual-looking animals?

- What things in nature happen over and over again?

- What kinds of natural disasters can you think of?

- What unusual plants can you name?

- What things always happen during special kinds of weather?

Look at your list of ideas about nature. Choose one idea to write about. Then write a question about your idea.

> Why do kangaroos hop?
>
> How did the rainbow get its colors?

Write the answer to your question in a few short sentences. Then write a short description of the setting and characters that will appear in your how and why tale.

Use Dialogue

Make your characters seem real by writing dialogue, or the words the characters say, in your story. Remember to use quotation marks around the characters' exact words.

> "Grasshopper, I wish I could jump like you," said Kangaroo.
>
> "Have you tried to jump?" Grasshopper asked.

Drafting

As you write your draft, remember that how and why tales are a special kind of folk tale. Folk tales are stories that have been handed down through the years. Make your how and why tale sound like an old story by beginning with phrases like these:

- Long ago, . . .
- When the world was very young . . .

The characters in a how and why tale are often, but not always, animals. They usually have a special character trait.

Sometimes it is a bad trait, such as lying or being vain. Sometimes the character is very brave or honest and wins a special gift, such as wings. In your how and why tale, make your main character's actions show his or her personality.

Develop the plot by showing how your character solves a problem, makes a decision, or faces danger.

The conclusion of your story will be the answer to the question you wrote to begin your prewriting notes.

Why Giraffes Are the Tallest Animals

Long ago, Giraffe had a very short neck. He was so small he couldn't even see himself. One day Giraffe complained to Elephant. Elephant told him about a pool that was so clear that Giraffe would surely be able to see himself.

Elephant and Giraffe dashed excitedly to the edge of the pool. But Giraffe's neck was so short, he could not see into the water.

"I have an idea," said Elephant, and he wrapped Giraffe's legs in his trunk. Giraffe stretched his head and neck out over the water and looked down.

"Oh, I am so beautiful!" exclaimed Giraffe, and he kept stretching and stretching until he had stretched himself right across the whole pool.

With his long, long neck, Giraffe was now taller than any other animal in the jungle. To this day, no animal is as tall as the giraffe.

Revising, Proofreading, and Publishing

Revising

A Time to Take Another Look

As you revise your how and why tale, imagine that you live in a long ago time. Pretend you are telling your story to entertain and teach your friends and family members as they sit around a glowing fire.

Use these questions to help you revise your draft.

- ❏ Does my title let my readers know what they are going to learn?

- ❏ Do I need to rewrite dialogue to show my main character's personality?

- ❏ Do the events of my plot follow each other in logical order?

- ❏ Do I need to replace boring, overused words with more interesting ones?

- ❏ Does my ending answer the question the title suggests?

Write the changes on your draft with a colored pencil. Then read over the revised draft to make sure all the changes are clear.

Listen to Your Story

Read your story into a tape recorder or ask a partner to read it aloud. As you listen, take notes about ways to make your story flow better, be clearer, or sound more exciting.

Proofreading

Time to Look at Capitalization, Punctuation, and Spelling

Before you write the final copy that will become part of the class book, check your capitalization, punctuation, spelling, and grammar to make your how and why tale look and read its best.

Use the checklist below to edit and proofread your work.

❑ Did I use marks of punctuation correctly?

❑ Did I use quotation marks correctly in my dialogue?

❑ Did I write clear and complete sentences?

❑ Did I spell all the words correctly?

Capitalize Character Names

Usually when you write the name of a kind of animal, you begin with a lowercase letter. But if you named your character Giraffe or Rabbit, be sure to capitalize the word whenever you use it as a name, as in the following sentence.

Because <u>R</u>abbit was so vain, all <u>r</u>abbits now have short, stubby tails.

 Publishing

Time to Share

Folktales are meant to be shared. Share your how and why tale by publishing it.

To publish, follow these steps:

1. Copy your revised draft in your neatest handwriting or type it on a computer.

2. Reread your final copy to be sure there are no errors.

3. Add an illustration if you wish.

Make a class How and Why book.

1. Collect all the tales.

2. Make a table of contents.

3. Make a book cover and bind the pages together.

4. Ask permission to read your book to a class of younger children.

5. Place your book in the class library so everyone can enjoy your tales.

Writing Letters

The Parts of a Social Letter

A social letter is made up of a heading, salutation, body, complimentary close, and signature.

Do you have a close friend who lives in another city? A favorite relative who lives hundreds or even thousands of miles away? Unfortunately, the people you like best do not always live near you. Even though you cannot see them often, you can keep in touch with friends and relatives by writing letters.

What are some of the things you can share in a letter? When you are with a friend, you probably tell stories and jokes, and you talk about new experiences and future plans. You can share the same things when you write a friendly letter. Letters can be enjoyable to write and to receive.

You probably have already written some, or even many, social letters. Let's review the parts of a social letter so that you will use the correct form. A social letter contains five parts.

1. heading
2. salutation
3. body of the letter
4. complimentary close
5. signature

Read the letter on page 158, and take careful note of each part.

About the Photograph

These girls became good friends at summer camp. They still keep in touch by writing letters. Do you have any friends you keep in touch with through letter writing?

2690 Rouen Street

Denver, CO 80220

December 3, 19_

Dear Roberta,

I enjoyed getting your letter last week. It really made me homesick for all my old friends in Houston. I am getting to like Denver, though. I especially like the Colorado Heritage Center. It has items from the early cliff dwellers who once lived in this area.

Another thing I like about Denver is the snow. I've never seen so much snow! I'm taking skiing lessons, and my mom is going to buy me a complete ski outfit for Christmas (I hope!). So far, this city seems as if it will be great to live in.

Write soon and let me know what's going on with all my Houston friends.

Your good friend,

Jenny

Heading

The heading of a letter contains the address of the writer and the date. It is usually written on three lines. The street address is written on the first line; the city, state, and zip code on the second line; and the date on the third line. The heading is written slightly to the right of the center of the paper, about an inch from the top of the sheet. If the letter is extremely short, the heading may be lowered. Ordinarily each line is written directly under the one above it. This is called block form.

Brief letters, or social notes, sometimes use only the date in the heading. Invitations, thank-you notes, and notes of acceptance or regret are examples of social notes.

Salutation

The salutation is the greeting at the beginning of a letter. It is only one line long and begins at the left-hand margin. The salutation varies, depending on the person to whom the letter is written. The first word and the person's name are always capitalized, and there is always a comma at the end of the salutation in a social letter.

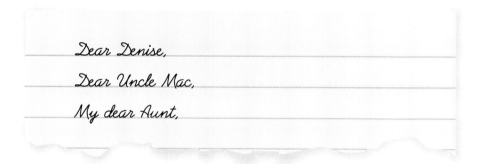

Dear Denise,

Dear Uncle Mac,

My dear Aunt,

Body

The body of the letter is the most important part because it contains the message. In this part, you write news about yourself that will be of interest to the person to whom you are writing. In the next lesson, you will learn more about writing the body of some special kinds of social letters.

Complimentary Close

The complimentary close lets the reader know that the letter is ending. The first word begins with a capital letter and should line up with (be exactly under) the first word of the heading. The complimentary close is always followed by a comma. Make sure that the complimentary close is appropriate for the person to whom you are writing.

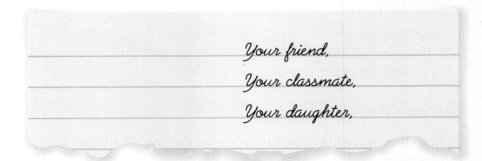

Your friend,

Your classmate,

Your daughter,

Signature

The signature is the name of the person who is writing the letter. When you are writing to relatives and close friends, use your first name only. If the person to whom you are writing does not know you very well, use your full name. The name always begins with a capital letter, and there is no punctuation mark after the name. Write your signature neatly under the first word of the complimentary close.

Activity A

Arrange each of the following addresses and dates in the proper form for the heading of a letter. Use the current year for the date in your headings.

1. April 27, 19__ , Anchorage, Alaska 99510, 123 Yukon Avenue
2. Chicago, Illinois 60613, June 29, 19__ , 3843 North Greenview Avenue
3. 438 North Street, June 10, 19__ , Norfolk, Virginia 23500
4. August 1, 19__ , Pennsbury Hospital, Jonesboro, Arkansas 72401

Activity B

Write the salutation for a letter written to each person listed below.

1. your mother
2. a very close friend
3. your cousin Teresa
4. Mrs. Gurek, a teacher in your school
5. your Aunt Sally
6. a classmate
7. Mr. Santelli, your coach
8. your brother

Activity C

Write the complimentary close for a letter written to each person listed below.

1. a classmate
2. your uncle
3. your brother
4. the captain of your soccer team
5. your teacher
6. a friend
7. your parents
8. your cousin Alan

Writer's Corner

▶ Think of three people you know who live too far away for you to visit very often. On a sheet of paper, write a heading, a salutation, and a complimentary close for a letter to each of them.

LESSON 2

Writing Social Letters

Types of social letters include the friendly letter, the invitation, and the thank-you letter.

The social letter is a form of writing that helps you keep in touch with people you know. The more you improve your writing skills, the more entertaining and informative your social letters will be.

Three types of social letters include the friendly letter, the invitation, and the thank-you letter. Remember the following points as you write each type of letter:

- Talk about one topic only in each paragraph and finish that topic before introducing a new one.
- Always write complete sentences.
- Indent the first sentence of each paragraph about one inch.

In friendly letters, friends exchange news about each other (just as the writer of the letter in Lesson 1 did). Read the friendly letter on the next page, in which a boy tells of his new hobby. Does the letter writer follow the rules of a good paragraph in describing his hobby? Does he write complete sentences? Is each paragraph indented?

Model: A Friendly Letter

105 Powder Boulevard

Dixon, IL 61021

December 17, 19__

Dear Jim,

It was really great to hear from you. Your drawing class sounds like lots of fun. I'm glad to hear that you saved up enough money to buy a drum set. It seems as if you're keeping very busy.

I've been quite occupied myself. You know that I was never the type to have hobbies, but in the past few months I've become a stamp collector. It started when my Uncle Ted sent me postcards as he traveled throughout Europe. I never realized before how many different stamps there were in the world. Now I look forward to the mail delivery and to each new collection that I have been able to order. Friends from all over have promised to watch carefully for any unusual stamps. Would you like to help me, too?

Say hello to your family, Jim. I'm glad you all like your new home.

Your friend,

Jason

An invitation should be as natural as a friendly letter. It should also state very clearly the kind of event, the day, the time, and the place. An invitation should be written so that the person who receives it will want to accept. Read this model invitation. Does it provide all the needed information? Does it make you want to attend the party?

Model: An Invitation

1666 Wall Street

Moline, IL 61265

December 5, 19____

Dear Anne,

Are the first blasts of winter's cold getting you down? Does the early darkness make you feel like hibernating until April? If that's how you feel (or even if it isn't), please join us in cheering up the season with a tree-trimming party and dinner on December 17. My family would love to have you come to our house at two o'clock.

Your friend,
Becky

A thank-you letter shows your appreciation for a favor you have received. In your letter, you should try to make the person feel good about what he or she did. Read the following and decide if it is an effective thank-you letter.

Model: A Thank-You Letter

99 Hamp Street
Denver, CO 80220
June 5, 19__

Dear Aunt Gail,

Thanks so much for giving me your old baseball card collection. It has many players that will make me the envy of all my friends who are collectors. Now I have cards of Roberto Clemente and Willie Mays!

Thank you again. We are all looking forward to your visit in July.

Your delighted niece,
Jayne

Activity A

Choose one of the following topics or one of your own, and write a paragraph that you might include in a letter to your cousin in another city. Include a heading, salutation, complimentary close, and signature.

A. a good book you have read
B. a sport you have been playing
C. a visit to a museum
D. your favorite TV program
E. a day when everything went wrong
F. a movie you liked
G. your favorite new CD

Activity B

From the topics listed below, write one letter of invitation and one thank-you letter. Include a heading, salutation, complimentary close, and signature.

INVITATIONS
A. an invitation to a birthday party
B. an invitation to your grandparents to attend a school play in which you will appear
C. an invitation to an evening of VCR movies at your house

THANK-YOU LETTERS
A. a thank-you note to your aunt and uncle after you spent a week of your summer vacation on their farm
B. a thank-you note to your best friend for visiting you while you were in the hospital
C. a thank-you note to a friend for a birthday gift

Writer's Corner

▶ Write a friendly letter to someone you would like to know: a book character, a movie or sports star, or a person from history. Tell this person why you are interested in him or her, ask questions, and comment on the things this person has done.

The Parts of a Business Letter

A business letter is made up of a heading, inside address, salutation, body, complimentary close, and signature.

Sometimes you need to write to a business to order a product, to request information, or to complain about an unsatisfactory product. Business letters have the same five parts as a social letter, as well as a part called the inside address.

1111 Tenth Street Memphis, TN 38109 February 10, 19__	HEADING
Carlson Stamp Shop 1425 Fifth Avenue Moline, IL 61265	INSIDE ADDRESS
Dear Sir or Madam:	SALUTATION
Please send me one package of five hundred stamps titled "World Collection" (#302 in your summer catalog). I am enclosing a money order for eight dollars ($8.00), which includes postage.	BODY
Very truly yours, *Barbara Cox* Barbara Cox	COMPLIMENTARY CLOSE SIGNATURE

Heading

The form for the heading of a business letter is the same as for the heading of a social letter. It contains the writer's street address, city, state, and zip code, and the month, day, and year. The heading is written slightly to the right of the center of the paper, about an inch from the top.

Inside Address

The inside address should begin on the left-hand margin, below the heading. It consists of the full name and address of the business or organization to which the letter is being sent. The inside address follows the same form and punctuation as the heading except for one difference. If the letter is being written to a specific person, that person's name and title are included on the first line of the inside address. The name of the business or organization then appears on the second line. Make sure that the inside address is the same as the address on the envelope.

Salutation

The salutation of a business letter is followed by a colon (:) and is made up of a formal phrase such as the following:

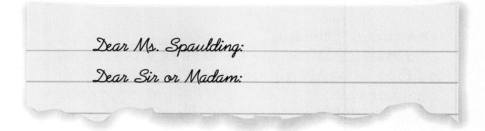

The salutation is directly below the inside address.

Body

The body of a business letter follows the same form as that of a social letter. It is short and courteous, and contains only necessary information.

Complimentary Close

The complimentary close of a business letter is more formal than that of a social letter. Such phrases as the following are used:

Yours truly,   Sincerely yours,

Very truly yours,   Respectfully yours,

The complimentary close is directly in line with the heading.

Signature

The signature of a business letter is also more formal. Directly below the complimentary close, sign your full name. Below that, you should type or neatly print your name. This form is necessary for the signature of a business letter so that your name is readable.

Business letters are often typed since typed letters are easier to read. However, it is acceptable for you to send handwritten business letters.

Activity A

Arrange each of the following addresses in the proper order for an inside address. Write a salutation to go along with each inside address.

1. 229 West Forty-third Street, *New York Times*, New York, New York 10000
2. Agriculture Department, Ames, Iowa 50010, University of Iowa, Professor Leslie Brock
3. Marshall Field and Company, Chicago, Illinois 60602, 111 North State Street
4. 3441 North Ashland Avenue, Managing Editor, Chicago, Illinois 60657, Loyola Press
5. New York, New York 10000, Program Director, National Broadcasting Company, 645 Third Avenue

Activity B

Copy this business letter on a sheet of paper and fill in the missing parts.

Marshall School
4358 Utica Avenue
Cheyenne, WY 82001

_____

Business Manager

_____

2120 Market Street
Cheyenne, WY 82001

_____

A recent article in your newspaper indicated that you offer guided tours in which you show grade-school groups how the <u>Cheyenne News</u> is written and printed. The sixth-grade class that I teach would be quite interested in taking such a tour sometime in April. _____

_____

_____ We need to make our plans by March 15.

_____

_____

Elizabeth Lopez
Teacher, Room 301

Writer's Corner

▶ Write a heading, inside address, salutation, complimentary close, and signature for a business letter to each of the following.

1. a local grocery store
2. a nearby department store
3. the mayor
4. the place of business of a family member
5. a business that you would like to visit

170

LESSON 4

Writing a Business Letter

A business letter should be short, courteous, and to the point.

A business letter is more formal than a social letter. A social letter helps people keep in touch and exchange various bits of news about each other. The purpose of a business letter is much more specific. The most common kinds of business letters do one of the following:

- order a product.
- make a request.
- complain about a product or service.

Since its goal is so specific, a business letter should be short and to the point. The letter writer must remember to be just as courteous in a business letter as in a social letter.

Letters Ordering a Product

One of the most common kinds of business letters is a letter in which the writer is ordering a product. It is important for the writer to give complete and precise information about what is being ordered. In addition, the writer should mention the method of payment.

Model: Placing an Order

110 George Street

Lynn, MA 01901

January 6, 19___

Inventors Supply Company

178 Tremont Street

Boston, MA 02180

Dear Sir or Madam:

Kindly send by mail as soon as possible one (1) Deluxe Young Inventor's Kit. Also, please include the complimentary Inventor's Notebook as advertised in your catalog.

I am enclosing a money order for ten dollars and twenty-five cents ($10.25), the price listed in your catalog. This includes postage and handling.

Very truly yours,

Carl Erley

Carl Erley

Notice that the letter is short and definite, with no unnecessary words or information.

Letters of Request

You may wish to make a request of a business firm, such as asking for permission to visit a broadcasting studio or a manufacturing plant. When writing a letter of this type, include a stamped, self-addressed envelope for the reply. Be specific as to the number of persons and the date.

Model: A Letter of Request

Henry W. Longfellow School
Salem, OR 97300
April 6, 19__

Kleen Dairy Company
475 Baker Street
Salem, OR 97300

Dear Sir or Madam:

Our class of twenty-five sixth-grade students is interested in the invitation you have extended to all schools to visit your dairy. We have been studying about the many products that a modern dairy supplies, and we welcome this opportunity to see a plant in operation.

Please let us know the earliest date convenient to you.

Very truly yours,
Kathleen Schultz
Kathleen Schultz (Secretary)

Letters Reporting Errors or Damage

There may be occasions when orders are not filled promptly or correctly, or when the articles received are damaged. When this happens, write a courteous letter to the company, calling attention to the error or damage and asking the firm to make the necessary adjustment.

Model: A Letter Reporting Damage

401 Wisconsin Avenue
Mill Valley, IL 60135
May 15, 19__

Practical Fishing Products, Inc.
106 South Lake Road
Westminster, MD 21157

Dear Sir or Madam:

    On April 29, I placed an order for the Friendly Fishing Pole and Reel set. On May 10, I received the set. Unfortunately, the reel arrived damaged. The handle had broken off from the body of the reel.

    Since the product is guaranteed, I am returning the damaged part, along with a photocopy of my original order. Please send a new reel as soon as possible.

Very truly yours,
Jason Cheng
Jason Cheng

Activity A

You want to visit a museum in your area. On a sheet of paper, write the following.

1. The heading: Use your address or your school's address.
2. The inside address: Use a real museum or make one up.
3. The salutation: Write one that is appropriate for this type of letter.
4. The complimentary close: Choose one that is appropriate.

Activity B

Now write a letter to the museum, requesting information about these points:

- a special exhibit that your class would like to see
- the days and times your class can visit
- the size of the group that can attend
- how to arrange a guided tour of the exhibit

Express your appreciation that the museum is available to student groups free of charge.

Writer's Corner

▶ Recently you ordered two CDs from the following company:

Golden Disc Music
1052 Record Avenue
Miami, Florida 33136

When the CDs arrived, one was broken. Write a letter telling the company what has happened. Explain that you would like the CD replaced or your money returned. Remember to be brief, to the point, and courteous.

Addressing the Envelope

The front of an envelope has the name and address of the person to whom the letter is being sent. It also has the return address of the sender.

You have probably addressed many envelopes. Let's review the layout of an envelope to make sure that you have been addressing them correctly. Look at the following example.

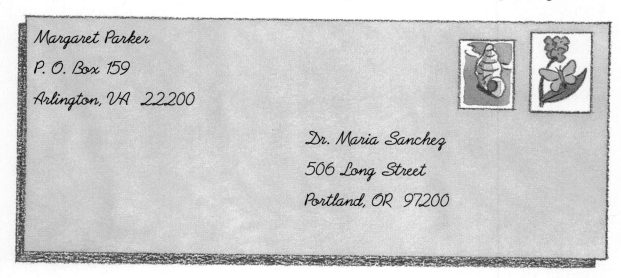

Margaret Parker
P. O. Box 159
Arlington, VA 22200

Dr. Maria Sanchez
506 Long Street
Portland, OR 97200

Note that the envelope contains the full name and address of the person to whom the letter is being sent, including a title such as Dr., Mr., Miss, Mrs., or Ms. The form and the punctuation should follow the style of the inside address of a business letter. The person's name should begin just above the center of the envelope and slightly to the right. The street address goes below the name, and the third line gives the city, state, and zip code. Each line in the address is exactly under the line above it. This is called block form.

The name and address of the person who wrote the letter appears in the upper left-hand corner of the envelope. The name goes on the first line, the street address on the second line, and the city, state, and zip code on the third line. (It is not necessary to write a title, such as Mr. or Ms.) This part is known as the return address. If for some reason the post office cannot deliver the letter, the return address will ensure that the letter comes back to the person who sent it.

The only punctuation used on an envelope is the period after abbreviations of titles and the comma before the name of the state. Be sure to use the correct two-letter abbreviation for the state. A complete list of these postal abbreviations can be found in this book on page 467.

Folding the Letter

A letter should be folded neatly before it is put into the envelope. Some notepaper is small and can be folded in half. Put the folded edge into the envelope first.

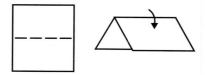

If you are using a large envelope and a typewriter-size sheet of paper, you can fold your paper into thirds. First, fold the bottom third of the paper a little more than half of the way up. Then fold the top third down. Be sure to keep the left and right edges even. Then place the letter into the envelope with the last fold at the bottom.

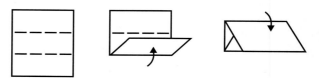

Activity A

Write the following names and addresses as they should be written on envelopes. Use your own return address and abbreviate the state. (Use page 467 to find the two-letter postal abbreviations.)

1. Juliet F. Jefferson, 724 Palm Street, Honolulu, Hawaii 96800
2. Dr. Chandra Singh, Saint Charles Hospital, 14 Front Street, Keokuk, Iowa 52632
3. Ms. Anne Gray, Rural Route 3, Big Bar, Idaho 83678
4. Mr. Roberto Flores, 5525 Penn Avenue, Pittsburgh, Pennsylvania 15201
5. Mrs. Howard L. Finkle, 123 Freeman Parkway, Providence, Rhode Island 02906
6. Thomas J. De Nero, 55 Flower Street, Santa Ana, California 92700
7. Ms. Carolyn Davis, 99 Hampshire Street, Denver, Colorado 80200
8. Mr. Paul Baird, University of Cincinnati, Cincinnati, Ohio 45201

Activity B

Bring in two envelopes from home. Using addresses from Activity A or addresses of friends, complete each envelope. Remember to include your return address. If necessary, draw horizontal lines on the envelope to help keep your writing straight.

Writer's Corner

▶ You have written social letters and business letters for this chapter. Once you are satisfied that one is ready to be "sent," address the envelope. Then fold the letter properly and put it into the envelope.

Filling Out Forms

Filling out a form is an orderly way of providing essential information.

As you have learned, letters to businesses and organizations must be short and to the point, providing necessary information with the fewest possible words. In this chapter, you have already seen sample business letters that request information and order products. Each letter is very specific and to the point.

Many businesses and organizations want to make sure that you tell them exactly what they need to know. To help you do this, they provide forms for you to fill out. A form is a document that asks you questions and leaves blank spaces for you to answer.

You have probably already filled out many forms. A coupon that you use to send away for something is a kind of form. When you join a community center or a little league, you fill out a form that provides necessary information. If you have ever opened a bank account, you filled out forms for that, also. As you grow older, you will fill out more and more forms. These include forms that help you do such things as pay taxes, give information about a change in your address, obtain a credit card, and apply for a job.

Activity

Copy the coupon below on a sheet of paper, and fill it out to order the package of ten baseball cards called "All-Stars, 1970s and 1980s." Use your own name and address.

THE BASEBALL CARD SHOP
1010 East Main Street
Madison, WI 53703

Please send me the following ten-card package(s), which are SPECIAL OFFERS for this month (December, 19___) only.

CHECK CHOICES · PRICE

	Old-Timers	**$4.95**
	Team pictures	**$4.95**
	All-Stars, 1970s and 1980s	**$4.95**
	Total	
	Postage	+ .70
	Total Enclosed	

SHIP TO:

Name _____

Address _____

City, State, Zip Code _____

Activity B

On a sheet of paper, complete the necessary information.

LAKESIDE PARK DAY CAMP

Application

Answer each question.

1. Name _____

2. Address _____

3. Phone number _____

4. Parents' names _____

5. Your age _____   6. Your birthday _____

7. Your height _____   8. Your weight _____

9. Your cap size _____   10. Your T-shirt size _____

Answer these questions by putting an *X* in the proper box.

11. I have attended summer day camp at Lakeside Park or at other parks for

   ❏ 0 years   ❏ 1 year
   ❏ 2 years   ❏ more than 2 years

12. I would be most interested in the following activities:

   ❏ baseball   ❏ singing
   ❏ volleyball   ❏ reading and storytelling
   ❏ soccer   ❏ hiking
   ❏ swimming   ❏ camping skills
   ❏ ceramics   ❏ others (please list below)
   ❏ woodworking   _____

Your signature _____

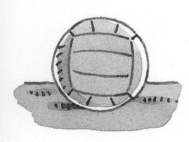

Writer's Corner

▶ Below is a form that Jorge used to order his soccer team's uniform. Now you find a form to fill out. It can be from a magazine, newspaper, local store, community center, post office, or anywhere else. Complete the form and share it with the class.

<table>
<tr><td rowspan="2">

Discount Outlet
Freeport, Maine 04033</td><td colspan="3">**Ship To:**
Jorge Gonzales
<u>Name</u>
901 Heathercrest Lane, #141
<u>Address</u>
Houston   TX   77008
City   State   Zip Code
(713)-555-0746
<u>Phone</u></td></tr>
</table>

Description	Qty.	Price Each	Total
Blue T-Shirt	*1*	*$15.99*	*$15.99*
White Tube Socks	*6 pr.*	*$1.99*	*$11.94*
		Total	*$27.93*

Homographs

Homographs are words that are spelled the same but that have different meanings and are often pronounced differently.

Homographs can be confusing because they are words that are spelled alike. You can identify a homograph only by the way it is used. For example:

> From the rocky cliff, Manolo *dove* into the ocean.
> (past tense of *dive,* pronounced dōv)

> As the sun broke through the clouds, a *dove* rested on the white picket fence in Jenny's yard.
> (a kind of bird, pronounced dəv)

Notice that the pronunciation of *dove* changes. There is a change in the vowel sound. The change in the vowel sound signals a difference in meaning. Look at the next two sentences:

> Akim takes pictures of any *object* that he finds interesting.
> (a thing that can be seen or touched, pronounced ŏb´ jĭkt)

> Does anyone *object* to spending the dues on a darkroom?
> (oppose, pronounced əb jĕkt´)

Here the pronunciation of the word changes because there is a definite change, or shift, in the accent. The shift in the accent signals a difference in meaning.

Activity A

Read the list of homographs below and pronounce each word. Tell whether each pair of homographs has a different pronunciation because of a vowel change or a shift in accent. Then give the meaning of each word. Use a dictionary if necessary.

1. **a.** bow (bō)   **b.** bow (baủ)
2. **a.** lead (lēd)   **b.** lead (lĕd)
3. **a.** live (līv)   **b.** live (lĭv)
4. **a.** present (prĕz´ nt)   **b.** present (prĭ zĕnt´)
5. **a.** record (rĭ kôrd´)   **b.** record (rĕk´ ərd)

Activity B

Complete each sentence with the correct homograph from the list in Activity A. Indicate whether the homograph you use is labeled *a* or *b* on the list.

1. I would like to _____ the new president of our class, Patty Layton.
2. The storm tossed the ship against a jagged rock, opening a massive hole in the _____ .
3. During the 1800s, Galena, Illinois, was a center for the mining of _____ .
4. Excitedly, Tina tore the wrapping off the unexpected _____ .
5. Charlie looked silly in that polka dot _____ tie.
6. Do any people _____ in Antarctica?
7. Jason will _____ his team to the playoffs.
8. Mary Lou will _____ today's important events in her diary.
9. The bank teller could not find a _____ of the deposit to my savings account.
10. The cat's toy looked so real that for a moment I thought it was a _____ mouse.

WRITER'S WORKSHOP

A Letter to the Editor

Are you proud of something that has happened in your community? Does something in your town make you really angry? Tell the world about your feelings with a letter to the editor. Write a letter to the editor of a local newspaper. Your letter may get published in the newspaper!

 Prewriting

Make a list of current events you have strong feelings about. Your feelings are the key to finding an issue for your letter to the editor.

Ask yourself questions like these to help you think of letter topics:

- Did something happen at your school that you think people should know about?

- Is there something you think your community needs?

- Is there something about your town that you're especially proud of?

- Did an elected official of your town do something you think was wrong?

- Would you like to thank anyone in your town for doing a great job?

Circle a topic on your list that you would like to write a letter about. Then give yourself ten or fifteen minutes of freewriting time to put down all your thoughts about the issue.

Where Will You Send Your Letter?

Get a copy of the newspaper you plan to mail your letter to. Turn to the Letters to the Editor section. On that page, you should find instructions for submitting a letter to the editor.

Drafting

Use your prewriting notes to plan your letter carefully. Remember, a newspaper often receives many more letters than it can print. To be published, your letter will have to be clearly written and to the point.

The beginning sentence of your letter should state your issue and tell how you feel about it. Read this example.

The children on the west side of town need their own playground.

Continue by listing at least three facts that support your main idea sentence. Write clearly and be brief.

End with a sentence that states the idea from your beginning sentence in a new way.

Remember to use the correct form for a business letter.

1234 North Avenue   HEADING
River Ridge, CA   95000
January 5, 19—

The Daily Times   INSIDE ADDRESS
5678 Washington Street
River Ridge, CA   95000

Dear Editor: SALUTATION
    The children on the west side of town need their own   BODY
playground. There are many children in our neighborhood
who have no safe place to play. To get to the town's only
park, we have to cross a busy, dangerous highway. We would
be safer and less likely to get into trouble if we had a place
to play near our own homes. We urge the city to build a park
on the west side in the near future.

Sincerely,   COMPLIMENTARY CLOSE
Joseph Jackson   SIGNATURE
Joseph Jackson

EDITOR'S WORKSHOP

Revising, Proofreading, and Publishing

Revising

Time to Take Another Look

Reread your draft to revise it. Make sure your issue is clear. Make sure you have presented your ideas in a thoughtful way.

Use these questions to help you revise your draft:

❑ Does my letter have all the parts a business letter needs?

❑ Does my beginning sentence clearly state my issue and my feelings about it?

❑ Do I need to rephrase my supporting arguments to make them clear?

❑ Do I need to rearrange my ideas to make them flow logically?

❑ Do I need to take out any unnecessary details?

❑ Do I need to choose more powerful words?

❑ Does my last sentence restate what I said in my beginning sentence?

Make your revisions with a colored pencil. Read your letter aloud to a friend and discuss your revisions together.

Read Published Letters
To get a better idea about what a newspaper editor looks for, read a few published letters from your local paper. Compare your letter with letters the editor selected for publication.

 **Proofreading**

Time to Look at Capitalization, Punctuation, and Spelling

When you've decided what to say, check your capitalization, punctuation, spelling, and grammar. Correct and careful writing shows that you have taken time and trouble with your letter.

❏ Did I use a colon after my salutation?

❏ Did I use capital letters and commas correctly in my heading and inside address?

❏ Did I use the correct mark of punctuation at the end of each part of my letter?

❏ Did I spell all the words correctly?

Read Aloud

Read aloud, exaggerating each punctuation mark. Make a long pause for each period and a short pause for each comma. Read sentences with exclamation marks with expression. If you've used too many commas or exclamation marks, you'll find out as you listen to your letter.

 Publishing

Time to Share

Publish your letter to call attention to an important issue.

To publish, follow these steps:

1. If you have access to a computer, type your letter.

2. If not, use your neatest handwriting to copy your revised draft.

3. Write your signature in your own handwriting.

4. Type or print your name below your signature.

Submit your letter.

1. Read your letter aloud to the class.

2. Use your best handwriting to address your envelope.

3. Add a stamp and mail your letter.

4. Read the editorial page every day to see if your letter is published.

Tools for Speaking Clearly and Correctly

Skilled speakers can use the tools of pitch, stress, and enunciation to speak more effectively and make their words come alive.

You have already learned a variety of ways to improve your writing. Although writing is an essential form of communication, it is not the only one. Can you imagine a waking hour when you do not express your thoughts and feelings through speech? Speech is such a common activity that you probably take it for granted. It includes a wide range of activities, such as casual conversation, reading aloud, introducing people to each other, debating, and making formal reports. The next few lessons will help you improve your skills of speaking and—just as important—listening.

Speaking requires many of the same skills as writing. A good speaker presents ideas in an organized and logical manner and makes these ideas more vivid by using language that "paints a picture." Speakers have another important tool—the voice. When you speak, you use the qualities of voice to make your words clearer and more vivid.

About the Photograph

Communicating, that's what it's all about! Whether reading aloud to a friend or sharing a joke, we are using speaking and listening skills.

Pitch

Pitch is the highness or the lowness of the speaker's voice. Variations in pitch can bring a spoken message alive. The speaker's voice becomes higher or lower in order to give the correct meaning to words.

Think about the following situation and listen to the pitch of your voice. Imagine that you have a role in a school play. The opening song is your cue that the play is about to begin. You hear the first notes of the song and say, "It's starting." You are stating a simple fact. The pitch of your voice is even. Now say the same sentence as a question, "It's starting?" The pitch of your voice is higher at the end. The meaning of the sentence is different. Through pitch, the listener understands that you are asking a question. Now say "It's starting!" with enthusiasm. The pitch of your voice starts high and then lowers. It shows your excitement.

Activity A

Read the following sentences in at least two different ways by varying the pitch. Then tell what kind of feeling you are expressing with each change in pitch.

1. It snowed last night.

2. This pizza's delicious.

3. Stop it.

4. Let someone else do it.

5. This music is too loud.

Stress

Stress is the emphasis or degree of force you put on a word. The meaning of a sentence can change depending on what words are stressed. Read the following sentences aloud, and listen to how different stress changes the meaning of the sentence. Put the emphasis on the italicized word.

Will *you* walk ten miles tomorrow?
   (This sentence emphasizes the person.)

Will you *walk* ten miles tomorrow?
   (This sentence emphasizes the action.)

Will you walk ten miles *tomorrow?*
   (This sentence emphasizes the time.)

Activity B

Read the following sentences in at least two different ways by varying the stress. Tell what meaning you are expressing with each change in stress.

1. Will you practice with me now?

2. Did you like that old movie?

3. Paula won first prize.

4. We planted those tomatoes yesterday.

5. Anna and Carlos went to the zoo.

Enunciation

Enunciation, or exact pronunciation, conveys the spoken message clearly. When you enunciate, you say vowels and consonants clearly and fully. Your listener can easily understand what you are saying.

Activity C

Now try some tuning-up exercises to practice proper breathing and enunciation.

1. Inhale through your nose and hold your breath for ten counts. Then exhale with the sound of *ah*. This opens your throat and helps to relax the muscles so that you may breathe more easily as you speak.

2. Practice the long and short sounds of *a*.

māy	măt
māte	măn
sāy	păn

3. Practice these consonant sounds. Concentrate on enunciating each consonant clearly.

d	The double dip delighted Donna.
t	Tinkering Tom took ten toadstools.
s	The sight of the sea surprised the sailor.
sh	Shall she shake the shawl?
z	Zebras zoom through Zanzibar.
zh	Azure sky measures pleasure.
j	Julie and Jason jumped for joy.
ch	The chattering chimps chuckled cheerily.
th	Theodore thought his thumb had thawed.

Activity D

Now that you have had a chance to practice pitch, stress, and enunciation, recite the two poems on pages 195 and 196 aloud. Be sure to pronounce all of the words distinctly. Use pitch and stress to make the poems sound interesting and to bring out the meaning of certain lines.

The Man in the Moon

The Man in the Moon as he sails the sky
Is a very remarkable skipper,
But he made a mistake when he tried to take
A drink of milk from the Dipper.
He dipped right out of the Milky Way,
And slowly and carefully filled it,
The Big Bear growled, and the Little Bear howled
And frightened him so that he spilled it!

Anonymous

Hector the Collector

Hector the Collector
Collected bits of string,
Collected dolls with broken heads
And rusty bells that would not ring.
Pieces out of picture puzzles,
Bent-up nails and ice cream sticks,
Twists of wires, worn-out tires,
Paper bags and broken bricks.
Old chipped vases, half shoelaces,
Gatlin' guns that wouldn't shoot,
Leaky boats that wouldn't float
And stopped-up horns that wouldn't toot.
Butter knives that had no handles,
Copper keys that fit no locks,
Rings that were too small for fingers,
Dried-up leaves and patched-up socks.
Worn-out belts that had no buckles,
'Lectric trains that had no tracks,
Airplane models, broken bottles,
Three-legged chairs and cups with cracks.
Hector the Collector
Loved these things with all his soul—
Loved them more than shining diamonds,
Loved them more than glistenin' gold.
Hector called to all people,
"Come and share my treasure trunk!"
And all the silly sightless people
Came and looked . . . and called it junk.

Shel Silverstein

Writer's Corner

▶ Reread the poem above. What do you think Hector's treasure trunk looked like? Write a description of Hector's trunk, then read your description to the class. Use pitch, stress, and enunciation to make your description sound interesting and to bring out the meaning of certain sentences.

Choral Speaking

Choral speaking is the art of speaking in a group.

Choral speaking is an enjoyable way to recite poetry. It is not a new discovery. The ancient Greeks were the first to use this manner of reciting poetry. In choral speaking, a chorus is a group of people who are divided into smaller groups according to the pitch of their voices. Do you think your voice is naturally high or low? If you have a low voice, the pitch of your voice is deep. If you have a high voice, the pitch of your voice is light. Many people fall in the middle and the pitch of their voices is medium. The natural pitch of one's voice is an essential element of choral speaking. Using the variety of voices of many students to recite a poem is fun to do and adds to the beauty and meaning of the words.

In this lesson, you will find certain markings that aid in the phrasing and inflection (rising or falling of the voice) of the poems you recite together in chorus.

Use a falling inflection of the voice (\) for important or emphatic words:

> I see the soldiers \ dressed in gray.

Use a rising inflection of the voice (/) when asking a question:

> Are you ill? /

Pause (//) at the end of a sentence or where the thought demands a pause:

> Why, say "Sail on! / sail on! / and on!" //

Tuning-Up Exercises

On page 194 in Lesson 1 of this chapter, you did some tuning-up exercises. Here are a few more to try before you begin your choral speaking.

Breathing

Inhale as if sipping. Hold your breath for ten counts, and exhale as if blowing a pinwheel. Imagine that you are making the wheel turn steadily and smoothly.

Enunciation

Practice the long and short sounds of *o* by saying the following words as they are arranged in columns. Then read across the page.

spōke	spŏt	hōpe	hŏp
lōaf	lŏt	mōde	mŏp
cōat	cŏt	rōde	rŏd

Consonant Sounds

Practice these consonant sounds. Say the sentences slowly the first few times, and then increase the speed.

Rory returned the record to Roberta.
Lilly lost her large yellow llama.
With radio and radium, we are really rich.
Lena likes luscious long licorice lollipops.

Activity A

Now you are ready to begin choral speaking. Each of the four poems on pages 199–202 has choral directions and inflection marks. Carefully follow the directions and the inflection marks as you read the poems in groups.

It Couldn't Be Done

LIGHT VOICES   Somebody said \ that it couldn't be done, //
        But he with a chuckle replied //

DEEP VOICES   That "maybe it couldn't," \ but he would be one \
        Who wouldn't say so \ till he'd tried. //

LIGHT VOICES   So he buckled right in \ with the trace of a grin \
        On his face. // If he worried \ he hid it. //

UNISON   He started to sing \ as he tackled the thing \
        That couldn't be done, // and he did it. //

LIGHT VOICES   Somebody scoffed: \
SOLO   "Oh, you'll never do that; \
        At least no one ever has done it"; //

DEEP VOICES   But he took off his coat \ and he took off his hat, //
        And the first thing we knew \ he'd begun it. //

LIGHT VOICES   With a lift of his chin \ and a bit of a grin, //
        Without any doubting or quiddit, //

UNISON   He started to sing \ as he tackled the thing \
        That couldn't be done, // and he did it. //

DEEP VOICES   There are thousands to tell you \ it cannot be done, //
        There are thousands \ to prophesy failure; //

LIGHT VOICES   There are thousands to point out to you, \ one by one, //
        The dangers that wait to assail you. //

DEEP VOICES   But just buckle in \ with a bit of a grin, //
        Just take off your coat \ and go to it; //

UNISON   Just start to sing \ as you tackle the thing \
        That "cannot be done," // and you'll do it. //

Edgar A. Guest

Velvet Shoes

UNISON　Let us walk in the white snow \
　　In a soundless space; //
With footsteps quiet \ and slow, \
　　At a tranquil pace, \
　　Under veils \ of white lace. //

LIGHT VOICES　I shall go shod in silk, \
　　And you in wool, //
White as a white cow's milk, \
　　More beautiful
　　Than the breast \ of a gull. //

DEEP VOICES　We shall walk \ through the still town \
　　In a windless peace; //
We shall step upon white down. /
　　Upon silver fleece, \
　　Upon softer \ than these. //

UNISON　We shall walk in velvet shoes: /
　　Wherever we go //
Silence \ will fall like dews \
　　On white silence below. //
　　We shall walk \ in the snow. //

Elinor Wylie

200

Mr. Nobody

GROUP **1:** I know a funny \ little \ man, /

2:   As quiet as a mouse, /

3: Who does the mischief that is done /

4:   In everybody's house! //

5: There's no one \ ever \ sees his face, /

6:   And yet / we all agree /

7: That every plate we break \ was cracked /

UNISON   By Mr. Nobody! //

GROUP **1:** 'Tis he / who always tears our books, /

2:   Who leaves the door ajar, //

3: He pulls the buttons \ from our shirts /

4:   And scatters pins afar; //

5: That squeaking door \ will always squeak /

6:   For, \ prithee, \ don't you see, /

7: We leave the oiling \ to be done /

UNISON   By Mr. Nobody. //

GROUP **1:** He puts damp wood upon the fire, /

2:   That kettles cannot boil; //

3: His \ are the feet that bring in mud, /

4:   And all the carpet's soil. //

5: The papers always are mislaid, /

6:   Who had them last \ but he? //

7: There's no one \ tosses them about /

UNISON   But Mr. Nobody. //

GROUP **1:** The finger-marks \ upon the door \

2:   By *none* of us / are made; //

3: We *never* \ leave the blinds unclosed, /

4:   To let the curtains fade. //

5: The ink we never spill, / the boots \

6:   That lying 'round you see /

7: Are *not our* boots; / they all belong /

UNISON   To Mr. Nobody.

Anonymous

Stopping by Woods on a Snowy Evening

LIGHT VOICES   Whose woods these are / I think I know. //
His house is in the village though; /
He will not see me stopping here \
To watch his woods \ fill up with snow. //

MEDIUM   My little horse must think it queer
VOICES   To stop \ without a farmhouse near \
Between the woods and frozen lake \
The darkest evening of the year. //

DEEP VOICES   He gives his harness bells a shake
To ask \ if there is some mistake. //
The only other sound's \ the sweep
Of easy wind \ and downy flake. //

UNISON   The woods are lovely, \ dark, \ and deep, //
But I have promises to keep. /
And miles to go \ before I sleep. //
And miles \ to go before I sleep. //

Robert Frost

Activity B

Decide as a class how you would like to read the next three poems, "The Camel's Complaint," "Raccoon," and "Wind Song." Choose which parts will be light, medium, and deep voices and which will be in unison. Plan where your voices will rise and where they will fall. Finally, think about the spirit in which each poem should be read.

The Camel's Complaint

Canary-birds feed on sugar and seed,
    Parrots have crackers to crunch;
And, as for the poodles, they tell me the noodles
    Have chickens and cream for their lunch.
        But there's never a question
        About MY digestion—
           ANYTHING does for me!

Cats, you're aware, can repose in a chair,
    Chickens can roost upon rails;
Puppies are able to sleep in a stable,
    And oysters can slumber in pails.
        But no one supposes
        A poor Camel dozes—
           ANY PLACE does for me!

Lambs are enclosed where it's never exposed,
    Coops are constructed for hens;
Kittens are treated to houses well heated,
    And pigs are protected by pens.
        But a Camel comes handy
        Wherever it's sandy—
           ANYWHERE does for me!

People would laugh if you rode a giraffe,
    Or mounted the back of an ox;
It's nobody's habit to ride on a rabbit,
    Or try to bestraddle a fox.
        But as for a Camel, he's
        Ridden by families—
           ANY LOAD does for me!

A snake is as round as a hole in the ground,
    And weasels are wavy and sleek;
And no alligator could ever be straighter
    Than lizards that live in a creek.
        But a Camel's all lumpy
        And bumpy and humpy—
           ANY SHAPE does for me!

Charles Edward Carryl

Raccoon

One summer night a little Raccoon,
Above his left shoulder, looked at the new moon.
    He made a wish;
    He said: "I wish
    I were a Catfish,
    A Blowfish, a Squid,
    A Katydid,
    A Beetle, a Skink,
    An Ostrich, a pink
    Flamingo, a Gander,
    A Salamander,
    A Hippopotamus,
    A Duck-billed Platypus,
    A Gecko, a Slug,
    A Water Bug,
    A pug-nosed Beaver,
    Anything whatever
Except what I am, a little Raccoon!"

Above his left shoulder, the Evening Star
Listened and heard the little Raccoon
    Who wished on the moon;
    And she said: "Why wish
    You were a Catfish,
    A Blowfish, a Squid,
    A Katydid,
    A Beetle, a Skink,
    An Ostrich, a pink
    Flamingo, a Gander,
    A Salamander,
    A Hippopotamus,
    A Duck-billed Platypus,
    A Gecko, a Slug,
    A Water Bug,
    A pug-nosed Beaver,
    Anything whatever?
Why must you change?" said the Evening Star,
"When you are perfect as you are?
I know a boy who wished on the moon
That *he* might be a little Raccoon!"

William Jay Smith

Wind Song

When the wind blows
The quiet things speak.
Some whisper, some clang,
Some creak.

Grasses swish.
Treetops sigh.
Flags slap
and snap at the sky.
Wires on poles
whistle and hum.
Ashcans roll.
Windows drum.

When the wind goes—
suddenly
then,
the quiet things
are quiet again.

Lilian Moore

Writer's Corner

▶ **What do you see and hear when the wind blows? Write a descriptive paragraph about your "Wind Song."**

Introductions

> **An introduction is a formal way of helping people become acquainted.**

Throughout your life, you will introduce many people to each other. A skillful introduction is important. It arouses people's interest and helps get a conversation started. To introduce people properly, begin by mentioning each person's name clearly and distinctly. Include some interesting fact about each person, such as "This is Ellen Jackson, the captain of our girls' basketball team." When you are introducing a young person to an adult, first identify the young person, as in the model below.

Model: An Introduction

LINDA (turning first to her father and then to her friend): Dad, this is Marilyn McKenna, our class president. Marilyn, this is my father, Doctor Baker.

FATHER (turning to Marilyn and putting out his right hand): How do you do, Marilyn. I've heard Linda speak about you often. I'm glad to meet you.

MARILYN (shaking hands with Doctor Baker): Thank you, Doctor Baker. I'm glad to meet you, too.

Activity A

Form groups of three and practice these introductions. You may add interesting facts about the people.

1. Susan Mercer is a new student in your school who is interested in gymnastics. Introduce her to Miss Shigota, the gymnastics coach.

2. You are going to an adventure movie with your friend, Billy Shaw. It is Billy's favorite movie, and he has seen it twice before. Introduce Billy to a classmate you meet in the theater lobby.

3. Introduce your uncle Ed Marino, a police detective, to your friend Chris Kellogg. Chris loves to read mystery stories.

4. At a charity dinner, you meet a famous hockey player. Introduce him to your best friend, who follows hockey very closely.

5. Your cousin Lelia Baez is visiting from Florida. Introduce her to Jeff Kerr, who vacationed in Florida last winter.

Writer's Corner

▶ Form groups of three. Have two students make up new names, interesting characteristics, and occupations for themselves. Have them give this information to the third person. Then have the third person introduce the two students to each other. The two who are introduced should courteously acknowledge the introduction and start a conversation based on what they have just learned about each other. Write your introductions on paper.

Listening to the Sounds Around You

Listening is a skill that helps you become aware of what is going on all around you.

Sit still and listen carefully for a moment. What do you hear? Birds singing? Rain on the windows? Traffic in the street outside? The clock ticking? Other students whispering and giggling? Think about what these sounds tell you. What can you say about your surroundings after hearing these sounds?

Listening closely to sounds is an important skill. In Chapter 4, you learned to use sensory impressions in your writing. Sound was one of those senses. The story of a camping trip can be brought to life, for example, with a description of crickets chirping, the campfire crackling, and perhaps even unexpected footsteps in the forest.

Listening carefully also helps you increase your awareness of what is going on around you. The sound of a car's horn as you cross the street warns you to be alert. The sound of a young child crying tells you to look and see what is wrong. People who listen attentively and who think about what they hear will also experience thoughts and emotions associated with the sound. These thoughts and emotions help you to understand, to act, to remember, and to describe.

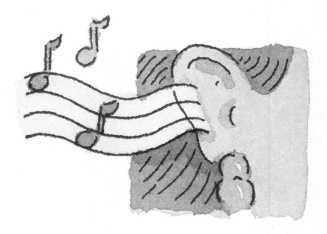

Activity A

Imagine that you hear each of the following sounds. Describe each sound and tell what thoughts come to mind.

1. Someone practicing the piano late in the evening
2. A motorized sound in the sky
3. Someone coughing loudly
4. A group of people laughing heartily
5. The thud of a snowball against a tree
6. A screeching car
7. Someone yelling your name
8. A telephone ringing unexpectedly in a crowded store
9. The splashing of a waterfall
10. Glass shattering

Writer's Corner

▶ Sit still for five minutes and listen to the sounds around you. List the different sounds you hear. When the five minutes are up, write the thoughts that each sound brings to your mind.

Listening for Information

In listening for information, take notes to remember important details.

In most of your everyday conversations, the details you need to remember stay in your mind. You remember what is essential. Other times, however, you may want to write down the information to help you remember it accurately. For example, you may be taking a telephone message, listening to your teacher lecture about the Civil War, or interviewing someone for your school newspaper. In such instances, you must take notes—written records of important details.

In Chapter 5, you learned about note taking for a written report. There are many other reasons for taking notes. Some of the notes you take may be brief, while others must contain a number of details. Often your notes will have to be rewritten later in a more readable form. Look at the following examples of notes.

Model: A Telephone Message Received by the Answering Service of a Busy Executive

CALL FOR: Ms. Tracy

FROM: Mr. Goodman
Goodman Limousine Service
Dallas, Texas

DATE: Tuesday, April 4, 19___

TIME: 8:30 A.M.

Your limousine will be waiting at the Dallas airport this evening. The driver will meet you at the baggage claim area at 7:30 P.M. If your plans change, call (214) 555-1200.

Model: A Telephone Message Received by Scott's Mother While Scott Was at the Doctor's Office

Message from Mike to Scott

- History quiz tomorrow, chapter on the Declaration of Independence.
- Math homework for tomorrow—Chapter 12, Exercises 1-7.
- Charity drive begins tomorrow. Bring your contribution.
- Trip to the Science Museum next Thursday, June 3. Be sure to pick up a permission slip.
- Practice for softball play-offs tomorrow at 3:00. Bring your bat.
- Hope you're feeling better. See you tomorrow.

Model: Classroom Notes

- Abraham Lincoln elected president in 1860.
- Many Southerners did not like Lincoln because of his stand against slavery.
- Soon after election, eleven states withdrew from Union and formed Confederate States of America.

Activity A

Imagine that you have just answered the phone. The caller has asked for your mother, but she is not at home. Your teacher will pretend to be the caller and give you the message. Listen carefully and jot down notes. Then write out the message as accurately as you can.

Writer's Corner

▶ Make up a realistic-sounding telephone message that includes names, dates, and times. Read the message to another student, and have that student take notes. After the notes have been rewritten as a reminder, or memo, check to see that the information is clear and accurate. Then reverse roles. You take notes as your partner gives a message.

Misused Words

Certain words that sound alike or that are similar in sound or spelling are often misused.

Pairs of similar words may cause confusion. One may be incorrectly used instead of the other. Some pairs are homophones, such as *passed* and *past*. Other pairs are words that are quite close in sound and in spelling, such as *were* and *where*. When you write, be careful to spell similar-sounding words correctly.

Activity A

The words in each set are often misused. Give the definition for the part of speech listed. Use the dictionary to complete the activity.

		PART OF SPEECH	DEFINITION
1.	accept	verb	_____
	except	preposition	_____
2.	its	adjective	_____
	it's	contraction	_____
3.	loose	adjective	_____
	lose	verb	_____
4.	passed	verb	_____
	past	preposition/adverb	_____
5.	quiet	adjective	_____
	quite	adverb	_____
6.	than	conjunction	_____
	then	adverb	_____
7.	right	adjective	_____
	write	verb	_____
8.	were	verb	_____
	where	adverb	_____

Activity

Complete each sentence with the correct word from the list of misused words in Activity A.

1. Be sure the numbers are _____ and _____ fill out the rest of the form.

2. Name one animal that is larger _____ an elephant.

3. _____ chilly outside today.

4. _____ _____ you when the electricity went out?

5. Mr. Pariser looked with horror at his new car and _____ dented fender.

6. When the bus was ready to leave, everyone was accounted for _____ Amy.

7. The operator asked, "Will you _____ a collect call?"

8. In 1863, Jules Verne began to _____ his fascinating science fiction stories.

9. Walking through the snow on Christmas Eve, Miguel noticed how _____ the neighborhood was.

10. The seaplane _____ over the shore and landed smoothly on the lake.

11. Did anyone here _____ a black-and-white ski mitten?

12. The two sprinters streaked _____ the finish line at the same time.

13. The doorknob on the old house was _____ , and it squeaked when I turned it.

14. Thomas Rockwell's book *How to Eat Fried Worms* is _____ popular with children.

15. Babies eat more frequently _____ adults.

WRITER'S WORKSHOP

An Oral History

All history is not written in books. History is also in the memories of the people who lived it. Collect a little piece of history for yourself. Interview an older friend or family member. Write a report about what you learn. Combine your report with your classmates' reports to make an oral history book.

 Prewriting

Decide what you want to learn from your interview. Then make a list of interview questions.

You may want to ask some of the questions below.

- When and where were you born?

- What did you do for fun as a child?

- Was the school you went to different from schools today? In what ways?

- What historic events have happened in your lifetime?

- How did those events change your life?

- How much did things cost when you were younger?

- What was the happiest time in your life?

- What was the saddest time in your life?

Make an appointment with your interviewee at a time and place that's convenient for both of you. Then gather your materials. Take a notebook, several pencils, and your list of questions. If you plan to use a tape recorder, ask permission to record the interview.

After your interview, write a thank-you letter. Offer to come back to share your report.

Guidelines for Interviewing

1. Greet your interviewee and then ask your first question.

2. Listen carefully and take notes as quickly as possible.

3. Ask your interviewee to repeat any details you miss.

4. Ask your interviewee to spell names of people and places.

5. If your interviewee doesn't want to answer a question, don't insist.

6. If your interviewee wants to talk about something that is not on your list, that is fine.

7. Review your notes while the interview is still fresh in your mind and fill in any missing details.

Drafting

When you write your draft, you don't need to use all the information you collected in your interview. Review your notes and circle the ideas you want to write about. Then number them in the order you plan to write them.

Begin with an interesting or surprising fact. Use the person's name in the first sentence and tell when he or she was born early in your report.

Expand your interview notes into sentences to write the body of your report. End with a statement that sums up what you wrote.

My Aunt Gerry's Life

Aunt Gerry was seven years old before her family got a television. That's because television had just been invented when she was a child. Aunt Gerry was born in 1946, so she is part of what people now call the "baby boom." There were many children in her Indiana neighborhood, and she and her friends spent a lot of time outdoors playing games like Red Rover and Freeze Tag.

Aunt Gerry has lived through many important historic events, such as the launching of the Sputnik satellites and the assassinations of President Kennedy and Martin Luther King, Jr. The event that affected her life the most was President Kennedy's death. "Before that," she says, "I felt safer. I thought assassinations only happened in books."

Aunt Gerry says she has had a happy and interesting life so far, and she thinks it will only get better.

EDITOR'S WORKSHOP

Revising, Proofreading, and Publishing

 Revising

Time to Take Another Look

Now is your chance to revise your oral history report. Make sure your report tells about personal memories. Make sure it adds life to the history you've read in books.

Use the checklist below to help you revise your oral history report.

❑ Does my oral history report sound like a conversation?

❑ Does it include the most interesting details from my interview?

❑ Do the details in each paragraph support the topic sentence?

❑ Do I need to substitute more exciting words for boring, overused words?

❑ Do I need to cut out unnecessary words, phrases, or sentences to make my oral history report flow better?

❑ Does my conclusion sum up my feelings or the feelings of the person I wrote about?

Use a colored pencil to revise your narrative so your revisions will stand out. Read your report to a partner. Ask your partner to tell you if any part of your report is not clear.

Add a Quotation
A quotation is a person's exact words enclosed in quotation marks. Add a quotation or two to make your writing come alive.

Use your interview notes or your tape-recorded interview to find interesting material to quote.

 **Proofreading**

Time to Look at Capitalization, Punctuation, and Spelling

Before you write your final copy, proofread your draft to check your capitalization, punctuation, spelling, and grammar.

Use the checklist below to proofread and edit your oral history report.

❏ Did I indent the first word of each paragraph?

❏ Did I begin each sentence and proper noun with a capital letter?

❏ Did I use marks of punctuation correctly?

❏ Did I spell each word correctly?

Take a Break
If you have time, take a long or short break before you begin proofreading. You can be more objective about your writing after a little time has passed.

 Publishing

Time to Share

Oral history is meant to be shared. Share your report by publishing it.

To publish, follow these steps:

1. Copy your revised draft in your neatest handwriting or type it on a computer.

2. After you finish, proofread your final copy one more time.

3. Check to be sure you did not leave anything out as you copied.

Make the oral history book.

1. Collect the reports and arrange them in order from oldest person to youngest.

2. Make a table of contents.

3. Design a cover and bind the pages together.

4. Place your book in the classroom library and refer to it as you learn more about history.

5. Borrow the book and read it to the person you interviewed.

Library Skills

The Organization of the Library

> **Knowing the arrangement of the library helps you to find information easily.**

Where would you go to find a good story to read at the beach or to find information on the latest explorations into space? Where could you obtain the answers to questions such as these:

- What did Jim Thorpe accomplish?
- Who wrote *Mrs. Frisby and the Rats of NIMH?*
- How does a newspaper story develop?

You can find answers to these questions—and a wealth of other information as well—in your community or school library.

Sometimes, it is enjoyable just to browse through a library and see what is there. However, if you have an assignment or report to complete by a certain date, you will want to find materials and information as quickly as possible. Therefore, you need to know what kinds of books and information your library contains and where these materials can be found.

In the library, books are classified into two major groups: fiction and nonfiction. The nonfiction group contains a special group of books called reference books.

About the Photograph

Did you know that there is unfamiliar territory for you to explore right in your library? Go exploring! Go to your library!

Fiction Books

The group of fiction books, or fiction collection, is found in a special section of the library. These books, which are made-up stories, are arranged alphabetically according to the author's last name. Most libraries identify fiction books with an *F* on the spine, or back edge. A shelf of fiction books, arranged in the correct order, would look like this:

Nonfiction Books

The difference between fiction and nonfiction books is the difference between a story (something a writer has made up) and facts (things that actually happen or have happened). Nonfiction can be the record of a person's experiences, the historical record of a nation, or a book on one of the many sciences that explain the world of nature.

In most libraries, the nonfiction collection is larger than the fiction collection. Nonfiction collections contain books from a vast number of subject areas. Because so many subjects are included in the nonfiction area, a system of classification is necessary for books to be located easily. In 1876, Melvil Dewey set up such a system. It is the most widely used library system in the world.

Dewey grouped all nonfiction books into ten major subject areas and assigned a group of numbers to each area. The system, which was named after him, is called the Dewey Decimal Classification System. The ten major areas and the range of their numbers are listed below. Subjects included in each of the areas are listed at the right.

Dewey Decimal Classification System

000–099	General Reference	Encyclopedias, almanacs
100–199	Philosophy and Psychology	Beliefs, morals, personality
200–299	Religion	Bible, mythology
300–399	Social Sciences	Education, government, law
400–499	Languages	Foreign languages, dictionaries
500–599	Sciences	Astronomy, math, zoology
600–699	Useful Arts	Business, cooking, medicine, sewing, television
700–799	Fine Arts	Acting, music, painting, photography, sports
800–899	Literature	Novels, plays, poetry
900–999	History	Biography, geography, travel

This numbering system is not limited to the three-place numbers from 000 to 999. Numbers can be expanded by placing a decimal point after the three-digit numbers. This "decimal" system helps to create subdivisions for each category. For example, under Useful Arts (the 600–699 range of numbers), there are many subdivisions that are not shown on the chart above. "Domestic animals" has the number 636. One subdivision is for Horses (636.1); another is for Dogs (636.7).

Activity A

Visit the fiction section of your library. Copy the titles and authors of ten fiction books that look interesting to you. List them alphabetically, using the last names of the authors.

Activity B

After studying the chart of the Dewey Decimal Classification System on page 221, decide to which group of numbers you would go to find a book on each of the following topics.

1. Greek mythology

2. Spanish

3. The paintings of Mary Cassatt

4. A biography of Bill Cosby

5. The sun and planets

6. A play to perform for Thanksgiving

7. Soccer

8. Learning to sew

9. Modern philosophy

10. Schools in America

Writer's Corner

▶ Pretend you are giving a tour of your local or school library to a friend who has never seen it. Write down clear directions that explain how to find your favorite sections of the library. Use the Dewey Decimal Classification System's numbers to make your directions clearer.

The Card Catalog

LESSON 2

The card catalog helps you to find books in your library quickly and easily.

Suppose your teacher assigns you a report on underwater exploration. In a conversation, your friend tells you that C. S. Lewis is a good author. Later, a classmate recommends the book *From the Mixed-up Files of Mrs. Basil E. Frankweiler.* Where can you find the information you need for your report, some books by C. S. Lewis, and *From the Mixed-up Files of Mrs. Basil E. Frankweiler?* The place to begin is the library's card catalog.

The card catalog may be a computer terminal, or it may be a cabinet with small drawers containing 3" x 5" cards. To use a computerized catalog, you type in the author, title, or subject to find information about the library's resources. In a cabinet, you will find the cards arranged alphabetically.

For fiction books, there are two listings: one lists the books by authors; the other, by titles. Each entry contains the same information about the book, but in a slightly different order.

If you know an author's name and want to find out the titles of his or her books, you should look up the last name of the author. Here are how the headings for two author cards for C. S. Lewis would look:

```
F
Lew        Lewis, C. S.
                  The Lion, the Witch, and the Wardrobe
```

```
F
Lew        Lewis, C. S.
                  Out of the Silent Planet
```

If you know only the title of a book, you have to consult the title card. The information is the same as on the author card except that the title is printed first. Title cards are arranged alphabetically according to the first word of the title. The words *a, an,* and *the* are not used for alphabetical arrangement. If you were looking for the title *The Lion, the Witch, and the Wardrobe,* you would look under the letter *L* for *Lion,* not *T* for *The.* A sample beginning of a title card is shown below.

The Lion, the Witch, and the Wardrobe

F

Lew   **Lewis, C. S.**

The letters "F Lew" appear on both the author card and the title card. To find this book by C. S. Lewis, you would go to the shelves where the fiction books are located. That is what the *F* for fiction tells you. Then you would look in the *L* section for Lewis. There you would find the C. S. Lewis books that are available. Sometimes the book you want is not on the shelf, but you know from the card catalog that the library has a copy. You might request that the librarian include your name on a waiting list for the book. You will then be notified when the book is available.

Nonfiction books have three kinds of cards: author, title, and subject. When you want to find information on a certain subject, such as underwater exploration, you need to refer to the subject card. There might be several subject cards for a particular subject, each listing a different book. After you checked all the cards on your subject, you would write down the titles and the identifying numbers of the books you wanted to use. At the top of the next page is a sample subject card for the subject "castles."

Castles

728.8
Sa5c **Sancha, Sheila**

      The Castle Story. Crowell, 1983.
        224p illus

      A reference that includes considerable
      information about types of castles.

      1 Castles   2 Buildings—Middle Ages
      3 Architecture—History of
      I. Sancha, Sheila   II. Title

In the upper left-hand corner of each card is the call number. The first line is the Dewey decimal number assigned to the book. This is the number you would use to find the book on the shelf. Most libraries have maps posted showing you where each group of numbers (200s, 400s, 700s, and so on) is located. Once you find the correct shelf, you then refer to the second line of the call number (*Sa* in the example) to find your book. The second line begins with the first letter or letters of the author's last name.

A helpful feature of most catalog cards is the cross-references. Cross-references are the numbered subject areas printed near the bottom of the card. These references suggest other topics you can explore for additional material.

For example, if you looked up the subject "spaceflight," you would probably find these cross-references:

1 Aviation   2 Astronauts
3 Project Apollo

Activity A

Visit the library and use the card catalog to complete this assignment.

1. List two books by each author.
   A. Ursula K. Le Guin
   B. Madeleine L'Engle
   C. Scott O'Dell

2. Locate the title card for each of the following books and name the author.
   A. *Charlotte's Web*
   B. *The Secret of Crossbone Hill*
   C. *American Tall Tales*

Activity B

Use the card catalog in your library to answer the following items.

1. Who wrote the book *Little Women?*
2. Name a book by Elizabeth George Speare.
3. Name a title and author from the subject area "transportation."
4. Who wrote *The Hobbit?*
5. Name two books written by Laura Ingalls Wilder.

Activity C

Visit your school or local library and look up the following subjects. List three cross-references for each.

1. Pets   2. Sports   3. Hobbies   4. Music

Writer's Corner

▶ Look up a book by title that you have already read. Read the short description of the book that is given. Write your own paragraph that more fully describes the book.

LESSON 3

Dictionary Skills

A dictionary is a book of words arranged in alphabetical order. A dictionary provides the correct pronunciation, spelling, and definition of each word.

There are many different kinds of dictionaries. There are pocket dictionaries. There are dictionaries just for grammar school students, for high school students, and for college students. There are dictionaries that list the names of famous people. Each kind of dictionary has a special purpose.

Dictionary writers, called lexicographers, include words that will fit the needs of the group for whom the dictionary is intended. A large dictionary may have more than one-half million words. A dictionary for beginning readers may have only 30,000 words. For example, the word *funambulist* (tightrope walker) would appear in an advanced dictionary but not in a dictionary for beginning readers. It would be considered too difficult and not very commonly used.

Alphabetical Order

Dictionary entries are arranged in alphabetical order. How well do you know your alphabet? Activity A will challenge you to alphabetize words as quickly as you can.

Activity A

Alphabetize the words in each set as quickly and accurately as you can.

1. BY FIRST LETTER
honorable
suite
windmill
criticism
venture
refund
luxury
keystone
goblet
journal

2. BY SECOND LETTER
persevere
profile
pagoda
piccolo
pyramid
plague
physical
positive
pulse
psychology

3. BY THIRD LETTER
devotion
decline
determine
defraud
deposit
destiny
derby

4. BY FOURTH LETTER
tricycle
trillion
triple
triumph
trial
trinket
tribute

Activity B

Make a list of eight to ten words beginning with *ar*. Each word should have a different third letter. Mix up the words and give them to another student to alphabetize. Do the activity again with words beginning with *do, mar,* and *sto*.

Guide Words

The two words printed at the top of every dictionary page are called guide words. They help you locate your word. The first guide word is the first entry on that particular page, and the second guide word is the last entry on that page. Any word coming alphabetically between these two guide words will be located on that page, too. Here are two sample pages from a dictionary showing guide words.

500 occasional/ointment   O.K./one 501

Off would be found on page 500 because *of* comes after *oc* and before *oi* in the alphabet. The word *old* would appear on page 501 since *ol* comes after *ok* and before *on.* The word *only* would come after page 501 because *onl* comes after *one,* and *one* is the last entry on page 501.

Activity C

Use the guide words shown on the dictionary pages above, and indicate whether each word would be located before page 500, on page 500, on page 501, or after page 501.

1. occupy
2. Oklahoma
3. onion
4. Olympic
5. obtain

6. octopus
7. ocean
8. occasion
9. omit
10. onlooker

Activity D

Set up *opossum* and *orchestra* as guide words. Write two words that would appear in your dictionary right before this page, four words that would appear on this page, and two words that would appear after this page. Do the activity again with *genealogy* and *gerbil* as guide words.

Reading a Dictionary Entry

Knowing all the parts included in a dictionary entry can help you discover important information about a word. The following sample shows you what is included in most entries.

A. division into syllables
B. pronunciation
C. accent
D. part of speech
E. definition
F. sample phrase or sentence

per mit (pər mĭt´ for 1, 2; pər´ mĭt or pər mĭt´ for 3) —v. 1 let; allow: *Her parents will not permit her to travel alone.* 2 give an opportunity: *If the weather permits, we'll head for the lake.* —n. 3 a license granted by one in authority: *Fishing permits are now available.*

Activity E

Refer to the sample dictionary entry above to answer the following questions.

1. How many parts of speech are listed for *permit* in the entry?
2. How many meanings are listed for *permit* as a noun?
3. When *permit* is used as a verb, which syllable is accented?
4. Write the second definition of *permit* as a verb.
5. How many pronunciations are listed for *permit* as a noun?

Writer's Corner

▶ A dictionary uses precise, often short definitions to explain what a word means. Your teacher will assign a word to you. Do more than what a dictionary does, and write a paragraph that fully defines the word.

Thesaurus

A thesaurus is a special reference book that lists synonyms.

A thesaurus is a special kind of book that lists synonyms. Synonyms are words that have the same or almost the same meaning.

Suppose you have written the following sentence:

> The carousel I rode in Santa Clara was *big*—it was ten stories high!

You decide that *big* is not a strong enough word to explain how big the carousel was. You look up the word *big* in a thesaurus, and you find the words *enormous, gigantic, huge,* and *large* as synonyms of *big.* You decide that *gigantic* is the best word to use to replace *big.*

In a thesaurus, words are generally arranged in alphabetical order, as in a dictionary. An entry might look like this:

bashful   shy, timid, modest   **bold**

The words *shy, timid,* and *modest* are synonyms for *bashful.* The word *bold* is an antonym for *bashful.* Often, antonyms, or words opposite in meaning, are given in a thesaurus. Look up in a dictionary any words you do not understand in the entry. Then, from the list of synonyms, choose the word that best fits the meaning of what you want to say.

In another kind of thesaurus, synonyms for a word would appear under a main entry. A sample entry would look like this:

> **BLOCK**
> As a verb, *block* means "to stop the movement of."
>
> **SYNONYMS**
>
> delay   To stop for a time
>   The teacher *delayed* the deadline for our reports.
>
> hinder   To slow down the movement of something
>   The bad weather *hindered* the construction of the skyscraper.
>
> prevent   To keep something from happening
>   Doctors try to *prevent* diseases from starting.
>
> prohibit   To refuse to allow to be done
>   The city *prohibits* swimming at public beaches after 8 P.M.

This kind of thesaurus usually has an index. It is often best to look in the index first. Many times the word for which you need a synonym will not appear as a main entry, but will appear as a synonym under a main entry.

Why is a thesaurus a helpful tool? A thesaurus can help you

- express yourself more exactly.
- build your vocabulary.
- improve your writing.
- avoid using the same word over and over in your writing.

Activity A

1. Look up each word below in a thesaurus. Write three synonyms for each.

    awful   eat   funny   speak

2. Look up each word below in a thesaurus. Write two antonyms for each.

    make   quiet   rough   old

Activity B

Find the synonym for *block* that best completes each sentence. Use the sample thesaurus entry on page 232.

1. I tried to catch the vase, but I could not _____ it from falling and breaking.
2. Because of rain, it was necessary to _____ the start of the baseball game.
3. The government does _____ private citizens from printing money.
4. Messy handwriting will _____ reading.

Activity C

Each pair of sentences has the same italicized word. Look up the italicized word in a thesaurus, and rewrite each sentence using a more exact synonym.

1. The commission will *plan* the Fourth of July celebration.
   Claudia and Jaime succeeded in their *plan* to spend a week in the museum.
2. Fred was *sad* when his friend moved away.
   The Baker family was *sad* at the loss of their grandmother.
3. Pennsylvania was *started* by the Quakers.
   A general meeting and social *started* our year.
4. He *ended* the test as the bell rang.
   Our class *ended* the year with a party.
5. I have a strong *belief* that an education is important.
   The teacher's *belief* in Adam helped him win the contest.

Writer's Corner

▶ Use a thesaurus to find one word that has at least three synonyms. Using the synonyms, write a paragraph that describes your word. Be creative. Use similes and metaphors to help you paint a vivid picture.

Using Other Reference Tools

Reference materials are books designed to give information and facts on a wide variety of subjects.

Each kind of reference material has its special purpose. There are three kinds of reference materials that you will be studying: encyclopedias, almanacs, and atlases.

Become familiar with these reference materials and where they are located in your library so you can use these materials effectively and your time in the library efficiently.

Using the Encyclopedia

An encyclopedia is a set of books containing articles, pictures, and maps. It gives general information about people, places, things, and events. People with special knowledge in each area provide the information. Therefore, hundreds of people contribute their knowledge, talent, and research to produce an encyclopedia.

Encyclopedia articles are arranged in alphabetical order. Guide letters on the spine of each volume inform you that articles beginning with that letter can be found in that particular volume. For example, an article on "Rome" could be found in the *R* volume of the encyclopedia.

Just as there are guide words in a dictionary, there are guide words in an encyclopedia to help you find articles. However, in an encyclopedia, there is only one guide word at the top of each page. Articles that fit alphabetically between the two guide words will be found on either of the two pages. Look at the two guide words in the illustration on the top of the next page.

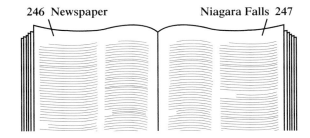

246 Newspaper   Niagara Falls 247

An article on "Newton, Sir Isaac" would be found on this set of pages since *Newt* comes after *news* and before *Ni.* An article on "Nicaragua" would come after page 247 since *Nic* comes after *Nia* in alphabetical order.

To find information in your encyclopedia, you might need to find the main idea of your topic. For example, if you were doing a report on "holiday customs in Japan," the main idea would be Japan. Articles that contain a great deal of information are usually divided into sections. For example, "Holidays and Customs" might be a subtitle under the general heading of "Japan." The most efficient way to use an encyclopedia is to find the general heading and then locate the specific subtitle.

Another important feature of the encyclopedia is the cross-reference section at the end of the article. These titles suggest other articles to which you can refer if you need more information. For example, if you looked up "Nursery School," the cross-references at the end of the article might be "Education," "History of Education," "Kindergarten," "Elementary School," and "Owen, Robert."

Activity A

Identify the main topic in an encyclopedia that would contain information on each of the following.

1. Name five aquariums in the United States.
2. How are photographs developed?
3. What are a few of the customs and ceremonies of Buddhism?
4. What are the capital, state bird, and state flower of Illinois?
5. Name some of the methods of food preservation.

Activity B

Consult your encyclopedia for the following articles. Name two cross-references for each topic that would give more information.

ENTRY	CROSS-REFERENCES
1. Olympic Games	
2. Heart	
3. Grand Canyon	
4. Alphabet	
5. Blindness	
6. Bees	

Using the Almanac

An almanac is a reference book with current general information. It contains facts, general data, and current statistics on many subjects. An almanac is published every year so that all its information is kept up to date. As a result, a 1999 almanac would contain world information, government data, and population statistics from 1998.

A table of contents and an index are provided to help you find your information.

The most commonly used almanacs are

- *The World Almanac and Book of Facts.*
- *Information Please Almanac.*
- *Guinness Book of World Records.*

Activity C

Study this section from the general index of *The World Almanac and Book of Facts*. To which pages would you refer if you were trying to answer the following questions?

1. What are the current world pole vault records?
2. If you looked up Pope John Paul II, to what entry in the index would you be referred?
3. What are the changing patterns in the United States' population?
4. Which playwright received the Pulitzer Prize last year?
5. What awards are given to poets?
6. What are the words of the Pledge of Allegiance?
7. Who discovered the North Pole?
8. What is the American Indian population of the United States?

Activity D

Make up a quiz that requires the use of the almanac. Think of some main topics that an almanac would contain—for example, state capitals. Then use the almanac to make a list of state capitals on a piece of paper. In a column across from this list, write the state for each capital, but mix up the order. Exchange papers with a partner. Use the almanac to match the pieces of information. Other quiz ideas are matching Olympic winners with the year or the field in which they won medals, or matching presidents with their birthplaces.

Using the Atlas

An atlas is a reference book with maps. You can use an atlas to locate cities, towns, countries, continents, bodies of water, islands, or mountains and to find geographical information about such places. In addition, most atlases also give information on population, climate, and products. A table of contents in the front of an atlas or an index at the back will help you find the information you need.

Activity ■E

For each statement or question below, tell which source listed here you would use to find the information. For some items, more than one source would be correct.

dictionary   encyclopedia
thesaurus   almanac
card catalog   atlas

1. If you spent your vacation in Wyoming, what national parks could you visit?
2. Give two antonyms for the word *hurry.*
3. Is the book *Bridge to Teribithia* in your library?
4. What is a *queue,* and how do you pronounce the word?
5. Give the definition of *marmoset.*
6. Give a few more exact words for *walking.*
7. What highway would you take from Atlanta, Georgia, to Montgomery, Alabama?
8. Does your library contain any books about knights in the Middle Ages?
9. What are the names of the present state governors?
10. What are the different varieties of apples, and which are the leading apple-producing states?

Writer's Corner

▶ Draw a map of your state. Label the major cities, bodies of water, boundaries, and the state capital. Pretend you are a travel agent who is promoting vacations in your state. Write a paragraph that explains why any family should vacation in your state.

Researching Your Roots

Knowing about your ancestors, the family members who came before you, helps you know yourself better. Research the country where your ancestors lived, and write a report about the information you find. Present your report orally.

 Prewriting

Ask family members where your ancestors are from. If you have ancestors from several countries, choose one to focus on.

Questions like these might help you plan your research.

- Where is my ancestors' country located?

- What is the climate like?

- What industries is the country famous for?

- What special traditions and holidays does the country have?

- What important historical events happened in the country?

Read an encyclopedia entry to get a general idea of what might be interesting about the ancestral country you chose for your report. Then choose two or three of your questions and research the answers.

Use various sources to find information. Write each fact you want to remember on a separate note card. At the top of the card, write the question it answers. At the bottom, write the name and author of the source and the page number of the fact.

Use Different Kinds of Sources

An encyclopedia is a good starting place, but short encyclopedia articles cannot give you all the specific information you need. Use a variety of sources including books, magazines, and interviews.

Drafting

When you've finished your research, use your questions to sort your note cards. Then make an outline of the information you plan to include in your report.

Write an introduction that will capture your reader's attention. You may want to begin with a story about one of your ancestors or start with an interesting fact from your research.

Each major topic in your outline will be a separate paragraph. Use the major heading to write the main idea sentence. Then expand your notes to write sentences about the supporting ideas. Be sure to use your own words, not the words of your sources.

End your report with a sentence that tells how you feel about the country of your ancestors.

Finally, write a title that will let your reader know at a glance what your report is about.

The Country of Thailand

I. Describing Thailand

  A. In Southeast Asia

  B. Bordered by Myanmar, Laos, Cambodia, and Malaysia

  C. Has tropical climate with monsoons and dry season

II. Resources and Industry

  A. Agriculture

    1. Rice is principal crop and leading export

    2. Also grow maize, cassava, and kenaf

  B. One of world's largest producers of rubber

III. People

  A. Thai is the official language

Revising, Proofreading, and Publishing

Revising

Time to Take Another Look

Revising your report is an opportunity to make your writing sound as interesting as a story. Make sure it flows smoothly and has strong, vivid verbs and adjectives. Ask yourself these questions to help you revise:

❑ Does my report begin with a fact or story that makes my reader want to read on?

❑ Do the details in each paragraph support the paragraph's main idea sentence?

❑ Do I need to rearrange paragraphs or details to make their order more logical?

❑ Does my report sound as if I wrote it in my own words?

❑ Do I need to replace overused words with more interesting ones?

❑ Does my ending sentence sum up my ideas or feelings?

❑ Do I need to add citations to show where I found my information?

You may need to verify some of your facts at this point. Check your original sources if something doesn't sound quite right. As you revise, use a colored pencil to make your revisions stand out.

CARS Can Help You Remember

Use the letters of the word CARS to help you remember what to do when you revise.

C hange a word or sentence to make it sound better.

A dd interesting details that you left out.

R emove unnecessary words by combining two short sentences.

S ubstitute more precise words for weak, overused verbs and adjectives.

Proofreading

Time to Look at Capitalization, Punctuation, and Spelling

Once you've revised the content of your report, proofread it to correct capitalization, punctuation, spelling, and grammar errors.

Use the checklist below to edit and proofread your report.

❏ Did I indent the first word of each paragraph?

❏ Did I use capital letters for the names of people and places?

❏ Did I follow the format for citing my sources?

❏ Did I spell all the names of people and places correctly?

> **Compare Final Copy and Draft**
>
> Ask a partner to follow along from your final copy as you read aloud your revised draft. Tell your partner to stop you if he or she hears any differences between your final copy and the revised draft.

Publishing

Time to Share

After all your hard work, you'll want to publish your report to share your new information.

To publish, follow these steps:

1. Copy your revised draft in your neatest handwriting or type it on a computer.

2. After you finish, proofread your final copy one more time.

3. Check to make sure you did not leave anything out as you copied your revised draft.

4. Add maps or pictures, if you wish.

Present your report orally.

1. Rehearse by reading your report aloud several times.

2. Ask your family for permission to bring in photos or artifacts from your ancestors.

3. Read your report in a firm, clear voice.

4. Make eye contact with your audience.

5. Show the maps, pictures, or artifacts you brought.

PART 2
Grammar, Usage, and Mechanics

244

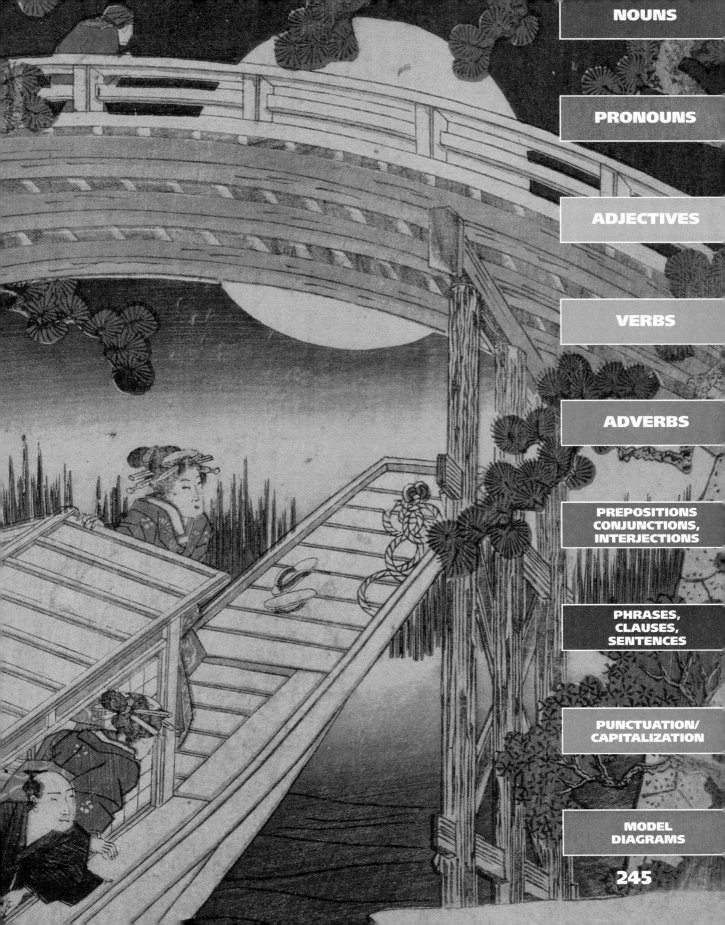

NOUNS

PRONOUNS

ADJECTIVES

VERBS

ADVERBS

PREPOSITIONS
CONJUNCTIONS,
INTERJECTIONS

PHRASES,
CLAUSES,
SENTENCES

PUNCTUATION/
CAPITALIZATION

MODEL
DIAGRAMS

Kinds of Nouns

A noun is a name word.

Read this paragraph. Each of the words printed in italics is a noun. Tell whether each names a person, place, or thing.

> The *sandwich,* which is easy to make and eat, is a common *food* in the *United States.* The *sandwich* is named after the *Earl of Sandwich.* This *aristocrat* lived in *England* two hundred *years* ago. The *earl* enjoyed *games* so much that he disliked stopping to eat. Then he had an *idea.* He had a *servant* put *meat* between *slices* of *bread,* and he ate this while playing.

Proper Nouns and Common Nouns

A proper noun names a particular person, place, or thing. A common noun names one member of a class of persons, places, or things.

	PROPER NOUNS	COMMON NOUNS
PERSON	Galileo	scientist
PLACE	Seattle	city
THING	*Voyager 2*	satellite

About the Photograph

Friends. School. Lunch. Sandwiches. You need nouns to name the people, places, and things in this photograph. What nouns tell about your lunchtime?

Proper nouns may contain several words. The important words in proper nouns are capitalized.

the Great Wall of China   the Rock of Gibraltar

Exercise 1

Find the nouns in these sentences. Tell whether each noun is proper or common.

1. Diana was a goddess of the Romans.
2. The attic of Greenwood Public Library is full of bats!
3. Christopher Columbus was always interested in ships.
4. Rhode Island is the smallest state in the United States.
5. The pyramids in Egypt are very old.
6. Imposing castles stand on the rugged hills of Belgium.
7. Beautiful lilacs bloom in our garden in May.
8. The teeth of a shark are as hard as steel.
9. The delicatessen bakes a giant cake each Fourth of July.
10. Buffalo Bill was a rider for the Pony Express.
11. Monica Carey lives in Chicago.
12. A storyteller from Ghana told a legend of the spider.
13. The glassware sparkled on the table.
14. The visitors were fascinated by the Cascade Mountains.
15. The tugboat chugged down the Mississippi River.

Exercise 2

Write a proper noun for each common noun.

Example: common noun, *state*
            proper noun, *Wisconsin*

1. river
2. island
3. book
4. ocean
5. street

6. building
7. hero
8. museum
9. holiday
10. explorer

11. teacher
12. author
13. friend
14. woman
15. team

16. park
17. city
18. boy
19. newspaper
20. continent

Exercise 3

Write a common noun for each proper noun.

Example: proper noun, *Poland*
            common noun, *country*

1. Kentucky
2. Mexico
3. Dodgers
4. Alps
5. Edison

6. Picasso
7. Labor Day
8. Amazon
9. *Santa Maria*
10. Paris

11. Mediterranean
12. Jackie Robinson
13. George Washington
14. Eiffel Tower
15. *Charlotte's Web*

16. White House
17. Amy
18. Disney World
19. Los Angeles
20. Saturn

Practice Power

▶ Write a paragraph that describes lunchtime at your school. As you reread your paragraph, circle all the common nouns you used and underline all the proper nouns.

Collective Nouns

A collective noun names a group of persons, animals, or things considered as a unit.

Our *class* is large.

This sentence names all the students in a grade as one group. *Class* is the name of a group of persons considered as one.

Here are some groups of persons or things that may be named by collective nouns.

GROUPS OF PERSONS OR THINGS	COLLECTIVE NOUNS
worshipers in church	congregation
ships of a navy	fleet
athletes who play together	team

Exercise 1

Find the collective nouns in these sentences.

1. A bear on roller skates juggled eggs for the crowd.

2. The storm took the crew of the sailboat by surprise.

3. The troop of scouts learned how to fold a tent.

4. The secretary of a club writes the minutes.

5. Today I saw a flock of geese flying south.

6. Tom's family wanted an apartment near the park.

7. A colony of bees produces wax and honey.

8. When the doors opened, the audience entered.

Exercise 2

Make two columns on a sheet of paper. In the first column, list all the collective nouns in these sentences. In the second column, list the group of persons or things named by each collective noun.

Example: The fleet sailed at dawn.

COLLECTIVE NOUN	GROUP OF PERSONS OR THINGS
fleet	ships

1. The shepherd took special care of his flock.

2. As the audience applauded, the cast bowed.

3. Ray directed the cowhands who were trying to stop the stampeding herd.

4. Is the band rehearsing this afternoon?

5. Our organization is raising money to help save the whales.

Practice Power

▶ Fold a piece of paper into fourths. In each section, draw a quick-sketch picture for each of the following four collective nouns. Then caption your drawings by using each collective noun in a sentence.

1. pod of whales   3. colony of rabbits
2. swarm of insects 4. troop of monkeys

Abstract and Concrete Nouns

Abstract Nouns

> **An abstract noun expresses a quality or condition. It names something that cannot be seen or touched.**

A marathon runner needs *strength* and *confidence* to finish a race.

Notice the abstract nouns in this sentence. They are *strength* and *confidence*. They name qualities a person can have.

Exercise 1

Find the abstract nouns in these sentences.

1. Kim showed her flying ability as she landed the plane in a rocky field.
2. We admired the beauty of the handmade quilt.
3. If goldfish are left in darkness, they may turn white.
4. Can anyone ever have complete freedom?
5. Perseverance helped Ricardo win the pie-eating contest.
6. It was Lloyd's idea to put the lobster in his mother's bathtub.
7. A cockroach will run to safety when the lights go on.
8. Joe spent most of his childhood on a reservation.
9. George loses his patience when the bus is late.
10. Mrs. Cowell's knowledge of giraffes amazed the zookeepers.
11. Since Madeline showed interest in Roald Dahl's *Charlie and the Chocolate Factory,* her teacher recommended *James and the Giant Peach.*

Exercise 2

Use these abstract nouns in sentences of your own.

1. love
2. democracy
3. independence
4. charity
5. sickness
6. patriotism
7. strength
8. truth
9. cleanliness
10. enthusiasm
11. pride
12. happiness
13. humility
14. cheerfulness
15. confidence
16. vitality
17. pleasure
18. bravery

Exercise 3

Many abstract nouns may be formed from other words by adding the suffixes *-hood, -ion, -ity, -ment, -ness, -ship*, or *-ty*. Make abstract nouns from these words by adding the proper suffix. Then use each of the nouns in a sentence.

1. friend
2. swift
3. moral
4. loyal
5. good
6. enjoy
7. kind
8. honest
9. leader
10. knight
11. thoughtful
12. truthful
13. bright
14. celebrate
15. major
16. disagree
17. companion
18. protect
19. rapid
20. entertain

Concrete Nouns

A concrete noun names a thing we can see or touch. Most of the nouns we use are concrete nouns.

Here are examples of concrete nouns.

bridge	violet	bus
pilot	seal	movie
Japan	Mount Everest	Dr. Seuss

Exercise 4

Find the concrete nouns in these sentences.

1. Who baked these delicious cookies?
2. The dictionary was so big the librarian could barely lift it.
3. Huge waves washed the rocky cliffs.
4. Larry stood on the icy sidewalk with a shovel.
5. The Hawaiian Islands are actually the tops of volcanoes.
6. A strange dog dashed through our yard.
7. Early hunters in the Philippine Islands used the yo-yo as a weapon.
8. Did you see the mischievous raccoon?
9. The young boy needed a map to find the subway.
10. The students could see Mars clearly through the telescope.
11. The plumber took the pipe apart and found a ring inside.
12. A book of poems was selected.
13. What is hidden in that old wooden trunk?
14. Some termites in Africa build very tall mounds!
15. Do you like jam on your bread?

Practice Power

▶ **Tell whether each noun is abstract or concrete. Then use each one in a sentence of your own.**

1. army	6. convoy	11. wisdom
2. nutrition	7. group	12. crew
3. privacy	8. hope	13. fleet
4. committee	9. ambition	14. band
5. carelessness	10. honesty	15. gratitude

LESSON 4 — Words Used as Nouns and Verbs

A noun is a name word. A verb expresses action or being. Many words can be used as either nouns or verbs.

We decided not to go to the *dance*. (noun)
I *dance* to all kinds of music. (verb)

Exercise 1

Tell whether each italicized word is a noun or a verb.

1. We left our blankets in the *shade* of the beach umbrella.
2. Elm trees *shade* Marina's prize-winning tulip beds.
3. Did Mark Twain really *pilot* a riverboat?
4. The *pilot* double-checked the map.
5. The Giorgio brothers still *work* in their Italian restaurant.
6. That *work* on the farm was harder than I expected.
7. We're planning a solar *experiment* for the first of May.
8. I *experiment* with color before I do a final design.
9. The top *step* was coated with ice.
10. Do not *step* on the mousetrap.
11. *Cover* the aquarium before you vacuum.
12. Kate drew a kangaroo on the *cover* of my notebook.
13. The *cut* required three stitches!
14. Paul Bunyan could *cut* a tree in half with one easy swing!
15. I *cut* the pieces of material for the dress.
16. During the winter, we use the fireplace to *heat* our house.
17. I won the first *heat* of the race.
18. It is important to drink water during the *heat* of the summer.

Practice Power

▶ What if last night you met a very unusual person in a dream? Write a short paragraph about this interesting character. Write your paragraph so that it includes words that are used as both nouns and verbs.

LESSON 5 · Qualities of Nouns

> **A noun has number, gender, and case. These are the qualities of a noun.**

In this lesson, you will study number. In the next lessons, you will learn about gender and case.

Number

> **Number shows whether a noun refers to one person or thing (singular number) or more than one (plural number).**

That *rose* is the most beautiful of all the *roses* in our garden.

Rose is singular; *roses* is plural. This change in the form of a noun to show whether the noun refers to one or more than one is called number.

Rules for Forming the Plural

Here are ten rules for forming the plural of nouns. If you want to use the plural of a noun that does not seem to be included in the rules, go to the dictionary for help. You will find that a choice of plural forms is given for some words. In such cases, more than one form would be correct: for example, *volcanos, volcanoes.*

1. Most nouns form the plural by adding *s* to the singular.

SINGULAR	PLURAL	SINGULAR	PLURAL
home	homes	book	books
nurse	nurses	song	songs

2. Nouns ending in *s, x, z, ch,* and *sh* form the plural by adding *es* to the singular.

SINGULAR	PLURAL	SINGULAR	PLURAL
fox	foxes	torch	torches
gas	gases	sash	sashes
topaz	topazes	wish	wishes
dress	dresses	box	boxes

3. Nouns ending in *y*

   a. Nouns ending in *y* preceded by a consonant form the plural by changing the *y* to *i* and adding *es*.

SINGULAR	PLURAL	SINGULAR	PLURAL
country	countries	baby	babies
melody	melodies	city	cities
duty	duties	fly	flies
colony	colonies	cry	cries

   b. Nouns ending in *y* preceded by a vowel form the plural by adding *s* to the singular.

SINGULAR	PLURAL	SINGULAR	PLURAL
day	days	pulley	pulleys
turkey	turkeys	play	plays
valley	valleys	chimney	chimneys
key	keys	attorney	attorneys

4. Nouns ending in *f* or *fe*

   a. Most nouns ending in *f* or *fe* form the plural by adding *s* to the singular.

SINGULAR	PLURAL	SINGULAR	PLURAL
roof	roofs	safe	safes

   b. Some nouns ending in *f* or *fe* form the plural by changing the *f* or *fe* to *ves*.

SINGULAR	PLURAL	SINGULAR	PLURAL
wolf	wolves	loaf	loaves
half	halves	shelf	shelves
knife	knives	scarf	scarves
life	lives	thief	thieves

Use a dictionary to check your spelling.

5. Nouns ending in *o*

    a. All nouns ending in *o* preceded by a vowel form the plural by adding *s* to the singular.

SINGULAR	PLURAL	SINGULAR	PLURAL
radio	radios	bamboo	bamboos
cameo	cameos	studio	studios
trio	trios	portfolio	portfolios

    b. Nouns ending in *o* preceded by a consonant generally form the plural by adding *es* to the singular.

SINGULAR	PLURAL	SINGULAR	PLURAL
tomato	tomatoes	hero	heroes
potato	potatoes	echo	echoes
mosquito	mosquitoes	torpedo	torpedoes

    c. Some nouns ending in *o* preceded by a consonant form the plural by adding *s* to the singular.

SINGULAR	PLURAL	SINGULAR	PLURAL
piano	pianos	alto	altos
solo	solos	silo	silos

6. A few nouns form the plural by a change within the singular.

SINGULAR	PLURAL	SINGULAR	PLURAL
man	men	woman	women
tooth	teeth	goose	geese
mouse	mice	foot	feet

7. A few nouns form the plural by adding *en* or *ren*.

SINGULAR	PLURAL	SINGULAR	PLURAL
ox	oxen	child	children

8. A few nouns have the same form in the plural as in the singular.

SINGULAR	PLURAL	SINGULAR	PLURAL
deer	deer	corps	corps
trout	trout	salmon	salmon
Chinese	Chinese	sheep	sheep
moose	moose	Japanese	Japanese

9. Compound nouns usually form the plural by adding *s* to the principal word.

SINGULAR	PLURAL
brother-in-law	brothers-in-law
editor in chief	editors in chief
drive-in	drive-ins

10. Letters and numbers

   a. Letters form the plural by adding *s* or *'s*. Lowercase letters and capital letters that would be confusing if *s* alone were added form the plural by adding *'s*.

SINGULAR	PLURAL
TV	TVs
a	*a*'s
I	*I*'s

   b. The plural of numbers is formed by adding *s*.

SINGULAR	PLURAL
1980	1980s
3	3s

Exercise 1

Write the plural of the following words. Then refer to the Rules for Forming the Plural (pages 257–260) to check your answers. Write the number of the rule that applies to each word.

Example: fife   fifes 4a

1. dish
2. grape
3. cherry
4. radio
5. door
6. church
7. sky
8. alto
9. vessel
10. daisy
11. monkey
12. roof
13. chief
14. lady
15. journey
16. piano
17. loss
18. dairy
19. ox
20. leaf
21. ostrich
22. hero
23. studio
24. fairy
25. *i*
26. 1970
27. match
28. hoof
29. candy
30. deer
31. birdhouse
32. wish
33. sister-in-law
34. alley
35. gulf
36. goose
37. family
38. child
39. Japanese
40. ax
41. moose
42. jury

Exercise 2

Make two columns on your paper and write *Singular* at the top of the first column and *Plural* at the top of the second. Then write each word in the singular or plural column. Complete the chart by writing the singular or plural form for each word.

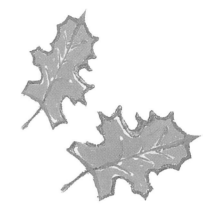

butterflies	leaves
sleigh	colonies
cities	bookcases
beet	kisses
surgeons	man
six-year-olds	squash
baseball	duty
chief	studio
blackberry	chalkboard
sheep	Vietnamese
ally	oxen
valley	sheriff

Exercise 3

Complete each sentence with the plural form of the noun in parentheses.

1. Falcons live on _____ (skyscraper) in _____ (city).
2. Paul always eats the _____ (*E*) in his alphabet soup first.
3. Both of my _____ (brother-in-law) are _____ (attorney).
4. Rivers make _____ (valley) as they flow through _____ (hill).
5. Are _____ (tomato) fruits or _____ (vegetable)?
6. In some states, sales _____ (tax) are placed on food.

Practice Power

▶ Look through old newspapers and magazines for headlines and titles, and cut out words that illustrate each spelling rule on pages 257–260. On a large piece of paper, make two columns, one headed *Singular* and the other *Plural*. Glue each word in the appropriate column and write the singular or plural in the other column.

Gender

Gender is that quality of a noun by which sex is distinguished. There are three genders: masculine, feminine, and neuter.

The masculine gender indicates males.

> The education of a *knight* began at the age of six or seven.

The feminine gender indicates females.

> The young page was placed under the guidance of the *lady* of the castle.

The neuter gender indicates objects.

> Every *castle* was a training school.

Some nouns may be either masculine or feminine.

> Every *servant* had duties to perform in the castle.

Many nouns that include both genders are now in common use.

TRADITIONAL	ALTERNATE FORM (BOTH GENDERS)
fireman	firefighter
policeman	police officer
chairman	chairperson
councilman	council member

How Gender Is Distinguished

Gender may be distinguished in three ways:

1. by using a different word.

MASCULINE	FEMININE	MASCULINE	FEMININE
son	daughter	gander	goose
nephew	niece	ram	ewe
stallion	mare	bull	cow
drake	duck	husband	wife

2. by using a different ending.

MASCULINE	FEMININE	MASCULINE	FEMININE
prince	princess	waiter	waitress
duke	duchess	emperor	empress

3. by changing part of the word.

MASCULINE	FEMININE	MASCULINE	FEMININE
landlord	landlady	grandfather	grandmother
grandson	granddaughter	stepfather	stepmother

Exercise 1

Tell whether each noun is masculine, feminine, or neuter. Remember, some nouns can include both masculine and feminine genders.

1. doctor
2. waitress
3. bicycle
4. astronaut
5. Alaska
6. computer
7. president
8. king
9. tomcat
10. nurse
11. mother
12. writer
13. lawyer
14. actress
15. lad
16. architect
17. uncle
18. ship
19. heroine
20. basketball
21. secretary
22. police officer
23. cook
24. hamburger
25. husband
26. artist
27. musician

Exercise 2

Write the feminine form for each masculine noun.

1. husband
2. son
3. hero
4. brother
5. waiter
6. grandson
7. male
8. man
9. rooster
10. stepfather
11. lion
12. brother-in-law

Write the masculine form for each feminine noun.

13. cow
14. princess
15. hostess
16. widow
17. bride
18. actress
19. landlady
20. girl
21. mare
22. ewe
23. niece
24. grandmother

Exercise 3

Complete each sentence by choosing the appropriate gender.

1. The _____ (prince, princess) wore a beautiful dress to the ball.
2. Since my father died, my mother is considered to be a _____ (widow, widower).
3. My sister moved to New York with dreams of becoming an _____ (actor, actress).
4. Most of the time, the _____ (groom, bride) walks down the aisle wearing a long, white gown.
5. A _____ (lion, lioness) has a full, flowing mane of coarse hair around the face.

Practice Power

▶ Work with a partner and choose one of the sentences from Exercise 3. Together, write a conversation between the masculine and feminine nouns named in parentheses in the sentence. For example, for sentence 1, write a conversation between the prince and the princess.

LESSON 7 — Nominative Case—Subject

The case of a noun shows its relation to some other word or words in the sentence.

Every noun in a sentence has a special use. For example, nouns can be used as subjects, subjective complements, direct objects, and objects of a preposition.

How a noun is used in a sentence tells the case of the noun. There are three cases of nouns:

- nominative.
- possessive.
- objective.

The first one you will study is the nominative case.

Subject

A noun used as the subject of a verb is in the nominative case.

> *Marcos* built a two-story tree house.
> *Lightning* struck the tree during a big storm.

The person, place, or thing talked about is the subject of a sentence. It may be determined by placing *who* or *what* before the verb. Look at the sentences above. Who built? The answer is *Marcos,* the subject of *built.* What struck? The answer is *lightning,* the subject of *struck.*

A noun used as the subject is in the nominative case.

Exercise 1

Find the subject in each sentence.

1. Lily feeds her kittens tuna every other day.
2. The acrobats perform their act without a safety net!
3. Rembrandt was one of the great painters of Europe.
4. My birthday is in August.
5. Some colonies have millions of ants!
6. A silent crowd gathered in front of the mine.
7. Adventurers from Spain explored South America.
8. Oysters produce fine pearls.
9. Sophie's skateboard slid out from under her feet.
10. At midnight, the weary soldiers reached camp.
11. In the 1920s, movies with sound first appeared in theaters.
12. Antonyms are words with opposite meanings.
13. In a rented car, the visitors toured the ancient city.
14. In the very strong gust of wind, Julian's new umbrella flipped inside out.
15. Every morning Mr. Stolz sets his plants in the sun.
16. In May, the teacher takes her science class to the planetarium.
17. Two teams practice basketball in the gym on Fridays.
18. Without a sound, the baby-sitter tiptoed away from the crib.
19. By accident, Maria hit the softball directly through the principal's window.
20. The veterinarian nervously bandaged the grizzly bear's leg.

Practice Power

▶ **Write ten sentences using the following nouns as subjects.**

1. vegetables
2. Abigail
3. tornado
4. computer
5. dentist
6. music
7. paper
8. summer
9. bicycle
10. Jerry

LESSON 8 Nominative Case— Subjective Complement

A noun used as a subjective complement is in the nominative case.

Beethoven was a famous *composer.*
Sally Ride was the first American *woman* in space.

A noun that refers to the same person or thing as the subject is a subjective complement. A subjective complement renames the subject.

SUBJECT		SUBJECTIVE COMPLEMENT
Beethoven	=	composer
Sally Ride	=	woman

A subjective complement follows a linking verb. The most common linking verb is *be* and its various forms: *am, is, are, was, were, being,* and *been.*

A subjective complement is in the nominative case because the subject is in the nominative case.

Exercise 1

Find the subjective complement in each sentence.

1. The Rhône is a river in France.
2. A spelunker is an explorer of caves.
3. Fitzgerald was a lizard with a very long tail.
4. Bill's mother is a successful lawyer.
5. The twins were members of a rock-climbing club.
6. My guitar teacher is Professor Frank.
7. Drums were early forms of communication.
8. This album is the nicest gift!
9. Last year Tammy was the best swimmer on our team.
10. *Treasure Island* is a story of adventure.

Exercise 2

Make two columns on your paper, labeled *Subject* and *Subjective Complement.* For each sentence, write the subject and the subjective complement in the correct columns.

Example: Those two boys are best friends.

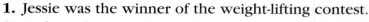

SUBJECT	SUBJECTIVE COMPLEMENT
boys	friends

1. Jessie was the winner of the weight-lifting contest.
2. A cheeseburger is Lou's favorite food.
3. This year the leader of our troop will be Mr. Duskin.
4. That dog is the noisiest animal in the shelter.
5. Yukio was the only skier on the mountain.
6. Photography is an interesting hobby.
7. Nana's voice was just a whisper.
8. Mules are often stubborn animals.
9. A sitar is a musical instrument.
10. The Sears Tower is the tallest building in Chicago.

Exercise 3

Complete each sentence by adding a subjective complement.

1. Michael is a _____ on the basketball team.
2. Someday Roberta will be a(n) _____ .
3. The mysterious package was a(n) _____ for Liza.
4. Gary was a(n) _____ at the Halloween party.
5. The last piece of fruit in the bowl was a(n) _____ .
6. Kareem's constant companion was his _____ .
7. My usual lunch is a(n) _____ .
8. Jennifer is the best _____ in the class.
9. The strange object in the picture was a(n) _____ .
10. My favorite subject in school is _____ .

Practice Power

▶ Write six sentences using the following nouns as subjective complements.

1. insects	3. hurricane	5. winter
2. Cathy	4. pencil	6. lawyer

Nouns in Direct Address

LESSON 9

A noun used in direct address is in the nominative case.

> *Carl,* Mr. Ramos is going to the game.
> There is no one home, *Inga,* at the Chens' house.
> I enjoyed reading your poem, *LaToya.*

In each sentence, the noun printed in italics is used independently to show the person addressed. A noun used in such a way is called a noun in direct address.

A noun in direct address is in the nominative case. It is set off by a comma or commas.

Exercise 1

Find the noun in direct address in each of these sentences. Explain the use of the commas.

1. Try to get all of us in the photograph, Jason, if you can.
2. Watson, I need you!
3. Didn't you beat Malik at the video game, Nina?
4. Hurry, Nat, and catch that hairy spider!
5. Connie, can you imagine living on a space station?
6. Your sister just ate the last french fry, Kip.
7. Thank you, Tony, for cleaning the computer area.
8. Who left these fingerprints, Mr. Vermeer?
9. Judy, a dance group will perform at school today.
10. Do you know what baklava is, Leo?
11. Wow, Elena, you received the highest grade in the class!
12. Lisa, your gerbil just escaped from its cage!
13. Will you help me with my math homework, Mother?
14. Congratulations, Melissa, for winning first place.
15. Please clean your room, Sarah, before you go outside to play.

Exercise 2

Copy the following sentences. Underline the noun in direct address in each and put commas where they are needed.

1. Jim did you get grape jelly on my diary?

2. I saw a shooting star last night Brigette.

3. Forrest please leave the skis outside!

4. Bonnie does your aunt feel any better?

5. Your paper airplane Pete just flew out the door.

6. Did your brother join an aerobics class Lonnie?

7. Agnes the soup of the day is minestrone.

8. Hitch up the horses Susan and we'll go for a ride.

9. Did you make that papier-mâché sculpture Mrs. Campbell?

10. Make a wish Terry and blow out the candles.

11. Get your raincoat Kris and we'll go to the store.

12. Ryan the turkey is ready to be carved.

13. Take out your books students and turn to Chapter Two.

14. Lauren did you find the information you needed?

15. Thank you Mia for watching my pet iguana while I was on vacation.

Exercise 3

Write nine sentences using these words as nouns in direct address.

1. Jill	4. Linda	7. Ray
2. Jack	5. boys and girls	8. Dad
3. Coach	6. Dr. Hancock	9. students

Exercise 4 REVIEW

Tell why the italicized nouns in these sentences are in the nominative case. The choices are subject, subjective complement, or noun in direct address.

1. *Hawks* are *birds* with excellent eyesight.

2. *Bruce*, have you seen our candle-making project?

3. Have you learned your part for the play, *Eileen?*

4. The very earliest *books* were *slabs* of stone.

5. *Nancy*, your *brother* was on the telephone all morning.

6. *Birds* have many different feeding habits.

7. The *currency* in Russia is the *ruble.*

8. *Leaves* floated lazily from the lower branches of the tree.

9. *Beverly Cleary* is a *writer* of children's books.

10. Early *dramas* took place in Greek theaters.

Practice Power

▶ To show your ability to use nouns in the nominative case, write two sentences using a noun as the subjective complement and two using a noun in direct address.

Possessive Case

> **A noun that expresses possession or ownership is in the possessive case.**

    Bill's voice announced the winners.

The voice that announced the winners belonged to or was possessed by Bill. The word *Bill's,* therefore, is in the possessive case. The sign of the possessive case is the apostrophe *s* (*'s*).

Rules for Forming the Possessive Case of Nouns

1. The singular possessive is formed by adding *'s* to the singular form of the noun.

    The *robin's* egg is in the nest.
    Listen to the *comedian's* joke.

2. The plural possessive of plural nouns ending in *s* is formed by adding the apostrophe only.

    The *robins'* eggs are blue.
    Listen to the *comedians'* jokes.

    If the plural form of the noun does not end in *s,* add *'s.*
    Ginny found the *children's* tickets.
    Did you see the display of *women's* gloves?

3. Proper names ending in *s* usually form the possessive case by adding *'s.*

    James's bicycle has just been repaired.
    Dickens's novels are widely read.

4. In compound nouns the *'s* is added to the end of the word.

POSSESSIVE SINGULAR	POSSESSIVE PLURAL
My *brother-in-law's* car is new.	My *brothers-in-law's* cars are new.

Exercise 1

**Find the nouns in the possessive case in these sentences.
Then tell what is being owned or possessed.**

1. Leon's shoes are lying in the middle of the hallway again.
2. A ptarmigan's feathers change from white in the winter to brown in the summer.
3. The knight's armor gleamed in the sunlight.
4. Ellen's new red sneakers lay at the side of the road.
5. The racers' cars were not damaged.
6. Shel Silverstein's humorous poems are popular with children and adults.
7. A person's eye blinks involuntarily.
8. Five of John's companions went with him to the dentist.
9. Our neighbors' cottages are covered with ivy.
10. Lizabel gave me the family's special recipe for perfect fudge.
11. On the calf's flank was the brand of the Rocking R Ranch.
12. Using Matt's compass, we managed to find our way back to the clearing.
13. The barks from the Harrisons' beagles warned us that someone was nearby.
14. Rising water slowly covered Annie McPhearson's cornfields.
15. Nicholas read all night to finish Ted's book.

Exercise 2

**Write the singular possessive and the plural possessive forms
for these nouns.**

1. baby
2. sparrow
3. wife
4. coach
5. astronaut
6. classmate
7. trout
8. nurse
9. artist
10. pharaoh
11. reindeer
12. woman
13. princess
14. snake
15. robot
16. uncle
17. carpenter
18. mouse
19. child
20. witness
21. dancer
22. hedgehog
23. owlet
24. stepsister

Exercise 3

Write each group of words in another way to show possession.

Example: trick of the magician
            the magician's trick

1. poems of Longfellow
2. wheelchair of Bobby
3. red nose of the clown
4. diary of the detective
5. hats of the cowboys
6. slipper of Cinderella
7. daffodils of Mr. Beetle
8. courage of the firefighters
9. colors of the chameleon
10. command of the sergeant
11. joy of the children
12. assignment of the reporter
13. pet shop of Uncle Louis
14. hiding place of the pirates

Practice Power

▶ Examine the picture below and write a paragraph that describes the situation. Be sure to include at least four singular possessive and four plural possessive forms of nouns.

LESSON 11 — Objective Case

NOUNS

Direct Object

A noun used as the direct object of a verb is in the objective case.

The championship team met the *governor.*
The school bought several *computers.*

The direct object of a verb may be determined by placing *whom* or *what* after the verb. The team met whom? The team met the governor. The school bought what? The school bought computers. The nouns *governor* and *computers* are, therefore, direct objects.

Exercise 1

Find the direct object in each sentence.

1. In the parade, Theresa twirled a baton.
2. At the Chinese restaurant, we ate spicy soup.
3. Who invented the zipper?
4. Kerry has moved the parsley from the windowsill.
5. I carry Mr. O'Connor's groceries upstairs to his room.
6. The Anasazi built their homes on the sides of cliffs.
7. Sergei slowly turned his flashlight toward the noise.
8. Did you see the double rainbow this morning?
9. A large dog patiently guarded the door.
10. Becky will weave these long strips into a basket.
11. The bricklayer pushed a huge wheelbarrow.
12. Lady Knotsworth sets a place at the table for the hound!

Exercise 2

Copy each sentence. Underline the verb and add a direct object.

1. Sometimes you can find a(n) _____ inside a shell.
2. Mr. Soon's art class made _____ for Ocean Awareness Week.
3. The crowd anxiously watched the _____ in the water.
4. Nora lost her favorite _____ at the beach.
5. Our class will visit a(n) _____ tomorrow.
6. A group of motorboats carries _____ to the island.
7. Earl read a(n) _____ about fish.
8. Evita wrote a(n) _____ about the dangers of polluting the ocean.
9. Roger dropped the squirming _____ into a huge bucket of water.
10. Divers gather unusual _____ from the ocean floor.

Practice Power

▶ Write six sentences using the following nouns as direct objects.

1. lobster
2. vacation
3. letters
4. ocean
5. mask
6. shell

Objective Case—
Object of a Preposition

> **A noun used as the object of a preposition is in the objective case.**

> Dr. Santilli lives and works in *Detroit.*
> On *Thursday,* there will be a lunar eclipse.
> During the *night,* rain washed away the snow.

In the first sentence, the noun *Detroit* is the object of the preposition *in.* In the second sentence, the noun *Thursday* is the object of the preposition *on.* In the third sentence, the noun *night* is the object of the preposition *during.* The nouns *Detroit, Thursday,* and *night* are in the objective case.

Exercise 1

Find the nouns that are objects of prepositions and name the prepositions.

1. The first Olympic Games were held in Greece.
2. The Venus's-flytrap catches insects in its spiked leaves.
3. We found the baseball mitt underneath the porch.
4. We watched the rat escape into the junkyard.
5. John's kite bobbed above our heads.
6. A clay flowerpot crashed on the sidewalk.
7. The longest day of the year is in June.
8. We get oxygen from the air.
9. Prairie dogs often dig tunnels under the surface of the ground.
10. The division problems on the chalkboard had mysteriously disappeared.

Exercise 2

Complete each sentence with a preposition followed by an object.

1. The snake slithered _____ .
2. _____ , Sadie received a present.
3. Have you ever seen a collection _____ ?
4. The Arabian colts were _____ .
5. Lennie found a large snake _____ .
6. Some pigeons wobbled _____ .
7. Most first graders like books _____ .
8. Not looking, Miguel ran _____ .
9. Fiona sang an Irish song _____ .
10. _____ , a herd of antelopes grazed.

Practice Power

▶ **Write sentences using each of the following prepositions and objects of the prepositions.**

1. up the stairs
2. beside the animals
3. between the trees
4. onto a horse
5. over the rainbow

6. on the grass
7. inside the barn
8. next to the fence
9. from the cow
10. above the door

LESSON 13 Objective Case— Indirect Object

> **A noun used as the indirect object of a verb is in the objective case.**

Some sentences contain two things—the direct object, or receiver of the action, and another object that tells to whom or for whom the action is done. The object to whom or for whom something is done is called the indirect object.

> The librarian gave an *award.* (direct object)
> The librarian gave *Amos* an award. (indirect object)

The direct object of the verb *gave* is *award. Amos,* the indirect object, tells to whom the award was given. The indirect object is ordinarily placed between the verb and the direct object. The preposition *to* or *for* can usually be placed before the indirect object without changing the meaning of the sentence.

> The librarian gave (to) Amos an award.

The following verbs may take indirect objects:

assign	hand	remit
bring	lend	sell
buy	offer	send
deny	owe	show
do	pardon	sing
forbid	pay	teach
forgive	promise	tell
get	read	wish
give	refuse	write
grant		

Exercise 1

The direct objects in these sentences are italicized. Find the indirect objects. Put the word *to* or *for* in front of the indirect object to check your answer.

Example: Michelle offered (to) her friend a *peach.*
Indirect object: friend

1. Leon sends my sister handmade *cards.*
2. The weaver sells tourists llama-hair *blankets.*
3. Frances wrote her father *directions* to the camp.
4. Mr. Key assigned the French class a three-page *report.*
5. I still owe my sister a *dollar* for Mother's present.
6. The mail carrier handed the clerk a large, oddly shaped *package.*
7. Our father denied Marty *permission* to swim.
8. You should give Jean some *advice* on the care of canaries.
9. Early bikes gave their riders a bumpy *trip.*
10. Ellen, tell the students the *story* of your kayak trip on the Haw River.
11. Mason handed the teacher the extra *copies* of the test.
12. Sandra gave her mother a microwave *cookbook.*
13. I'll read the class a *haiku* about snowflakes.
14. Jason lent his brother his *skates.*
15. Show Maggie your new *parakeet.*

Exercise 2

Copy each sentence. Add an indirect object and underline the direct object.

1. Andrew writes _____ letters in code.
2. One Girl Scout sold _____ thousands of boxes of cookies!
3. Donnie will buy _____ a newspaper at the corner.
4. A seismologist gave _____ an explanation of the Richter scale.
5. Who taught _____ that card trick?
6. Dorothy sent _____ an invitation to her birthday party.
7. Ms. McIver tells _____ unbelievable stories about the Loch Ness monster!
8. I am happy to lend _____ my telescope.
9. First, read _____ the directions on the box.
10. Give _____ the grasshopper before it escapes!

Exercise 3

Copy each sentence. Add a direct object and underline the indirect object.

1. José must bring Julie a(n) _____ for her birthday.
2. Ann gave her friend a(n) _____ on the last day of school.
3. Paul sold his neighbor the _____ at his family's garage sale.
4. Who owes me _____ for the sandwiches?
5. The delivery boy offered me _____ with our pizza order.

Practice Power

▶ Use five of the verbs listed on page 279 in sentences of your own. Be sure to include an indirect object and a direct object in each sentence.

LESSON 14

Nouns in Apposition

Appositive in the Nominative Case

> A noun in apposition is in the same case as the noun it explains. An appositive that explains the subject is in the nominative case.

A word or group of words that explains a noun is said to be in apposition with that noun. It is called an appositive.

> Jack Lane, the *wrestler,* weighs almost three hundred pounds.
>
> My older sister, *Cecilia,* built a mobile as an art project.

In the first sentence, *wrestler* explains the noun *Jack Lane.* It is an appositive. Since *Jack Lane* is the subject of the sentence and in the nominative case, *wrestler* is also in the nominative case. In the second sentence, *Cecilia* explains the noun *sister.* Since *sister* is the subject of the sentence and in the nominative case, *Cecilia* is also in the nominative case.

Here are some characteristics of appositives.

- The appositive may be omitted from the sentence and a complete thought remains.
- The appositive follows another noun.
- The appositive has the same meaning or refers to the same person or thing as the noun it explains.
- The appositive is frequently set off by commas.

Exercise 1

Copy these sentences. Draw two lines under each appositive and one line under the noun it explains.

1. Clair, the lifeguard, rescued a toddler from the pool.
2. Wilma Rudolph, a famous American track-and-field star, won three gold medals in the 1960 Olympics.
3. Jai alai, a Spanish game, uses small wicker baskets.
4. Harry Houdini, a magician, would free himself from a locked box underwater.
5. The Cape May Cyclists, a new club, will have daily rides.
6. Leif Ericson, a bold Viking, visited North America.
7. The pyramids, royal tombs, were built thousands of years ago in Egypt.
8. Mrs. Clarkton, the mail carrier, doesn't like loose dogs.
9. Pennsylvania, the Keystone State, produces coal.
10. Theta Carson, a beekeeper, sells honey during the summer.

Exercise 2

Copy these sentences. Put commas where they are needed to set off the appositives.

1. The Eiffel Tower a popular tourist attraction is in Paris.
2. The South Pole the coldest place on earth has snow all year.
3. My second cousin Barry raises peacocks.
4. Chris Stevens a textile worker lost his job when the factory closed.
5. Gray Dove Chief Lone Star's daughter built her own tepee.
6. Mrs. Vance the newspaper's proofreader checks for errors.
7. Harriet Tubman a former slave helped many slaves escape to freedom before the Civil War.
8. Jason a young inventor is trying to think of a new use for paper clips.
9. Saturn the second largest planet takes almost thirty years to orbit the sun.
10. *A Wrinkle in Time* a book by Madeleine L'Engle tells of a girl traveling into another dimension.

Exercise 3

Rewrite each sentence and put an appositive after the subject. Remember to use commas to set off the appositives. Choose from these appositives.

the witch of Clearwell   our cook
the longest-living animals   an artist
the constellation

Example: Roy asked his track coach to accept the trophy.
          Roy, the winner, asked his track coach to accept the trophy.

1. Tortoises have been known to live up to 152 years.

2. Jack found an opossum asleep in the vegetable bin.

3. Pegasus is seen in the night sky of the Northern Hemisphere.

4. Arnold Lovitt draws cartoons for a children's magazine.

5. Grizelda cast a spell on the vain prince.

Appositive in the Objective Case

> **A noun in apposition is in the same case as the noun it explains.**

We cannot see oxygen, a colorless *gas.*
The players have confidence in Maria Ciardi, their *center.*

When you studied the nominative case, you learned that an appositive explains a noun. The appositive is in the same case as the noun it explains.

Appositives that explain nouns in the objective case are in the objective case. In the examples above, *gas* explains *oxygen,* the direct object. Therefore, *gas* is in the objective case. *Center* explains *Maria Ciardi,* the object of a preposition. Therefore, *center* is also in the objective case.

An appositive is usually set off by commas.

Exercise 4

The appositives in these sentences are italicized. Name the noun that each appositive explains. Give the case of the appositive and the reason it is in that case.

1. Bonnie did the Highland fling, a lively Scottish *dance*.

2. The boy jumped onto the junk, a small wooden *sailboat*.

3. The visitors fed the noisy mallards, brightly colored *ducks*.

4. The scientist spoke to Eliza, a talking *robot*.

5. I just met my new boxing coach, *Glenn Reilly*.

6. A local lawyer saved Old Baldy, a hundred-year-old *lighthouse*.

7. We often buy flowers from Mr. Golgi, the street *vendor*.

8. Lynn played the part of Billie, the mysterious *stranger*.

9. A herd of deer appears every winter on Mr. Fenton's property, a Christmas tree *farm* near the state line.

10. King Arthur valued Excalibur, his magical *sword*.

Exercise 5

Copy these sentences. Set off the appositives by adding commas where they are needed.

1. The librarian showed the class a copy of *Knights* a magazine about the Middle Ages.
2. Have you met Annabelle Hart the princess?
3. Ann's favorite movie of all time *Star Wars* is on TV tonight.
4. Kim uses pork in *thit nuong cha* Vietnamese meatballs.
5. The setting of *The Incredible Journey* a classic children's novel is the Canadian wilderness.
6. George Washington was inaugurated in New York City the nation's first capital.
7. Ana gives Wiggin her parakeet speaking lessons daily.
8. Brett bought his mother a gift an ink pen a week ago.
9. Winnie works at the Bookshelf a shop on Lang Street.
10. Allen met my older sister Dana at the airport.
11. Lindsey brought her brother Larry to the park to play with his friends.
12. Julio's favorite food spaghetti is being served for dinner.
13. Suzanne and Samantha gave Mrs. Sellers their teacher their science project.
14. In 1957, Russia launched its first satellite *Sputnik I* into space.
15. I saw the runaway animal a dragon.

Putting It All Together

With a partner or small group, write ten nouns on separate cards or slips of paper. Include proper and common nouns. Also include singular, plural, and possessive forms of nouns. Place all the nouns in a box or hat and exchange them with another pair or group.

Reach into the box or hat you have received and withdraw a noun. Write a story about the noun. Place the noun in the objective and nominative cases. Use direct address. Also use the singular, plural, and possessive forms of the noun. Then read your story to the group.

Chapter Challenge

Read this paragraph carefully and answer the questions.

¹Would you rather watch a television program or listen to the radio? ²To some people, news on the radio is dull. ³They prefer to see a television reporter's videotape. ⁴To many people, plays on television are more interesting since the audience can see as well as hear. ⁵Some people, however, say that listening to a play on the radio allows them to use their imagination. ⁶Both television and radio have advantages and disadvantages. ⁷Television presents pictures to its audience. ⁸Radio, the earlier invention, gives its listeners only sound. ⁹Radio, however, is more portable. ¹⁰You can be doing chores or traveling and still listen to the radio.

1. Why is *radio* in sentence 1 in the objective case?

2. Why is *news* in sentence 2 in the nominative case?

3. Name two nouns in the objective case in sentence 2.

4. What is the gender of *reporter's* in sentence 3?

5. What is the case of *reporter's* in sentence 3?

6. Name two plural nouns in sentence 4.

7. Name an abstract noun in sentence 5.

8. Name a collective noun in sentence 7.

9. What is the direct object in sentence 7?

10. What is the object of the preposition in sentence 7?

11. What is the indirect object in sentence 8?

12. Name the appositive in sentence 8.

13. In sentence 9, *radio* is in what case?

14. In sentence 10, *radio* is in what case?

15. Write the plural of the noun *radio*.

PRONOUNS

Personal Pronouns

A pronoun takes the place of a noun.

Read the following paragraph.

> Chester Greenwood was a boy with a problem. Chester suffered from cold ears. To make matters worse, Chester lived in Maine, where winter can be very cold. Then an idea occurred to Chester. The idea made Chester the inventor of earmuffs. Chester asked his grandmother to sew fur and velvet on metal loops that would fit against his ears.

The noun *Chester* is used six times in the above paragraph. The noun *idea* is used twice. Now read this paragraph.

> Chester Greenwood was a boy with a problem. He suffered from cold ears. To make matters worse, he lived in Maine, where winter can be very cold. Then an idea occurred to him. It made him the inventor of earmuffs. He asked his grandmother to sew fur and velvet on metal loops that would fit against his ears.

In the second paragraph, pronouns take the place of many of the nouns. As a result, the second paragraph sounds smoother than the first. In the second paragraph, the pronouns *he* and *him* take the place of the noun *Chester*. The pronoun *it* is used in place of the noun *idea*.

About the Photograph

A smooth ride down a slippery slope is lots of fun. Writers can smooth bumpy sentences by replacing some of the nouns with pronouns.

The word to which a pronoun refers is its antecedent.

Margery Facklam wrote the book but did not illustrate *it*.

In the sentence above, the antecedent of *it* is the noun *book*.

Since pronouns take the place of nouns, they have the same qualities as nouns: gender, number, and case. You will study more about the qualities of pronouns in this chapter.

Person

A personal pronoun shows by its form
- **the speaker (first person).**
- **the person spoken to (second person).**
- **the person or thing spoken about (third person).**

I have a birthday party on Saturday. (first person)
Pam said *you* knew about the party. (second person)
They were very excited about the party. (third person)

Pronouns that indicate the speaker are not the same as pronouns that indicate the person spoken to or the person spoken about. Since the forms of pronouns change in this way, personal pronouns are said to show person.

- The personal pronouns of the first person (speaker) are *I, me, we,* and *us.*

    I wonder what this gift could be?

- The personal pronoun of the second person (person spoken to) is *you.*

    You wrapped my gift with pretty paper.

- The personal pronouns of the third person (person or thing spoken about) are *he, she, it, him, her, they,* and *them.*

    He enjoys the birthday gift.

Exercise 1

Find the personal pronouns in these sentences. Give the person of each: first, second, or third.

1. During hibernation, bears are deep in sleep, but they wake up for food.
2. Did you know that they have storerooms underground?
3. Ground squirrels also have them.
4. Yesterday I saw a chipmunk carrying food to a burrow.
5. Can you show me where it went?
6. In winter you rarely see a northern chipmunk.
7. Do we know of any other hibernators that live in this area?
8. Raccoons hibernate, too, but they awaken to get warm.
9. Look! The mother raccoon has three babies with her.
10. He told me that animals dream.
11. They went inside the hole to hide!
12. The mother raccoon will find food for the young raccoons.
13. They will often find food alone.
14. Will you please tell me more about hibernation?
15. I will gladly give them information.

Complete each sentence with personal pronouns. Give the person of each.

16. Have _____ read any books by Margery Facklam?
17. Yes, _____ have read *Frozen Snakes and Dinosaur Bones.*
18. _____ worked at the Buffalo Museum of Science.
19. _____ also worked at the Aquarium of Niagara Falls.
20. Did _____ know that clown fish wear pajamas?
21. Kendall said that _____ will go with _____ to the book fair.
22. Please allow _____ to play with _____ .
23. Will _____ help _____ carry these heavy boxes?
24. _____ know that Hawaii became the fiftieth state in 1959.
25. _____ gave _____ a new sweater for Christmas.

Number

A singular pronoun takes the place of a singular noun.

A plural pronoun takes the place of a plural noun.

The singular personal pronouns are *I, me, you, he, she, it, him,* and *her.* These pronouns refer to one person or thing.

The plural personal pronouns are *we, us, you, they,* and *them.* These pronouns refer to more than one person or thing.

Gender

A pronoun that refers to males is masculine gender.

A pronoun that refers to females is feminine gender.

A pronoun that refers to an object is neuter gender.

Only pronouns in the third person singular change form to show gender. The masculine pronouns are *he* and *him.* The feminine pronouns are *she* and *her.* The neuter pronoun is *it.* In the plural, the pronouns *they* and *them* are used for all three genders.

Exercise 2

Find the personal pronouns in these sentences and tell whether each is singular or plural.

1. He sent us a burlap bag full of oysters.
2. Don't blame me if the power goes off!
3. They yelled at him from across the crowded sidewalk.
4. The race began when he set off the cannon.
5. We will hang bunches of mistletoe from the rafters.
6. They left a message on the electronic bulletin board for us.
7. They strung together the turquoise beads for her.
8. Maria, you have been chosen by them to head the cleanup committee.
9. I plan to take it to obedience school.
10. She fell asleep in the grass as bagpipes droned in the distance.

Exercise 3

Give a pronoun that will take the place of each of the following nouns. For some nouns, more than one pronoun can replace the noun.

1. Rick
2. campfire
3. carpenter
4. aunt
5. arcade
6. hairbrushes
7. refrigerator
8. pilots
9. screams
10. Kevin
11. brothers
12. Maggie
13. stereo
14. men
15. nephew
16. pasta
17. giraffe
18. apartment
19. newspaper
20. scissors
21. travelers
22. gossip
23. mother
24. necklace
25. joke
26. keyboard
27. actor
28. clerk
29. clown
30. grandmother

Practice Power

▶ Choose any ten nouns from Exercise 3. Write sentences using both the noun and the pronoun in two related sentences.

Example: The *pasta* was difficult to eat. *It* kept wiggling off my fork.

Compound Personal Pronouns

Compound personal pronouns end in *-self* or *-selves*.

	SINGULAR	PLURAL
FIRST PERSON	myself	ourselves
SECOND PERSON	yourself	yourselves
THIRD PERSON	himself, herself, itself	themselves

Andrea *herself* met us at the pet store to pick out our new cat.

My cat plays with yarn by *himself.*

My cats groom *themselves* thoroughly.

Exercise 1

Find the compound personal pronouns in these sentences.

1. Sea urchins move themselves by using the spines on their bodies.

2. We made the antismoking posters ourselves.

3. Freddie will have to do the dishes by himself.

4. Mickey Mouse himself greeted us at Disney World.

5. Sally wrote the award-winning play herself.

6. Did you hurt yourself in the sledding accident?

7. I myself will play the drum and trumpet at the same time.

8. Please relax and make yourselves comfortable.

9. The cat itself opened the cabinet door!

10. You should give yourselves extra time for this math quiz.

Exercise 2

Complete each sentence with the correct compound personal pronoun.

1. We decided to dig up the treasure _____ .

2. The children _____ pulled the heavy crate up from the basement.

3. Couldn't you keep _____ from opening the present before your birthday?

4. Nancy _____ kept the fire burning through the night.

5. Mr. Mackie _____ saw the Loch Ness monster.

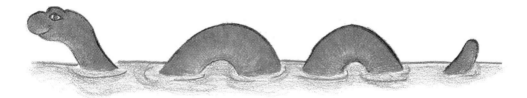

Practice Power

▶ With a partner, discuss the advantages and disadvantages of having a pet. Then, using compound personal pronouns, each of you write a paragraph explaining your own and your partner's opinion.

Personal Pronouns— Nominative Case

Subject of a Verb

> **A pronoun used as the subject of a verb must be in the nominative case.**

Grace and (I, me) went to the circus last night.

Here is the correct form: Grace and *I* went to the circus last night.

The pronoun *I* is in the nominative case because it is the subject of the verb *went* together with the noun *Grace.*

Here are the nominative case personal pronouns.

	SINGULAR	PLURAL
FIRST PERSON	I	we
SECOND PERSON	you	you
THIRD PERSON	he, she, it	they

Exercise 1

Choose the correct form of the personal pronoun for each sentence.

1. The McLeans and (we, us) went to the circus.

2. Justin and (me, I) tried on the clown's hat.

3. Trinh and (he, him) are watching the monkeys race.

4. Tommy and (her, she) climbed up on the Indian elephant.

5. The boys and (us, we) tried the cotton candy.

6. (They, Them) will try to ride their bikes around the arena.

7. My sister and (I, me) are excited about seeing the lions.

8. Tyler and (him, he) watched the trapeze artists.

9. Rosario and (she, her) like to sit in the front row.

10. Did (them, they) catch the monkey's toy?

Complete each sentence with the correct form of a personal pronoun. Be sure to vary your choice of pronouns.

11. Marian and _____ will be at the circus early.

12. You and _____ need to pay Mr. Collins for the tickets.

13. Did Elizabeth and _____ go to the snack bar?

14. He and _____ will feed the animals.

15. Jean and _____ want to see your program.

16. The twins and _____ enjoyed the blue poodles.

17. Carl and _____ went to the circus, too.

18. Tonya and _____ will wait until next year to attend.

19. Will Julio and _____ watch the TV special tonight instead?

20. Tuan and _____ bought a program at the circus to share with Julio and Tonya.

Subjective Complement

> A pronoun used as a subjective complement is in the nominative case.

The girl on the Ferris wheel is (she, her).

Here is the correct form: The girl on the Ferris wheel is *she*.

She is in the nominative case because it is the subjective complement. *She* follows the linking verb *is* and refers to the same person as the subject, *girl*.

Exercise 2

Choose the correct form of the personal pronoun for each sentence. Notice that the subject and the subjective complement can often be switched.

Example: The winner was *he.*
             He was the winner.

1. The farmhand who swept the barn floor was (she, her).

2. That is (him, he) without the sunglasses.

3. The best car washers were (they, them).

4. Was it (her, she) on the phone?

5. The first ones to get tickets were (us, we)!

Complete each sentence with the correct form of a personal pronoun. Be sure to vary your choice of pronouns.

6. The man in the pinstripe suit must be _____ .

7. Was that _____ in the wrinkled photograph?

8. The most impressive hula dancers were _____ .

9. Which one of you made this mess? It was _____ !

10. That was _____ with the stack of books.

Exercise 3

Choose the correct form of the personal pronoun for each sentence. Tell whether the personal pronoun is the subject or the subjective complement.

1. My friend and (me, I) baked a cake.

2. Aren't those bakers in the kitchen (they, them)?

3. Carlos and (him, he) bought all the ingredients to bake the bread.

4. Is that (she, her) in front of the stove?

5. Margie and (me, I) made the whole wheat bread.

6. That was (we, us) making the bread.

7. Was it (he, him)? No, it was (me, I)!

8. Either Adriana or (I, me) will clean the cookie sheet.

9. Has (her, she) sent her a sample to taste?

10. (Them, They) gave us the wrong directions to the bakery.

11. Eddie and (he, him) created a new recipe.

12. It is (him, he) who made the bread.

13. This is (her, she) baking.

14. That is (they, them) in the Swedish bakery.

15. Helen and (him, he) will make muffins tonight.

Practice Power

▶ Write a paragraph about an activity you have done with someone else, such as going to the circus or baking a cake. Reread your paragraph and circle all the pronouns you used as subjects or subjective complements.

Personal Pronouns— Objective Case

Object of a Verb

> A pronoun used as the direct object of a verb is in the objective case.

Dorothy invited (I, me) to the rock concert.

Here is the correct form: Dorothy invited *me* to the rock concert. *Me* is the direct object of the verb *invited*.

Here are the objective case pronouns.

	SINGULAR	PLURAL
FIRST PERSON	me	us
SECOND PERSON	you	you
THIRD PERSON	him, her, it	them

Exercise 1

Choose the correct form of the personal pronoun used as the direct object of a verb for each sentence.

1. Max will have to call (he, him) about our lunch order.
2. They sent Armand and (me, I) to the citywide math contest.
3. The white laboratory mice fear (them, they).
4. I know (she, her) from somewhere, I'm sure!
5. A carpenter helped (we, us) with the doghouse blueprints.
6. Jenna admires Pat and (him, he) for their knowledge of antique toys.
7. The smell of smoke in the room alarmed (we, us)!
8. Did the talent scout choose (her, she)?
9. Whitney blamed Meryl and (I, me) for that mix-up!
10. Jonathan wants (they, them) on his soccer team.
11. Lila admired (he, him) when he scored a touchdown.
12. Mrs. Hensen asked (us, we) to mow her lawn.
13. We need (they, them) to give us a ride.
14. The cashier thanked (she, her) for shopping in the store.
15. My teacher sent (me, I) a get-well card.

Complete each sentence with the correct form of a personal pronoun. Be sure to vary your choice of pronouns.

16. Did the snake handler impress _____ ?
17. The class election results surprised the principal and _____ .
18. Of all of the science fiction writers, I like _____ best.
19. The baby lions amused Ramona and _____ .
20. The roller coaster car slowly carried Sally and _____ to the top.
21. The police officer found Benny and _____ .
22. My family took _____ on vacation.
23. Celia told _____ to stand in line.
24. Megan introduced Erik and _____ .
25. A school of fish followed Alex and _____ as they snorkeled.

Object of a Preposition

> **A pronoun used as the object of a preposition is in the objective case.**

Directions for feeding the hamsters came with (they, them).

Here is the correct form: Directions for feeding the hamsters came with *them*.

The pronoun *them* is the object of the preposition *with*.

Exercise 2

Choose the correct form of the personal pronoun for each sentence.

1. Can she show the shortcut to (we, us)?
2. That is a secret between my mom and (I, me).
3. Did you leave the leftovers in the microwave for (they, them)?
4. The new pitcher threw a fast ball to (she, her).
5. On the stairs, I could hear heavy footsteps above (me, I).
6. A slow-footed donkey trailed behind Frank and (him, he).
7. Is this bunch of mail from Alicia and (her, she)?
8. The house was painted last summer by (they, them).
9. I hope the skywriter will speak to Ted and (we, us).
10. Please save the leftover plum pudding for Marsha and (I, me).

Complete each sentence with the correct form of a personal pronoun. Be sure to vary your choice of pronouns.

11. The restless crocodile gnashed its teeth at _____ .
12. Cheryl offered to toast pumpkin seeds for Brigid and _____ .
13. The ice-cream vendor stopped near _____ .
14. The hall monitor held the jump rope for Curtis and _____ .
15. We'll learn to play the lute with _____ .

Exercise 3

Choose the correct form of the personal pronoun for each sentence. Tell whether the personal pronoun is the direct object or the object of a preposition.

1. The librarian asked the children to sit beside (she, her).
2. Dominique rolled the baby carriage toward (them, they).
3. Tony's grandfather will help (I, me) with repairing the rocking chair.
4. Won't you take (we, us) to the horror movie?
5. That cornhusk doll was made by (him, he).
6. Coach Simmons hurled the basketball down the court to (she, her).
7. Did you see Roland and (they, them) up on the roof?
8. Kyle practiced his bird calls for (us, we).
9. We found (they, them) in the garden beside the scarecrow.
10. Don't touch that diary! It belongs to (me, I)!

Complete each sentence with the correct form of a personal pronoun. Be sure to vary your choice of pronouns. Tell whether the pronoun is the direct object or the object of a preposition.

11. Emilie brought _____ to Mr. Fred's Fudge Factory.
12. Joan knit a heavy sweater for _____ last winter.
13. I quilted a simple pattern on the pillow top for _____ .
14. Mom sent _____ to the store for cayenne pepper.
15. A tall man sat in front of _____ just as the movie began.
16. Rosaura's favorite books have many illustrations in _____ .
17. Did Jason take all twenty pints of blueberries with _____ ?
18. Frances, Jan will take _____ to the store
19. The boys dragged the bag of newspapers behind _____ .
20. Ruby's canary landed on top of _____ .

Exercise 4

Find the personal pronoun in each sentence. Then give the case of each pronoun and tell how it is used: subject, subjective complement, direct object, or object of a preposition.

1. I looked around the firelit cabin.
2. They read the newspaper from front page to back.
3. That child without a scarf is she.
4. The blue envelope was addressed to her.
5. We deserve the tug-of-war prize!
6. The lion tamer warned them to stay away from the animals.
7. Marilyn did not recognize him in a coat and tie.
8. The Frisbee spun straight toward me!
9. He ate every chocolate chip in the cookie dough.
10. Paula rowed the boat through the marsh for us.

Exercise 5 REVIEW

Choose the correct form of the personal pronoun to complete each of these sentences. Give the reason for your choice.

1. Fran and (her, she) are paper carriers.
2. The pilot spoke to Karen and (him, he).
3. The tent will shelter my brother and (I, me).
4. Allan and (I, me) offered to work backstage for the play.
5. Ted and (she, her) will work together.
6. I bought the book on genealogy for (they, them).
7. Richard and (they, them) forgot their gym clothes.
8. Alicia and (he, him) saw a bear across the lake.
9. The woman asked (us, we) how to get to the beach.
10. The person flipping the pancakes was (she, her).

Complete each sentence with the correct form of a personal pronoun. Give the reason for your choice. Be sure to vary your choice of pronouns.

11. Una and _____ spent two hours watching the game.
12. The acrobats' stunts really amazed _____ .
13. Was it _____ who burned the popcorn?
14. Ryan and _____ are about to leave for the game.
15. Grace, give the paintbrush to _____ .

Practice Power

▶ Complete each sentence with a personal pronoun. The person, number, and gender to use for each pronoun are given in parentheses. Be sure to use the correct case.

Example: Greta blew the balloon so much that ____it____ burst. (third, singular, neuter)

1. Where are _____ ? (third, plural, masculine/ feminine)

2. The librarian told _____ about the new riddle books. (first, plural, masculine/feminine)

3. _____ was large, dark, and loud. (third, singular, neuter)

4. _____ saw lovebirds in the open-air market. (third, singular, masculine)

5. Garrison brought a copy of the contest rules for _____ . (third, singular, feminine)

6. _____ explained that the koala is really not a bear. (third, plural, masculine/feminine)

7. _____ baked a batch of soft pretzels for the yard sale. (first, singular, masculine/feminine)

8. The mechanical mouse rolled into _____ . (third, singular, masculine)

9. The baby-sitter called _____ about ten o'clock. (third, plural, masculine/feminine)

10. _____ plans to grow petunias in the window box. (third, singular, feminine)

Possessive Pronouns and Contractions

Possessive Pronouns

> Possessive pronouns are used to show possession or ownership by the speaker, the person spoken to, or the person or thing spoken about.

The yellow bag is *mine,* and the white one is *yours.*

Here are the possessive pronouns.

	SINGULAR	PLURAL
FIRST PERSON	mine	ours
SECOND PERSON	yours	yours
THIRD PERSON	his, hers, its	theirs

Exercise 1

Find the possessive pronouns in these sentences.

1. Stephen found a ferret. Has Michiko lost hers?
2. I put mine in the closet last week.
3. His is playing the piano.
4. We got ours from a traveling circus.
5. Yours is hiding underneath the bed.
6. I just saw theirs in the refrigerator.
7. Hers just arrived in the mail.
8. This one can't be mine!
9. David has his on a leash.
10. Those must be its!
11. Mine will not eat split-pea soup.
12. The Nguyens took theirs to Alaska.
13. The one climbing out of the basket must be yours.
14. Hers is purple with orange stripes.
15. Ours was wearing Joanie's new hat.

Exercise 2

Complete each sentence with an appropriate possessive pronoun. Be sure to vary your choice of pronouns.

1. This is _____ , not _____ .
2. It has to be better than _____ .
3. Everyone will be impressed by _____ .
4. Keep a lookout for _____ .
5. All this strange equipment must be _____ .
6. If _____ is fixed, then please fix _____ .
7. Collect _____ and store the rest in the barn.
8. Let's make a new one and pretend it's _____ .
9. The flying saucer is _____ .
10. _____ has already been to outer space.

Contractions Containing Pronouns

> **The personal pronouns are used with verbs to form contractions. The apostrophe (') is used to show where a letter or letters have been left out.**

Study the spelling and meaning of these contractions.

CONTRACTION	MEANING	CONTRACTION	MEANING
I'll	I will	it's	it is
they're	they are	they'll	they will
I've	I have	they've	they have
we're	we are	you'll	you will
I'm	I am	he'll	he will
you're	you are	she'll	she will

Exercise 3

Find the contraction in each sentence and tell what pronoun and verb have been used to form it.

1. It's time for the leaves to start changing colors.
2. You're going to walk into a huge, sticky spiderweb!
3. I'll stir this bubbling pot of spaghetti sauce.
4. Boyd said that he'll finish the soap carving tomorrow.
5. We're learning origami, Japanese paper folding.
6. They'll be happier if they can run through the sprinkler.
7. I'm looking for a suspenseful mystery story.
8. You'll be late if you watch one more TV program.
9. Elena, you're holding the marshmallows too close to the fire!
10. They're on their way to a surprise party.

Exercise 4

Complete each sentence with an appropriate contraction.

1. _____ planning a trip to Timbuktu!
2. Did you know that _____ be in a three-legged bag race?
3. _____ try to answer your questions.
4. The builders report that _____ found a hole in the roof.
5. _____ already put two coats of paint on the motorcycle.
6. I believe that _____ the first person to discover this.
7. _____ going to be guests of the governor!
8. _____ happy to see the crocuses bloom.
9. The weather reporter promised that _____ not going to rain.
10. Fatima hopes that _____ buy a subscription to the newspaper.

Practice Power

▶ Write five sentences using the two-word meanings of the contractions listed on page 307. Exchange your sentences with a partner and rewrite each other's sentences using contractions where you can.

LESSON 6

Correct Use of Possessives and Contractions

Possessives are often confused with contractions because they sound alike. Possessives express ownership or possession. They do not use apostrophes.

Its flower is yellow. (possessive)

A contraction is one word made from two words. The apostrophe is used in a contraction to show where a letter or letters have been left out.

It's time to mow the lawn. (contraction—*it is*)

Study these possessives and contractions and learn the difference between them.

POSSESSIVES	CONTRACTIONS
its roof	it's (it is) sleeping
your lawn	you're (you are) late
their house	they're (they are) not here

Exercise 1

Tell whether each italicized word is a possessive or a contraction.

1. *It's* the biggest bullfrog that is the loudest croaker!
2. *Their* basketballs are in the equipment room.
3. A sunflower will turn *its* head to follow the sun.
4. What would you trade for *your* latest baseball card?
5. Children used to do *their* handwriting with quill pens.
6. Helena, *you're* not going to believe this!
7. *Your* sister is digging earthworms for her fishing trip.
8. *They're* going to learn a new song in music class today.
9. *It's* a huge bowl of steaming chili.
10. André says that *it's* too stormy to fly a kite.

Exercise 2

Choose the correct word for each sentence.

1. (You're, Your) painting must be dry before you frame it.
2. Pandas try to limit (their, they're) diet to bamboo shoots.
3. (You're, Your) wearing my new sneakers again.
4. (They're, Their) ready to start the backgammon game.
5. An oil-covered bird cannot clean (its, it's) own feathers.
6. (You're, Your) next in line, Elijah.
7. Do snakes really shed (they're, their) skins?
8. (Its, It's) a good time to try that new brownie recipe.
9. The men left (their, they're) work boots at the front door.
10. How is (you're, your) headache?
11. (They're, Their) the biggest apples I've ever seen!
12. Large acorns fell from (it's, its) gnarled branches.
13. If (your, you're) finished, I'll take a turn.
14. The turtles climbed out of (their, they're) box.
15. We heard that (its, it's) going to snow all day!

Practice Power

▶ Imagine that you and your friend(s) are dressed nearly alike for a costume party, but there are some differences in your costumes and makeup. Write five sentences comparing theirs (his or hers) with yours. Make sure you use possessive pronouns.

LESSON 7

Interrogative Pronouns

An interrogative pronoun is used in asking a question.

The interrogative pronouns are *who, whom, which, what,* and *whose.* Study the following examples.

- *Who* is used in speaking of persons.

    Who opened the umbrella first?

    Who is the subject of *opened.*

- *Whom* is used in speaking of persons.

    Whom did they see in the rain?

    Whom is the direct object of *see.*

- *Which* is used in speaking of persons or things.

    Which is your favorite umbrella?
    Which of the umbrellas did you forget?

    In the first sentence, *which* is the subject of *is.* In the second sentence, *which* is the object of *did forget.*

- *What* is used in speaking of things and in asking for information.

    What will you do?

    What is the object of *will do.*

- *Whose* is used in speaking of persons.

    Whose is the pink-striped umbrella?

    Whose shows possession.

Exercise 1

Find the interrogative pronouns in these sentences. Tell whether they refer to persons or to things.

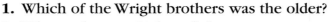

1. Which of the Wright brothers was the older?
2. What makes an airplane fly?
3. For whom was the Taj Mahal built?
4. Which would you choose to put in a time capsule—a photograph or a diary?
5. Who brought an early version of the hamburger to the United States?
6. What would a podiatrist check?
7. Which of these writers created Frankenstein?
8. What should a first-aid kit contain?
9. Whose were the words "All the world's a stage"?
10. What does the Richter scale measure?

Exercise 2

Complete each sentence with an interrogative pronoun, *who, which,* or *what*. Use *who* for persons, *which* for persons or things, and *what* for things or general information.

1. _____ invented the safety match?
2. _____ is the duty of a forest ranger?
3. _____ of the deserts is largest?
4. _____ are the three primary colors?
5. _____ wrote *Alice in Wonderland?*
6. _____ was Duke Ellington's full name?
7. _____ mountain has the higher peak, Mount McKinley or Mount Everest?
8. _____ of the jewels is the most valuable?
9. _____ was Anne Frank?
10. For _____ is the Red Sea named?
11. _____ is a synonym for *zephyr?*
12. _____ did Jack Sprat not eat?
13. _____ of the Native American chiefs wrote an alphabet for his people?
14. _____ would you measure with a craniometer?
15. _____ is the name of our galaxy?

The Use of *Who* and *Whom*

> The interrogative pronoun *who* is used when the sentence requires a pronoun in the nominative case.
>
> The interrogative pronoun *whom* is used when the sentence requires a pronoun in the objective case.

Who may be used as a subject. *Whom* may be the direct object of a verb or the object of a preposition.

> *Who* was present at the meeting?   (*Who* is the subject.)
>
> *Whom* did the class elect?   (*Whom* is the direct object.)
>
> To *whom* was the trophy awarded?   (*Whom* is the object of the preposition.)

Exercise 3

Complete each sentence with *who* or *whom.*

1. _____ is the guitarist in that group?
2. _____ was that man in the stovepipe hat?
3. For _____ did the dance troupe perform?
4. By _____ was the self-defense class taught?
5. Lem, _____ invited the ants to our picnic?
6. To _____ was the stamp catalog sent?
7. For _____ are you writing that note?
8. By _____ was the pantomime performed?
9. _____ wants to photograph wolves in the wilderness?
10. To _____ did you tell my secret?
11. _____ did you invite?
12. _____ tossed this paper airplane on my desk?
13. Marty, _____ should we ask for permission?
14. _____ is the person wearing the bicycle helmet?
15. _____ is the stargazer in your family?

Practice Power

▶ Write four sentences with the interrogative pronouns *who, whom, which,* or *what.* Use social studies, science, or math topics for your questions.

Distributive and Indefinite Pronouns

Distributive Pronouns

A distributive pronoun refers to each person, place, or thing separately.

Each has to give a short talk before the election.
Neither likes butter on popcorn.

The distributive pronouns are *each, either,* and *neither.*
They are singular in number.

Exercise 1

Find the distributive pronouns in these sentences.

1. If we divide the fifteen cherries evenly, each of us will get seven and a half of them.
2. Neither could remember the address of the pet shop.
3. Do you like either of these modern paintings?
4. Neither of your brothers has red hair like you.
5. You should feed each a can of food a day.
6. We concluded that neither would win the frog-jumping contest of Calaveras County.
7. Have you read either of the assigned stories yet?
8. Each of the jockeys wore bright colors.
9. I think that neither of the clocks is correct.
10. Each will wear an armband and carry a banner.
11. Either of us will be meeting you at the airport.
12. Anna gave each of her classmates an invitation to her birthday party.

Indefinite Pronouns

> **An indefinite pronoun refers to no specific person, place, or thing.**

Many plan to attend the party at the park.
Everyone wonders who dressed like a gorilla for the party.

Here are some singular indefinite pronouns.

anybody	everybody	nobody	somebody
anyone	everyone	no one	someone
anything	everything	nothing	something

Some indefinite pronouns are usually plural.

both	many
few	several

Some indefinite pronouns may be singular or plural.

all	some

Exercise 2

Find the indefinite pronouns in these sentences.

1. Somebody keeps sounding a car horn.
2. Everyone has signed Felicia's leg cast.
3. Would someone take this computer back to the lab?
4. This hot curry is ordered by very few.
5. Many complain about the weather, but no one can do anything about it.
6. Everyone must complete a map showing the state's products by Friday.
7. Does anyone you know have an unusual hobby?
8. We went to the zoo to see snakes, and we saw several in the reptile house.
9. Crossword puzzles and hangman are popular word games, and I like doing both.
10. All of the red balloons were sold before we arrived.

The Correct Use of Indefinite Pronouns with Negatives

When a sentence contains a negative such as *not* or *never,* use *anything* or *anyone* to express negation.

Didn't (nobody, anyone) bring pickles for the picnic?

Here is the correct form: Didn't *anyone* bring pickles for the picnic?

The sentence has one negative word, *didn't,* the contraction of *did* and *not.* To choose another negative word, *nobody,* would be incorrect. The use of double negatives is incorrect.

Exercise 3

Choose the correct indefinite pronoun to complete each sentence.

1. There was (nothing, anything) left in the cookie jar.
2. The canary doesn't have (nothing, anything) to eat.
3. I have never seen (anything, nothing) so colorful.
4. The camp counselor told us not to bring (nothing, anything) except our lunches.
5. I have never met (anyone, nobody) as tall as Mr. Ortiz.
6. (Nobody, Anybody) on our team had bowled before.
7. I promise not to tell (nobody, anybody) your secret.
8. (Nothing, Anything) makes me scratch more than a mosquito bite!
9. (Nobody, Anybody) in our class knew the password.
10. There wasn't (nobody, anyone) at the beach.

Putting It All Together

Form a group of five students. As a group, make up a story using singular, plural, and possessive pronouns. Then assign roles: one student will play pronouns related to *I,* one or two will play pronouns related to *you,* one will play pronouns related to *he, she,* and *it,* and everyone will play pronouns related to *they.* The fifth student will be the storyteller. As the storyteller tells the story to the class, the players will stand up each time their assigned pronoun is mentioned.

Chapter Challenge

Read this paragraph carefully and answer the questions.

¹Helen Keller was less than two years old when she was afflicted by a serious disease. ²It left her blind and deaf. ³For the next five years, she wasn't able to speak. ⁴She was a frightened and bewildered child who couldn't understand the strange silence around her. ⁵Helen's life began to change when Anne Sullivan, from the Perkins Institute for the Blind, became her teacher. ⁶Helen learned to understand the names of objects spelled into her hand. ⁷A whole new world opened up for her. ⁸She proved that every struggle could end in victory. ⁹Few have had to overcome the enormous obstacles she faced. ¹⁰Helen herself enjoyed a brilliant career helping those who were deaf and blind.

1. Find the personal pronouns in sentences 1 and 2.

2. Give the case of each of the pronouns in sentences 1 and 2.

3. What is the antecedent of the pronoun *It* in sentence 2?

4. What pronoun is the subject of sentence 3?

5. How is the pronoun *She* in sentence 4 used?

6. In which case is the pronoun *her* in sentence 4? Why?

7. In which case is the pronoun in sentence 7? Why?

8. Name the person, number, and gender of the pronoun in sentence 8.

9. Name the compound personal pronoun in the paragraph.

10. Name the indefinite or distributive pronoun in the paragraph.

318

LESSON 1 — Descriptive Adjectives

An adjective describes or limits a noun or a pronoun.

There are two main kinds of adjectives: descriptive and limiting. In Lessons 1–3, you will study descriptive adjectives. In Lessons 4–6, you will learn about limiting adjectives.

A descriptive adjective describes a noun or a pronoun.

Read these sentences.

> The dolphins jumped through the ring.
> The sleek, playful dolphins jumped through the red ring.

In the second sentence, notice how the words *sleek* and *playful* describe the noun *dolphins*. The word *red* describes the noun *ring*. These words are descriptive adjectives. A descriptive adjective modifies a noun or pronoun. It usually tells *what kind* about the noun or pronoun it modifies.

There are two classes of descriptive adjectives: proper adjectives and common adjectives. A proper adjective is formed from a proper noun. A common adjective is any adjective not formed from a proper noun.

PROPER ADJECTIVES	COMMON ADJECTIVES
American artist	*popular* artist
French paintings	*colorful* paintings
European exhibition	*international* exhibition

About the Photograph

What descriptive adjectives can you think of to describe this familiar lunchroom scene?

ADJECTIVES

Exercise 1

Find the descriptive adjectives in these sentences.
Tell whether they are common or proper.

1. In the trunk, we found a red Spanish scarf.

2. The uniforms were decorated with bright buttons.

3. Beautiful grounds surround the old mansion.

4. Skillful Belgian needleworkers make fine lace.

5. *Don Quixote* is an inspirational story.

6. Have you ever seen a double rainbow in a stormy sky?

7. Toads move in short, clumsy hops.

8. A silver moonbeam fell on the narrow path.

9. Brazilian coffee is imported by the United States.

10. The ancient Peruvian city bustled with curious tourists.

Complete each sentence with a common or proper adjective according to what is indicated in parentheses.

11. A *(common or proper)* guide showed us the sights of the *(common)* city.

12. It is hard to find real *(proper)* spaghetti sauce.

13. The *(common)* cookie jar fell from the kitchen shelf.

14. A *(proper)* ship cruised up the Mississippi River.

15. The *(common)* seagulls swooped down onto the *(common)* beach.

Exercise 2

Form proper adjectives from each of these proper nouns.
Use a dictionary to check your spelling.

Example: proper noun, *China*; proper adjective, *Chinese*

1. Spain
2. Arabia
3. Greece
4. Japan
5. Africa

6. Italy
7. France
8. Europe
9. America
10. Denmark

11. Alaska
12. Ireland
13. Peru
14. Switzerland
15. Egypt

Exercise 3

Form common adjectives from each of these common nouns.
Use a dictionary if you need help.

Example: common noun, *winter*; common adjective, *wintry*

1. wind
2. wood
3. silk
4. athlete
5. joy
6. love
7. magic
8. noise

9. gold
10. fun
11. luck
12. storm
13. cloud
14. sun
15. friend
16. color

17. truth
18. hero
19. mountain
20. skill
21. courtesy
22. mystery
23. mischief
24. courage

Exercise 4

Write one synonym for each of these adjectives.

1. comical
2. faithful
3. ignorant
4. dangerous
5. expensive
6. angry
7. confident
8. peaceful
9. huge
10. graceful
11. brilliant
12. selfish
13. enormous
14. honest
15. clever
16. amiable
17. sincere
18. famous
19. ancient
20. clumsy
21. beautiful
22. odd
23. lively
24. furious
25. hilarious
26. unusual
27. serious

Exercise 5

Write one antonym for each of these adjectives.

1. ugly
2. enormous
3. awkward
4. strong
5. sweet
6. proud
7. dull
8. swift
9. kind
10. clean
11. early
12. distant
13. incorrect
14. idle
15. silent
16. rich
17. coarse
18. careless
19. beneficial
20. tame
21. plentiful
22. dark
23. brave
24. flimsy
25. high
26. friendly
27. shallow

Practice Power

▶ Think of three items you use that were made in another country. Think of at least two descriptive adjectives for each item. Use both common and proper adjectives. Then use the adjectives and nouns in sentences.

LESSON 2 — Position of Adjectives

> **The usual position of the adjective is before the noun.**

The *agile* gorilla amazed the audience.

In this sentence, *agile* comes right before *gorilla,* the noun it describes.

> **Some adjectives follow and complete a linking verb. Such adjectives are called subjective complements.**

The gorillas are *funny.*

That gorilla looks *intelligent.*

The first sentence describes *funny* gorillas, and the second sentence describes an *intelligent* gorilla. In both of these sentences, the adjective does not come before the noun. Instead, it follows a linking verb. The most common linking verb is *be.* An adjective that completes a linking verb modifies the subject. It is called a subjective complement.

Chapter 11   **323**

Exercise 1

Find the adjective used as the subjective complement in each sentence and tell which noun it modifies.

1. This jar of peanut butter was full yesterday.
2. The chairs for dollhouses are tiny.
3. The plan for a bake sale might be workable.
4. This velveteen seems smooth.
5. Suddenly the wind was silent.
6. A trip into the haunted house could be dangerous.
7. Frances Hodgson Burnett's novels remain popular with children and adults.
8. The lemonade tasted bitter.
9. The noses of the presidents on Mount Rushmore are really gigantic!
10. The basket of laundry is heavy.

Complete each sentence with an adjective used as a subjective complement.

11. Buck's saddlebags are _____ .
12. The mountains ahead of us appear _____ .
13. Those mugs are _____ .
14. Mr. Graham's antique sleigh looks _____ .
15. The chimes from the cathedral are _____ .

Exercise 2

Tell whether each italicized adjective comes before a noun or is a subjective complement.

1. The Taj Mahal in India is an *exquisite* building made with *white* marble.
2. The *natural* beauty of Switzerland is described in this book.
3. Becky is planning a *big* party for her cat.
4. The results of Arno Sierra's experiment were *remarkable*.
5. These streets are *narrow* and *steep*.
6. She heard a *weird* sound.
7. We gazed upon *endless* miles of *dusty* desert.
8. Abebe Bikila was *barefoot* when he won the Olympic marathon in 1960.
9. The *ordinary* incident was described in an *exaggerated* manner by Rodney.
10. Can you name the *smallest* ocean?
11. Sean will travel through *Italian* vineyards.
12. The Assyrians were *firm* rulers.
13. Mr. and Mrs. Seton have been *generous* neighbors.
14. *Twenty* guards have already surrounded the *open* vault.
15. The *large* praying mantis on the vine was *motionless*.
16. The *brave* performer jumped over *twelve* people.
17. The results of our *scientific* experiment were *predictable*.
18. It was *amazing* when Orville and Wilbur Wright flew the *first* airplane in 1903.
19. During the *violent* storm, that *huge* tree almost fell on our house.
20. Leo's *helpful* teacher told him that his work was *satisfactory*.

Practice Power

▶ Write two sentences for each of the following adjectives. In one sentence, use the adjective before a noun. In the other sentence, use the adjective as a subjective complement.

1. delicious
2. courageous
3. colorful
4. windy

LESSON 3 Words Used as Nouns and Adjectives

> **The use of a word in a sentence determines its part of speech. Some words can be used as nouns or adjectives.**

It frequently happens that the same word may be used as different parts of speech. Notice the use of the word *light* in the following sentences:

> Ron extinguished the *light*. (noun)
> I couldn't find the *light* switch in the dark. (adjective)

A noun is a name word. An adjective describes or limits a noun.

Exercise 1

Tell whether each word in italics is a noun or an adjective.

1. Her fingers flew over the *ivory* keys on the piano.
2. Elephant and walrus tusks are made of *ivory.*
3. Marbles are sometimes made by melting scraps of *glass.*
4. The old books are protected in a *glass* case.
5. Early trains were often called "*iron* horses."
6. The *iron* left a brown spot on my shirt.
7. The swimming pool should reopen in *May.*
8. Because of the harsh winter, I don't think there will be many *May* blossoms.
9. Paintings created by *cave* dwellers were discovered in France by four boys looking for their dog.
10. By the entrance to the magical *cave* was a small dragon.
11. I can't write my report if I don't have any *paper.*
12. Some potato chips are packaged in *paper* cans.
13. This *country* road will lead you through wheat fields.
14. Can you name the smallest *country* in the world?
15. My uncle has a *country* house in Wisconsin.

Exercise 2

Rewrite the following paragraph and add descriptive adjectives. Try to add at least five descriptive adjectives.

The sun shines through the water near the shore. Here the floor of the sea is a garden. Stones and shells and coral rest on the bottom. Schools of fish flitter past. Seaweed moves with the waves. In places, a can or an object shows the presence of people on the beach nearby.

Practice Power

▶ Write five descriptive sentences about the picture on this page. Try to include at least two nouns used as adjectives.

LESSON 4 · Limiting Adjectives

A limiting adjective either points out an object or indicates number.

The jar was full of jellybeans. (points out an object)

There are *twenty* jellybeans in the jar. (indicates number)

This gift arrived from the candy store. (points out an object)

You will learn about the most important kinds of limiting adjectives in this lesson and in Lessons 5 and 6.

Articles

The articles are *the, a,* and *an.*
The is the definite article. A and an are indefinite.

The clock woke me up. (definite: refers to a specific clock)

An ostrich is exciting to watch. (indefinite: refers to any ostrich)

The following rules apply to articles.

- The definite article *the* may be used with either singular or plural nouns: *the* ship, *the* brushes.
- The indefinite articles *a* and *an* may be used only with singular nouns: *a* clock, *an* ostrich.
- The article *an* is used before a vowel sound: *an* apple, *an* hour.
- The article *a* is used before a consonant sound: *a* feather.

Numeral Adjectives

> **A numeral adjective indicates exact number.**

I have *one* sandwich and *two* cookies in my lunch bag.
The *first* day of the week is Sunday.

Numeral adjectives may refer to the number of things or to the arrangement of things in numerical order.

Exercise 1

Use an indefinite article before each of these nouns.

1. festival
2. eggshell
3. pueblo
4. umbrella
5. hour
6. hammer
7. curb
8. actor
9. apron
10. eagle
11. relative
12. opening
13. villager
14. antler
15. kingdom
16. engineer
17. football
18. Icelander
19. oboe
20. bonfire

Exercise 2

Complete these sentences by adding definite or indefinite articles.

1. _____ player kicked _____ football down _____ field.
2. _____ unusual sight greeted us when we opened _____ door.
3. With bursts of speed of over sixty miles _____ hour, cheetahs are _____ fastest four-footed animals.
4. _____ Missouri River is _____ longest river in _____ United States.
5. _____ dog walked slowly along _____ railroad tracks.
6. _____ designs inside _____ kaleidoscope are formed from _____ reflections of plastic chips in small mirrors.
7. _____ crocodile slipped into _____ shallow water.
8. _____ skinny dog followed Ms. Lopez into _____ butcher shop.
9. We did not have _____ answer to _____ riddle.
10. I felt _____ tremor from the distant earthquake.

Exercise 3

Find the numeral adjectives in these sentences. Tell which noun each adjective modifies.

1. One American flag waved in the breeze.

2. After the first wolf howls, the rest of a pack often joins in.

3. We celebrated my sister's fifth birthday by baking a peppermint cake.

4. You need the fourth edition of this thesaurus.

5. On July 20, 1969, two Americans walked on the moon.

6. Four airplanes from the Blue Angels performed maneuvers.

7. All forty-one men on the ship were experienced sailors.

8. On their twentieth anniversary, our parents bought their second car.

9. Name the five contestants remaining in the spelling bee.

10. Aren't there eleven days left in this month?

11. Alfredo sat in the second row of the empty auditorium and sang aloud.

12. If the thirteenth day of a month is on Friday, some people actually believe they'll have bad luck.

13. We saw seven small kayaks going down the river.

14. Two cars limped from the racetrack toward the pit.

15. The third little pig was smart to build its house out of brick.

Practice Power

▶ Write two or three sentences about going to a grocery store, and use four indefinite articles in your sentences. Now rewrite the sentences using numerical adjectives.

Demonstrative Adjectives

A demonstrative adjective points out a definite person, place, or thing.

The demonstrative adjectives are *this* and *that.* The plural of *this* is *these,* and the plural of *that* is *those.* *This* and *these* refer to persons or things that are near at hand. *That* and *those* refer to persons or things that are farther away.

> *This* jar of ink is fairly dry. (near at hand)
> *That* park has many bicycle trails. (farther away)
> *These* machines will be very useful. (near at hand)
> *Those* spectators will be late. (farther away)

Each of the italicized adjectives points out a definite person, place, or thing. A demonstrative adjective agrees in number with the noun it modifies. This is usually the noun closest to it.

Those and *Them*

Those is used to point out something. *Those* may be an adjective or a pronoun. *Them* is always a pronoun. It can never be used as an adjective.

> Don't pick *those* flowers. (adjective)
> She likes these, but I prefer *those.* (pronoun)
> Do you like *them?* (pronoun)

Exercise 1

Put the correct demonstrative adjectives before the names of the following objects, which are near at hand.

1. _____ sandwiches
2. _____ doughnuts
3. _____ dollar
4. _____ size of shoe

5. _____ kinds of problems
6. _____ style of car
7. _____ color of ink
8. _____ styles of hair

Exercise 2

Put the correct demonstrative adjectives before the names of the following objects, which are far away.

1. _____ game
2. _____ saxophones
3. _____ kinds of traps
4. _____ sorts of pencils
5. _____ pineapple
6. _____ type of work
7. _____ brands of butter
8. _____ kinds of sports

Exercise 3

Find the demonstrative adjectives in these sentences.
Tell whether each is singular or plural.

1. My mother uses this brand of flour for biscuits.
2. We won the game because our shortstop fielded that last grounder.
3. This shield made of feathers belonged to an Aztec king centuries ago.
4. Amanda took these pictures of her relatives in Venice.
5. What were those strange sounds?
6. Kenneth brought this crystal radio to show to the class.
7. Cotton will not grow in that hard soil.
8. The Beebes planted those kinds of vegetables last spring.
9. These colors are our school colors.
10. The scientist explained this symbol on the chart.
11. That tongue twister is a tough one.
12. I didn't order this kind of soft drink.
13. These people are the hardest workers.
14. That stage is beautifully decorated with flowers.
15. Are those model trains on sale?
16. Are those children going with our class to the Smithsonian Institution?
17. These gerbils belong to Mr. Roma.
18. I've never tasted anything better than this biscuit.
19. What is wrong with that dog?
20. These countries are located in Africa.

Exercise 4

Choose the correct word to complete each sentence.

1. Who knows how to handle (them, those) snapping crabs?
2. I watched (those, them) sky divers jump from the plane.
3. We plan to invite (them, those) to a jazz concert in the park.
4. Mr. Ziegler is going to move (those, them) bales of hay with a tractor.
5. Where did you buy (them, those) hockey sticks?
6. Dietra bought a pet mongoose from (those, them) yesterday.
7. The yard was bright with the flickering of (those, them) fireflies.
8. (Them, Those) toy cars have windup spring motors.
9. Whitney presses (those, them) flowers in a book.
10. Ms. McKay met (them, those) on a streetcar in San Francisco.

Complete each sentence with the correct word, _those_ or _them_.

11. _____ boiled ears of corn are dripping with butter.
12. Did you meet _____ after their concert?
13. Who will carry _____ bags of cement to my car?
14. Henry found _____ old photographs in a shoe box.
15. Scuba divers removed _____ sunken treasures from the ocean floor.

Practice Power

▶ **Find the words that describe or limit nouns in these sentences.**

1. These trees are sturdy and strong.
2. A black spaniel jumped from the car!
3. These modern highways actually follow old Native American trails.
4. Those small white boats will try to dock at the busy harbor.
5. We believe the Babylonians made wise laws.
6. Those villagers have a Dutch tulip festival in the spring.
7. That hungry squirrel thought the small toy was an acorn.
8. Three players have already fouled out.
9. Brown bears climbed over the wooden fence.
10. An oasis is a fertile spot in a desert.
11. Do these notebooks belong to the children?
12. An angry elephant began to charge at the frightened tourist.
13. We saw three dinosaur exhibits at the museum.
14. Which of these instruments can you play alone?
15. I prefer them with white frosting, rather than chocolate frosting.
16. Carpenters must use precise measurements when building a house.
17. Those determined ducks would not leave the picnic area until the bread was gone.
18. This recipe calls for two cups of flour, one cup of sugar, and an egg.
19. The muscular man lifted that heavy box.
20. An informative paper on humpback whales would be interesting.

More Limiting Adjectives

Possessive Adjectives

A possessive adjective indicates ownership.

> *My* dress is green.   *Our* car is in the garage.
> The ribbon is in *her* hair.   I met *your* uncle.
> *Its* wing is broken.   *Their* house is new.

Because the italicized words in these sentences modify nouns, they are adjectives. Since they show possession, they are called possessive adjectives.

The possessive adjectives are

	SINGULAR	PLURAL
FIRST PERSON	my	our
SECOND PERSON	your	your
THIRD PERSON	his, her, its	their

Interrogative Adjectives

An interrogative adjective is used in asking a question.

Which, what, and *whose* are interrogative adjectives when they modify nouns and ask questions.

> *Which* flags are on that stadium? *What* colors are they?
> *Whose* suitcase has brown straps?

Exercise 1

Find the possessive adjectives in these sentences. Tell what noun each adjective modifies.

1. Why is our dog under the bench?
2. Young people all over the world read her book.
3. I want May Nguyen to sample my rice with saffron.
4. Carolyn painted her boat a soft shade of gray.
5. An oystercatcher slides its beak into the shell of an oyster, and then it cuts the muscle and pulls the meat out.
6. Did your brother bring his mitt to the ballpark?
7. Graham crackers got their name from Sylvester Graham, an early nutrition expert.
8. My friends are arriving from Australia next month.
9. This is our chance to see the world!
10. Ella stretched her long trunk to reach the marshmallow.

Complete each sentence with an appropriate possessive adjective. Be sure to vary your choices.

11. _____ new coat is made of wool.
12. Helen is named after _____ aunt.
13. We should spend more of _____ time baby-sitting for Katrina.
14. Grandfather and I enjoy sitting on _____ back porch while the sun sets.
15. Mr. Wilson is _____ candidate for president of the Senior Citizens' Craft Guild.
16. _____ son became a wise and powerful emperor.
17. The sparrow hawk missed _____ prey as it swooped down.
18. The woman felt that _____ voice was a musical one.
19. Have you seen _____ new stereo?
20. Little Gordon Schuster likes to wear _____ cowboy outfit.

Exercise 2

Find the interrogative adjectives in these sentences. Tell the noun that each modifies.

1. What tree grows to be the tallest?

2. Whose first novel was called *The Pickwick Papers?*

3. Which artist did a series of water lily paintings?

4. What sound does a kookaburra make?

5. In what place did salsa music originate?

6. In which city in France was Renoir born?

7. Whose speech is known as "I Have a Dream"?

8. Which early Impressionist often painted ballerinas?

9. Which leaves do silkworms eat?

10. Of what fruit is guacamole made?

Complete each sentence with an interrogative adjective.

11. _____ picture was on America's first postage stamp?

12. _____ animal is called a leviathan?

13. _____ painting is called *American Gothic?*

14. _____ materials does a painter use?

15. _____ painting *Mona Lisa* hangs in the Louvre?

Practice Power

▶ How many answers do you know to the questions in Exercise 2? If you don't know the answer, where do you think you can find the information? Do you like quiz questions? Think of three quiz questions to ask your classmates. Use interrogative adjectives, and in at least one of your sentences use a possessive adjective. Use the encyclopedia or other research books if you need to!

LESSON 7

Using Adjectives to Compare

Comparison is the change that adjectives undergo to express different degrees of quality, quantity, or value.

Most adjectives have three degrees of comparison: the positive degree, the comparative degree, and the superlative degree.

The positive degree shows a quality.

> That horse is *slow.*

The comparative degree shows a quality in a greater or lesser degree.

> Of the two, it is the *slower* horse.

The superlative degree shows a quality in the greatest or the least degree.

> There goes the *slowest* horse of all.

The comparative degree is used when speaking of two persons or things. The superlative degree is used when three or more persons or things are compared.

How Adjectives Are Compared

1. Most adjectives of one syllable and some adjectives of two syllables form the comparative degree by adding *-er* to the positive. They form the superlative degree by adding *-est* to the positive.

POSITIVE	COMPARATIVE	SUPERLATIVE
tall	taller	tallest
rich	richer	richest
dark	darker	darkest
clear	clearer	clearest
quick	quicker	quickest
bright	brighter	brightest
soft	softer	softest
narrow	narrower	narrowest

   a. If the positive degree of the adjective ends in *e*, the comparative degree is formed by adding *-r.* The superlative degree is formed by adding *-st* to the positive form.

POSITIVE	COMPARATIVE	SUPERLATIVE
safe	safer	safest
wise	wiser	wisest
brave	braver	bravest
ripe	riper	ripest
pure	purer	purest
large	larger	largest
tame	tamer	tamest

   b. If the positive degree of an adjective of one syllable ends in a single consonant preceded by a single vowel, the consonant is doubled before adding *-er* and *-est.*

POSITIVE	COMPARATIVE	SUPERLATIVE
slim	slimmer	slimmest
hot	hotter	hottest
sad	sadder	saddest
big	bigger	biggest

c. If the positive degree of the adjective ends in *y* preceded by a consonant, the *y* is changed to *i* before adding *-er* and *-est*.

POSITIVE	COMPARATIVE	SUPERLATIVE
noisy	noisier	noisiest
lazy	lazier	laziest
funny	funnier	funniest
friendly	friendlier	friendliest
happy	happier	happiest
pretty	prettier	prettiest
wealthy	wealthier	wealthiest
easy	easier	easiest

2. Adjectives of three or more syllables, and some of two syllables, form the comparative degree and the superlative degree by adding *more* and *most* or *less* and *least* before the positive form of the adjective.

POSITIVE	COMPARATIVE	SUPERLATIVE
courteous	more courteous	most courteous
generous	more generous	most generous
difficult	less difficult	least difficult
famous	less famous	least famous

3. Some adjectives may be compared by both methods: *worthy, worthier, worthiest; worthy, more worthy, most worthy.*

4. Certain adjectives are compared irregularly.

POSITIVE	COMPARATIVE	SUPERLATIVE
little	less	least
bad	worse	worst
good	better	best
many, much	more	most
late	later, latter	latest, last
far	farther	farthest
old	older, elder	oldest, eldest

5. Some adjectives cannot be compared: *dead, perpendicular, eternal, circular, four, fifth, round, golden, this, that, square, every, all, triangular, whole, several.*

Exercise 1

Give the comparative and the superlative degrees of each of these adjectives by using *-er* and *-est.*

1. young
2. brave
3. mild
4. hazy
5. glad
6. lucky
7. glossy
8. cheap
9. dreary
10. handy

11. tough
12. thick
13. gentle
14. rude
15. wet
16. shady
17. dim
18. poor
19. juicy
20. strange

Exercise 2

Compare each of these adjectives by using *more* and *most* or *less* and *least.*

1. beautiful
2. thoughtless
3. gracious
4. reliable
5. brilliant

6. common
7. successful
8. fruitful
9. dependable
10. comfortable

11. industrious
12. generous
13. charitable
14. familiar
15. valuable

16. numerous
17. helpful
18. sensitive
19. interesting
20. fortunate

Exercise 3

Find the adjectives that can be compared, and tell the degree of comparison of each: positive, comparative, or superlative.

1. Sir Galahad was a brave knight.
2. I prefer the smaller pumpkins for making pies.
3. You gave a good description of the ghost town, Pete.
4. Courageous firefighters entered the burning building.
5. Did you see the rugged mountains in the distance?
6. *Tyrannosaurus rex* was the fiercest dinosaur.
7. Let's walk down the sunnier side of the street.
8. Much fruit is grown in California.
9. These rocks are more difficult to climb over than the ones we just climbed.
10. It's a common mistake in multiplication.
11. *The Blue Room* is the most beautiful painting I have ever seen.
12. A python is longer than a boa constrictor.
13. According to the latest report, we can expect snow.
14. Is Sadie's car reliable?
15. The most widely distributed book in the world is the Bible.
16. Bicycle shops are busier in the summer than in the winter.
17. Clovers with four leaves are less numerous than those that have three.
18. We found interesting designs on the Easter eggs.
19. The longest cave is 330 miles of passages.
20. The ripest blueberries will make the best pies.

Practice Power

▶ Write your own sentences using each of the adjectives given.

1. sweetest
2. braver
3. useful
4. most thoughtful

Correct Use of the Comparative and Superlative Degrees

Use the comparative degree when two persons or things are compared. Use the superlative degree when more than two are compared.

Miles is the *better* swimmer of the two. (two compared)

Miles is the *best* swimmer on the team. (more than two compared)

The comparative degree is often used with the word *than*.

Oranges are generally *larger than* limes.

For the comparative form, do not use *-er* and the word *more* (or *less*) at the same time.

INCORRECT: more noisier

For the superlative form, do not use *-est* and the word *most* (or *least*) at the same time.

INCORRECT: most noisiest

Exercise 1

Choose the correct word(s) to complete each sentence.

1. Lincoln is considered by many historians to be the (taller, tallest) president.

2. Which is (older, oldest)—the telegraph or the radio?

3. It is (colder, coldest) in Antarctica than it is here.

4. Of the triplets, Kip is the (less mischievous, least mischievous).

5. Which is (thinner, thinnest), a needle or a pin?

6. Jeanette is the (better, best) driver in her family.

7. The triangle is the (simpler, simplest) instrument in an orchestra.

8. Which subject is (less difficult, least difficult), math or science?

9. China has the (greater, greatest) population in the world.

10. Lilly thinks koalas are (cuter, cutest) than pandas.

Exercise 2

Complete each sentence with the correct form of the adjective in parentheses.

1. The Amazon River is the (long) river in South America.
2. This problem is (difficult) than the other one.
3. Shrews are the (small) living mammals.
4. *Home Alone* is the (funny) movie Christopher has ever seen.
5. This book is the (good) one that Andy has read.
6. Moles spend (much) time underground than any other place.
7. Rhode Island is (small) than Delaware.
8. Wyatt grew the (big) pumpkin of all.
9. The diamond is the (hard) of all stones and will even cut glass.
10. Was J. P. Morgan (wealthy) than John D. Rockefeller?
11. The Sears Tower in Chicago is the (tall) building in the United States.
12. This clown is (thin) than the other one.
13. My cat, Sam, is the (curious) cat I've ever known.
14. Venus is the (close) in size to Earth.
15. Juan feels that Benjamin Franklin is the (famous) inventor of all time.

Write a sentence showing the correct use of these adjectives.

16. more cheerful	21. safest
17. worst	22. wiser
18. warmest	23. least difficult
19. better	24. funnier
20. most delicate	25. much

Putting It All Together

With a partner, plan the retelling of a daring adventure or an escape from danger. On one sheet of paper, write the basic story. On another sheet, list adjectives. Include limiting, demonstrative, possessive, interrogative, and comparing adjectives.

Stage a performance in which one person tries to tell the story in a serious way. The second person should interrupt to add funny or ridiculous details.

Chapter Challenge

Read this paragraph carefully and answer the questions.

The harbor is alive with ships from around the world. Several freighters rock on the tide, graceful liners glide up to the piers, and tugs wander in and out of the harbor. The tugs, which are smaller than the other vessels, look tiny compared to the black hulls of the freighters. Two pleasure boats cruise up the river. Strains of cheerful music from their orchestras float toward shore. What a busy picture of life on American waters this port shows!

1. Name an adjective used as a subjective complement in sentence 1.

2. What noun does this subjective complement modify?

3. Name a limiting adjective in sentence 1.

4. Name an adjective in the comparative degree in sentence 3. Write the two other degrees of this adjective.

5. Name the three descriptive adjectives in sentence 3.

6. Find a numeral adjective in the paragraph.

7. What noun does the numeral adjective modify?

8. Is the word *pleasure* used as a noun or an adjective in sentence 4?

9. Is *cheerful* in sentence 5 a descriptive or limiting adjective?

10. Find a proper adjective in the paragraph.

11. Name an indefinite article in sentence 6.

12. Find a demonstrative adjective in sentence 6.

13. Does the demonstrative adjective modify a singular or plural noun?

14. Write the comparative and the superlative forms of *cheerful* in sentence 5.

15. Does the paragraph contain any adjectives in the superlative degree?

Working with Verbs

A verb is a word used to express action or being.

In her seventies, Grandma Moses *started* a new hobby. She *sewed* pictures with yarns. Then the rheumatism in her hands *worsened*. Needlework *was* now difficult for her. At her sister's suggestion, she *switched* to painting as a pastime. Some of her paintings on display in a drugstore window *attracted* the attention of an art collector. Several years later, there *was* an exhibit of her paintings in New York City, and Grandma Moses *gained* fame by the age of eighty-five. Grandma's paintings *remain* popular. People *admire* them for their simplicity and charm. Her paintings *show* the American countryside in all its bright colors and throughout its changing seasons. Grandma once *wrote* that her choice of a hobby *was* chicken farming until she *began* painting. Many people *are* happy that she *began* her new hobby.

Look at the italicized words in the paragraph. Some express action. They are the verbs *started, sewed, worsened, switched, attracted, gained, admire, show, wrote,* and *began*. Some express being. They are the verbs *was, remain,* and *are*.

Without a verb, there can be no sentence.

> *Find* a cool, shady spot for our picnic. (a sentence—with the verb *Find*)
>
> In the shade of the elm tree. (not a sentence—no verb)

About the Photograph

You are never too young or too old to begin a hobby. These children are painting. What verbs tell about your hobby?

Verb Phrases

A verb phrase is a group of words that does the work of a single verb.

The verb in some sentences consists of only one word. In many sentences, however, the verb is made up of two or more words, as in these examples:

> Marsha *has received* a certificate for free ice cream.
> The glasses *were resting* on Grandfather's stomach.
> The baby *was named* Leo.

The words in italics are all verb phrases since they do the work of single verbs.

The words that make up a verb phrase are usually written together. In some sentences, however, particularly in interrogative and negative sentences, the parts of the verb phrase may be separated.

> *Have* you *read* about the adventures of Tom Sawyer?
> When *did* you *live* in Italy and Japan?
> My name *was* not *called* by the leader.

Have read, did live, and *was called* are verb phrases. The principal verbs in these sentences are *read, live*, and *called*. The other words—*have, did*, and *was*—are auxiliary verbs.

Any verb used with the principal verb is called an auxiliary verb.

Here are common auxiliary verbs.

am	could	had	is	shall	were
are	did	has	may	should	will
can	do	have	might	was	would

Exercise 1

Make a sentence from each group of words by adding one action verb or verb of being.

1. German music boxes _____ several tunes.
2. My little brother _____ only the green jellybeans.
3. The airplane _____ over the Grand Canyon.
4. Grandpa Walsh _____ an expert fiddle player.
5. A hungry tabby cat _____ in our yard.
6. White _____ a good color to wear in hot weather.
7. My sisters _____ popcorn in front of the TV.
8. Yesterday the crowd in Carter Stadium _____ through the gates.
9. Aunt Elise's story about the disastrous camping trip _____ everyone.
10. Hermit crabs _____ along the rocks in the tide pools.
11. The instructor at the YMCA _____ the basic pool safety rules.
12. The Scottish word for a lake _____ *loch*.
13. Leonardo da Vinci _____ some of the world's most beautiful art.
14. The puzzle _____ five thousand pieces.
15. These drawings _____ of the first bathing suits.

Exercise 2

Some of these groups of words are sentences. Others are not because they do not have a verb. For those that are sentences, name the verb.

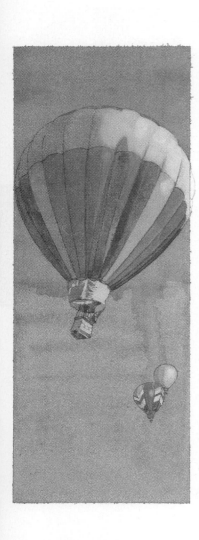

1. A colorful hot-air balloon drifted overhead.
2. The graceful skaters circled the ice rink.
3. Here nearly three hundred years ago.
4. Without a shadow of doubt!
5. Adam typed forty-five words in one minute.
6. Straight black hair, blue eyes, and high cheekbones.
7. Thousands of buffalo roamed the open prairie.
8. At the first eerie sound, the tired camper crawled quickly out of her tent.
9. On the top of the huge mountain.
10. The beagle chased the squirrel under the towels on Mrs. Pettigill's clothesline.
11. The mess on the table and in the sink.
12. Larry shoved the canoe into the muddy currents.
13. We slid across the lake on the slippery ice.
14. Marian tiptoed through the vegetable garden.
15. Down the street and around the corner.
16. My uncle handed me a foreign coin as a souvenir from his trip overseas.
17. A parade of children marched proudly.
18. Because of all their creative, exciting ideas.
19. The first weavers, shoemakers, and other such craft workers.
20. After takeoff, Mikhail relaxed.

Exercise 3

Find the verb phrases in these sentences. Tell which verb is the principal verb and which one is the auxiliary verb.

1. Have you ever watched dolphins in the ocean?
2. A thousand weeds are growing in our garden—and only one flower!
3. Two tourists had lost their way among the winding streets.
4. Ellen will explain the dance steps.
5. Tom has tried several cleaners on this chocolate stain.
6. You might enjoy the pyrotechnics display.
7. These topics were arranged in alphabetical order.
8. Frankly, I could eat four more hot dogs!
9. The trunk of an African baobab tree can measure more than thirty feet in diameter.
10. After that tumble, I am seeing stars.
11. How do people get those model ships into bottles?
12. Our track coach has developed special exercises for us.
13. You will always find the definition in a dictionary.
14. Tall Gothic cathedrals were built during the Middle Ages.
15. We shall help with the charity carnival.
16. Hans was secretly hoping for a postponement of his dental appointment.
17. Do you know the second verse of "Jingle Bells"?
18. Have you ever traveled to Paris?
19. Coral reefs have changed the geography of the world.
20. Can you tell me the difference between a fruit and a vegetable?

Practice Power

▶ Choose any nine common auxiliary verbs from the list on page 350. Write nine sentences using these auxiliary verbs with the principal verbs listed below. Include at least two sentences that are interrogative as well as two with adverbs that divide the verb phrase.

1. excavate	4. launch	7. scamper
2. giggle	5. surprise	8. gaze
3. pretend	6. interrupt	9. juggle

LESSON 2

Principal Parts of Verbs

The principal parts of the verb are the present, the past, and the past participle.

These three parts are so important that they are called the principal parts. If you know the principal parts, you can use any form of the verb correctly.

The past never takes an auxiliary or helping verb. The past participle is always used with an auxiliary or helping verb.

> They *flipped* a coin for the last cupcake. (past tense)
>
> My cousins *have lived* in Australia for three years. (past participle with auxiliary verb)

Regular and Irregular Verbs

A regular verb forms its past and its past participle by adding *d* or *ed* to the present.

The following verbs and many others add *d* or *ed* to the present to form the past and past participle. They are regular verbs.

PRESENT	PAST	PAST PARTICIPLE
bake	baked	baked
call	called	called
like	liked	liked
offer	offered	offered
play	played	played

> **An irregular verb does not form its past and its past participle by adding *d* or *ed* to the present.**

The principal parts of irregular verbs are formed in various ways, generally by a change in the word itself. That is why they are called irregular verbs. There is no general rule for forming the principal parts of such verbs. It will be necessary for you to learn the principal parts in order to use the different forms of the verbs correctly.

PRESENT	PAST	PAST PARTICIPLE
buy	bought	bought
sit	sat	sat
wear	wore	worn
write	wrote	written

The past and the past participle of irregular verbs are often confused. Remember, the past never takes an auxiliary or helping verb. The past participle is always used with an auxiliary or helping verb.

Notice the irregular verbs in the following examples:

Eddie *bought* a new watch for his dad on Father's Day.

Bridget *drank* the rest of the milk yesterday.

Steve *tore* a hole in his new shorts climbing over a fence today.

Our dog *hid* under a chair when we wanted to take him to the veterinarian.

Here are the principal parts of the more common irregular
verbs. They should be carefully studied.

PRESENT	PAST (These stand alone.)	PAST PARTICIPLE (These require a helping verb, such as *have*.)
am (is, be)	was	been
beat	beat	beat, beaten
begin	began	begun
bend	bent	bent
bet	bet	bet
bind	bound	bound
bite	bit	bitten
blow	blew	blown
break	broke	broken
bring	brought	brought
build	built	built
burst	burst	burst
buy	bought	bought
catch	caught	caught
choose	chose	chosen
come	came	come
do	did	done
draw	drew	drawn
drink	drank	drunk
eat	ate	eaten
fall	fell	fallen
fight	fought	fought
find	found	found
flee	fled	fled
fly	flew	flown
forget	forgot	forgotten
freeze	froze	frozen
give	gave	given
go	went	gone
grow	grew	grown
have	had	had
hear	heard	heard
hide	hid	hidden
hurt	hurt	hurt

PRESENT	PAST	PAST PARTICIPLE
keep	kept	kept
know	knew	known
lay	laid	laid
leave	left	left
lend	lent	lent
let	let	let
lie (recline)	lay	lain
lose	lost	lost
make	made	made
meet	met	met
ride	rode	ridden
ring	rang	rung
rise	rose	risen
run	ran	run
see	saw	seen
send	sent	sent
set	set	set
shake	shook	shaken
sing	sang	sung
sink	sank	sunk
sit	sat	sat
speak	spoke	spoken
spend	spent	spent
stand	stood	stood
stick	stuck	stuck
swim	swam	swum
swing	swung	swung
take	took	taken
teach	taught	taught
tear	tore	torn
tell	told	told
think	thought	thought
throw	threw	thrown
wear	wore	worn
win	won	won
write	wrote	written

Exercise 1

Complete each of the following sentences with the past tense or the past participle of the irregular verb at the left. If an auxiliary verb is given, the past participle is to be used.

come
1. A thundercloud _____ across the valley at thirty miles an hour.

burst
2. After the party, Teddy _____ every blue balloon.

eat
3. I _____ caviar for the first and last time yesterday.

see
4. Yes, I _____ him perform in a concert.

wear
5. People _____ beautifully decorated masks for the Mardi Gras festival.

send
6. The magazine _____ over a thousand valentines to subscribers.

make
7. Toby had _____ three different cakes for the baking contest.

ride
8. Have you ever _____ on the back of a camel?

freeze
9. It's so cold that the water in the birdbath has _____ .

ring
10. Has the fire alarm _____ yet?

grow
11. The banana plant has _____ a foot every month.

lose
12. The tourists have _____ their map and their guidebook.

write
13. Al _____ about the customs of the early Greeks.

hide
14. Where have they _____ the colored eggs?

go
15. Who has _____ to look for Ed?

tear
16. The bird _____ the paper into strips for its nest.

throw
17. I have _____ those dirty sneakers into the washer.

shake
18. After climbing from the pond, the wet dog _____ water on everybody.

fall
19. Six inches of snow had _____ while we slept.

begin
20. The seminar _____ at noon.

sing
21. The court jester _____ a riddle for the king.

take
22. We have _____ this rocky path as a shortcut.

find
23. Archaeologists have _____ many fossils in Tanzania.

give	24. This bag of peanuts _____ me a burst of energy.
draw	25. Ron _____ cartoons for the class newspaper.
ride	26. The Lone Ranger always _____ a white horse.
break	27. Walt has _____ his big toe.
see	28. Have you _____ a falling star?
run	29. The sprinter _____ to the end of the track.
teach	30. Jess _____ me how to fix my bicycle.
do	31. What have you _____ with the keys?
know	32. I have _____ Fenster, the handyman, for years.
win	33. Who _____ the new sports car?
drink	34. Pearl's dog _____ all the lemonade!
hear	35. We have _____ the warning siren before.
stand	36. The giraffes _____ around the acacia trees.
buy	37. I _____ a musical birthday card for my piano teacher.
choose	38. Bonita has _____ to study aikido, a Japanese art of self-defense.
hear	39. The park ranger had already _____ the tornado warnings.
build	40. Ancient people _____ Stonehenge, a mysterious group of large stones in England.
sit	41. The cowardly lion _____ down behind the knight.
grow	42. The lawn _____ several inches in one week.
forget	43. Roberto has _____ where he left his jacket.
bend	44. The blacksmith slowly _____ the horseshoe.
hurt	45. Ms. Graystone _____ her back pulling weeds.
fly	46. The birds have _____ north for the summer.
sink	47. My feet _____ into the sand.
lose	48. Who _____ the presidential election for 1984?
think	49. Sally _____ of a new use for her computer.
stand	50. On the top of the hill _____ the observatory.

Practice Power

▶ Choose two regular verbs from the list on page 354 and two irregular verbs from the list that begins on page 356. Then write three sentences for each verb using the present, past, and past participle forms.

Troublesome Verbs

Lie and *Lay*

> The verb *lie* means "to rest or recline." The principal parts are *lie, lay,* and *lain.*

> The verb *lay* means "to put or place in position." The principal parts are *lay, laid,* and *laid. Lay* is usually followed by a direct object.

The boy *lay* on the beach. (=rested)

The boy *laid* the radio on the sand. (=put)

Study the chart below.

	REST OR RECLINE	PUT OR PLACE
PRESENT	lie	lay
PAST	lay	laid
PAST PARTICIPLE	(have) lain	(have) laid

Sit and *Set*

> The verb *sit* means "to have or keep a seat." The principal parts are *sit, sat,* and *sat.*

> The verb *set* means "to place or fix in position." The principal parts are *set, set,* and *set. Set* usually has a direct object.

The monkey *sits* on a rock. (=has a seat)

Tom *set* the chicken in the nest. (=placed)

Rise and *Raise*

> The verb *rise* (*rise, rose, risen*) means "to ascend."

> The verb *raise* (*raise, raised, raised*) means "to lift."
> *Raise* usually has a direct object.

The smoke *rose* from the chimneys. (=ascended)

Patti *raised* her hand to answer the question. (=lifted)

Let and *Leave*

> The verb *let* (*let, let, let*) means "to permit or allow."

> The verb *leave* (*leave, left, left*) means "to abandon" or "to depart."

Let Monica play her violin. (=permit or allow)

We *left* for the parade early. (=departed)

Teach and *Learn*

> The verb *teach* (*teach, taught, taught*) means "to give instruction."

> The verb *learn* (*learn, learned, learned*) means "to receive instruction."

I *taught* them how to yodel. (=gave instruction)

I've already *learned* how to yodel. (=received instruction)

Exercise 1

Choose the correct verb form of *lie* or *lay* to complete each sentence.

1. Amelia (lies, lays) down for a nap every afternoon.
2. Now (lie, lay) your hands on your head and run in place.
3. Three yellow rosebuds (lay, laid) in the wicker basket.
4. Where have you (lain, laid) Aunt Aggie's cowboy hat?
5. Corinne (lain, laid) a towel over the kneaded dough.
6. Your skates have (lain, laid) there for a week!
7. Who will (lie, lay) the foundation of this house?
8. The leopard (lies, lays) behind the bushes.
9. Where should I (lay, lie) in the tent?
10. Julianna likes to (lie, lay) in the sun and listen to the radio.
11. Do you think the mail carrier (lay, laid) this package here?
12. Thomas, (lie, lay) on this cot and rest.
13. The carpenter (lay, laid) a hammer on the table.
14. How long has it (lain, laid) there?
15. A huge tree, felled by beavers, (laid, lay) across the pond.

Exercise 2

Choose the correct verb form of *sit* or *set* to complete each sentence.

1. Louie and Huey (sat, set) in the sandbox this morning.
2. Please (sit, set) the pancakes in front of me.
3. Bonnie (sat, set) on the porch and looked at the stars.
4. (Sit, Set) those lightbulbs down carefully.
5. Let's (sit, set) where we can see the stage.
6. The old hen (sits, sets) on any nest except her own.
7. (Sit, Set) the groceries in the back of the car.
8. Who (sat, set) this piece of bubblegum on his plate?
9. Our cat (sets, sits) in the window and stares at the birds.
10. (Sit, Set) here until you give your speech.
11. She made the child (set, sit) under the beach umbrella.
12. We (sat, set) on a log at the edge of the forest.
13. Dwayne (sit, set) his plate of cookies in the kitchen.
14. The hikers (sat, set) under the stone bridge.
15. (Sit, Set) the alarm for six o'clock.

Exercise 3

Choose the correct verb form of *rise* or *raise* to complete each sentence.

1. The speaker (rose, raised) to address the cheering crowd.
2. Helena slowly (rose, raised) her hand.
3. The camels (raised, rose) from their knees.
4. Caleb's hang glider had (risen, raised) above the treetops!
5. The captain of the boat (rose, raised) the flag.
6. Jeff (rises, raises) before five o'clock.
7. The Chinese kite (rose, raised) rapidly.
8. She (rose, raised) her eyebrows at the question.
9. A plume of smoke (rose, raised) from the campfire.
10. Cane Creek was (raising, rising) because of heavy rain.
11. (Rise, Raise) the freezer lid so we can get the meat out.
12. The temperature has (risen, raised).
13. The startled crows (rose, raised) from the cornfield.
14. Yoshi (rose, raised) the magnifying glass from the table.
15. Many people (raise, rise) earlier in the summer.

Exercise 4

Choose the correct verb form of *let* or *leave* to complete each sentence.

1. (Let, Leave) the bird's eggs alone!
2. The express bus (lets, leaves) at three o'clock.
3. (Let, Leave) those pennies in the fountain!
4. Diego (let, left) his backpack behind the old shed.
5. (Leave, Let) me go with you on the nature walk!
6. Don't (leave, let) anyone eat my french fries!
7. Why has Deirdre (let, left) the room?
8. Ross (let, left) me help paint the Earth Day mural.
9. The plane does not (let, leave) until noon.
10. Has he (let, left) his new address with you?
11. We shall (let, leave) the children name the new park.
12. (Leave, Let) Miguel try it first!
13. I promise that I'll (let, leave) you use my mitt.
14. The puppy (let, left) a trail of cookie crumbs.
15. He (let, left) all the dinosaur bones undisturbed.

Exercise 5

Choose the correct verb form of *teach* or *learn* to complete each sentence.

1. The coach (taught, learned) me how to spin a basketball on my finger.

2. Our dog, Sauerkraut, (taught, learned) to beg for German food.

3. I (teach, learn) about the world economy by reading the newspaper.

4. Abraham Lincoln (taught, learned) himself by reading borrowed books.

5. Baby woodpeckers watch their parents and (teach, learn) how to find worms.

6. Linda, (teach, learn) me how to play boccie.

7. Did the scouts (teach, learn) you how to tie a half hitch?

8. Each student (teaches, learns) a first-aid procedure to a younger partner.

9. Will you (teach, learn) your lines in the play by tonight?

10. Please (teach, learn) me how to adjust the gears on my bike.

Practice Power

▶ You had a very unusual dream last night. Write a short paragraph describing your dream. Use at least five of the troublesome verbs from this lesson.

Transitive and Intransitive Verbs

Transitive Verbs

A transitive verb expresses an action that passes from a doer to a receiver.

DOER	ACTION	RECEIVER
Mary	read	the book.

In this sentence, the action *(read)* passes from the doer *(Mary)* to the receiver *(book)*. The verb *read* is, therefore, a transitive verb.

To determine the receiver of the action, ask the question *whom* or *what* after the verb. Mary read what? The word that answers the question is the receiver of the action. It is called the direct object of the verb. The direct object of the verb *read* in this sentence is *book.*

The verbs in the sentences below are transitive.

> Stella *delivers* the newspaper. (The word *newspaper* is the direct object.)
>
> Charlie *caught* a firefly. (The word *firefly* is the direct object.)

VERBS

Intransitive Verbs

> **An intransitive verb has no receiver of its action.**

Franklin *lived* on the seventy-fifth floor.

The action of this verb, *lived,* begins and ends with the doer. There are no answers to the questions "Franklin lived whom?" or "Franklin lived what?"

An intransitive verb may be followed by a prepositional phrase or an adverb. The phrase or adverb does not receive the action.

The scouts hiked *in the canyon.* (prepositional phrase)

The ice melted *quickly.* (adverb)

Exercise 1

The verb in each sentence is transitive. Identify the verb. Then name the doer and the receiver of the action.

1. With a steady hand, Mariah carefully lit the candle.
2. Jenny cleaned her room very thoroughly.
3. We baked the brownies just a little too long.
4. In the 1890s, Dr. James Naismith invented basketball.
5. The chickadees ate the seeds from the feeder.
6. You tore a valuable piece of paper.
7. The tourists stalked the lions with their cameras.
8. The tailor made clothes for everyone but himself.
9. The Great Wall of China protected that country for centuries.
10. My dog makes spectacular catches of my stick.
11. Galileo studied the planets with a telescope.
12. The winner broke the record for the school.
13. My friend wrote this letter in our secret code.
14. The class celebrated everyone's birthday on one day.
15. Carolyn learned violin when she was only six years old.

Exercise 2

The verb in each sentence below is intransitive because there is no receiver of the action. Find the verb. Then name the doer in each sentence.

1. Skiers raced recklessly down the icy slope.
2. An excited fan leaned forward.
3. Christmas Island lies in the Indian Ocean.
4. Those astronauts spoke about their next spaceflight.
5. Finally beside a warm fire, Andrea whistled happily.
6. The entire group of seals plunged beneath the waves.
7. The snowy ground glistens in the early morning sun.
8. The bells on Karin's costume jingled softly.
9. A Moroccan flag floated in the warm breeze.
10. The starlings nest in these trees every night.
11. James went to countless baseball and soccer practices.
12. Children walk toward the school bus.
13. Uranus travels around the sun every eighty-four Earth years.
14. The president resides in Washington, D.C.
15. A moose suddenly appeared at the edge of the lake.

Practice Power

▶ Write a sentence for each of these transitive verbs. The verb may be in present, past, or past participle form.

    1. set   **2.** lay   **3.** destroy   **4.** run

▶ Write a sentence for each of these intransitive verbs. The verb may be in present, past, or past participle form.

    5. sit   **6.** lie   **7.** sparkle   **8.** disappear

Verbs That Are Transitive or Intransitive

Some verbs may be either transitive or intransitive, according to their use in the sentence.

TRANSITIVE	INTRANSITIVE
Orlando *counted* the pennies.	Orlando *counted* carefully.
Jean *painted* stars on the ceiling.	Jean *painted* all day.
The rock *broke* the window.	The glass *broke*.

Exercise 1

The verbs in these sentences can be used as transitive or intransitive verbs. Find the verb in each sentence, and tell whether it is transitive or intransitive.

1. My aunt grows prizewinning tomatoes.
2. The alfalfa sprouts grew in a glass jar on the windowsill.
3. Chandra entered a bubblegum-blowing contest.
4. We entered quietly through the back door.
5. Joe and Carlos seldom lose in chess competitions.
6. My uncle flew an antique plane in the air show.
7. For our class project, we wrote a complicated program on the computer.
8. George always writes with a sharp pencil.
9. Carita lost the tennis match to her best friend.
10. I actually flew in a helicopter.

Exercise 2

Find the verb in each sentence. Name the doer of the action. Name the receiver if there is one. Tell if each verb is transitive or intransitive.

1. Sir Spencer answered the wizard's question correctly.
2. The cold winds howl fiercely through the cracks in the wall.
3. The hot-air balloonist postponed his flight until a sunny day.
4. Cut daisies wilt quickly.
5. The fast train runs between Paris and Lyons.
6. Our dog likes caramel, bananas, and peanut butter!
7. That factory recycles old newspapers.
8. The marching band plays during halftime.
9. Fresh sawdust completely covered the floor of the workshop.
10. My mother hurried into the grocery store.
11. We saw the old ship on display in the harbor.
12. Mitchell's cousin came from New Zealand.
13. Vacationers see active volcanoes in Hawaii.
14. The excited puppy bounded after the red car.
15. During the day, hippopotamuses spend their time in water.

Practice Power

▶ Write two sentences for each of these verbs. Use the verb first as a transitive verb and then as an intransitive verb. The verb may be in present, past, or past participle form.

1. talk   3. explore   5. bounce   7. decorate
2. play   4. paint   6. relax   8. fly

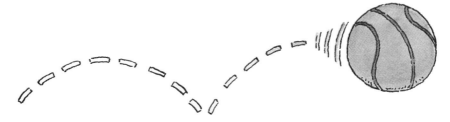

Linking Verbs

A linking verb links the subject with a noun,
pronoun, or an adjective. The word that follows
a linking verb is called a subjective complement.

SUBJECT	LINKING VERB	SUBJECTIVE COMPLEMENT
Those girls	are	*members.* (noun)
That bee	is	*it.* (pronoun)
Ted	was	*enthusiastic.* (adjective)

Each of the verbs in these sentences needs a complement to
complete its meaning. The verb links this complement with
the subject. The verb *are* links the complement *members* with
the subject *girls.* The verb *is* links the complement *it* with the
subject *bee.* The verb *was* links the complement *enthusiastic*
with the subject *Ted.*

The noun, pronoun, or adjective that completes the meaning
of these verbs is called a subjective complement.

The forms of the verb *be* are the most common linking verbs.

am	be	being	was
are	been	is	were

The following verbs also can be used as linking verbs.

appear	feel	remain	sound
become	grow	seem	taste
continue	look	smell	

When these verbs are used as linking verbs, a form of the verb
be can be substituted for the original verb.

John *looked* healthy.	John *was* healthy.
The whistles *sounded* shrill.	The whistles *were* shrill.
The day *grew* hot.	The day *was* hot.

Exercise 1

Find the linking verb in each sentence. Tell whether the italicized complement is a noun, a pronoun, or an adjective.

1. Prizes at rodeos were often *buckles* for the cowboys' belts.
2. The girl in the chemistry class is *she*.
3. These handwoven Navajo blankets are very *warm*.
4. The platypus is an egg-laying *mammal*.
5. Trojans were *enemies* of the ancient Greeks.
6. The tour through Mavis Hargrove's old mansion was *scary*.
7. The lumberjack in the red plaid jacket was *he*.
8. The beach was *sunny* all morning.
9. The poppy-seed bagels are still *warm*.
10. A bookmobile is a *library* on wheels.

Exercise 2

Find the linking verb and the complement in each sentence. Then substitute a form of the verb *be* for the original verb.

1. Somehow, Ramona remained calm throughout the Olympic competition.
2. This grapefruit ice cream tastes unique.
3. Ms. Lee, the librarian, seems knowledgeable about cats.
4. The Red Sea appears reddish—but only at certain times.
5. Five blocks away, the siren still sounds clear.
6. The sky looks cloudy today.
7. Uncle Jack's fried crawfish smell appetizing.
8. We feel happy about the election results.
9. Irene Ross became our class president.
10. The cornstalks in Kansas grow very tall.

Exercise 3 REVIEW

Find the verbs in these sentences. Tell whether each is transitive, intransitive, or a linking verb.

1. The ferocious tiger and the friendly cat are members of the same family.
2. Louis was friendly to the new boy down the street.
3. The runaway toboggan slid down the hill.
4. Mr. Waldorf saw the Coast Guard cutter in the harbor.
5. Beavers build new dams across Lumbee Creek every year.
6. A balloon pops in a tiny fraction of a second.
7. A computer chip is tiny.
8. Many wild animals never grow completely tame in captivity.
9. Harriet trudged to the farmhouse.
10. A brightly uniformed band leads the parade.
11. We heard the call of a blue heron from the marsh.
12. Nearly twenty million people live in Malaysia.
13. Many Spaniards danced in the streets of Pamplona.
14. An usher in a tuxedo conducted us to our seats.
15. Sir Arthur Conan Doyle wrote many famous detective stories.
16. The kite rose above the pine trees.
17. Louisa became an excellent gymnast.
18. The photographer waited patiently for a zebra.
19. I eagerly pulled the bundle of letters from the mailbox.
20. General Ulysses S. Grant was the commander of Union armies during the Civil War.

Practice Power

▶ You have just walked into the world-famous shop, the Sweet Tooth. What kind of food do you think this shop sells? Describe the shop. Write sentences using some form of these six linking verbs.

taste   look   feel   smell   appear   seem

Simple Tenses

The tense of a verb shows the time of the action or being.

> You *walk* the dog today.
> Calvin *walked* the dog yesterday.
> Myra *will walk* the dog tomorrow.

Today is present time, *yesterday* is past time, and *tomorrow* is future time. Notice how the verb *walk* changes in form when used to show these various times. This quality of a verb is called tense. The word *tense* means "time."

The present tense shows action or being in present time.

> Apples *grow* in our backyard.
> Apples *are* a very healthful snack.

If the subject is a singular noun or a pronoun in the third person singular, the verb form ends in *s* in the present tense.

> Josie *acts* in all the school plays.

The past tense shows action or being in past time.

> He *sang* last night.
> We *were* members of the drama club this year.

The future tense shows action or being in future time.

> He *will sing* tomorrow.
> They *will be* members of the drama club next year.

The auxiliary verb *shall* or *will* is used to form the future tense.

Exercise **1**

Find the verb in each sentence and give its tense.

1. I love the song playing on the radio!
2. Felix found his key on the dusty shelf.
3. The boxer jumps rope as part of his practice routine.
4. What time is my piano lesson today?
5. The surfers were disappointed by the small waves.
6. I play classical music for my plants every morning.
7. Paige will perform a solo on the grand piano.
8. Our mail carrier delivers the mail at ten o'clock every day.
9. Juan lives in a two-story house in Dallas.
10. The pipe organ is the largest musical instrument.
11. The dancer twirled close to the edge of the stage.
12. We froze two trays of ice cubes for our lemonade stand.
13. Will you watch the last golfers tee off?
14. My cousins catch mackerels from the pier at night.
15. Chan painted the fence with short, quick strokes.
16. Some redwood trees live more than one thousand years.
17. Will there be a holiday tomorrow?
18. The soapy water bubbled merrily over the sides of the washing machine.
19. Frankie will write a complaint to the president of the soft-drink company.
20. In 1889 and 1890, the reporter Nellie Bly traveled around the world in seventy-two days.
21. My father rode his bike to work yesterday.
22. The swimming pool opens at noon today.
23. Alexander Graham Bell invented the telephone in 1876.
24. Simona's brother cuts his hair at least once a month.
25. The gymnast flips through the air.

Exercise 2

Complete these sentences by supplying the tense indicated in parentheses for the verbs listed.

Talk

1. The club members _____ about their favorite books. (present)
2. You _____ on the telephone for over an hour! (past)
3. James _____ about nothing but his new motorcycle for a week. (past)
4. The fire chief _____ to our class next week. (future)
5. Mrs. Takada _____ quickly when she is excited. (present)

Bring

6. My sister _____ my lunch to school when I forget it. (present)
7. I _____ my bicycle inside whenever it looks like rain. (present)
8. They _____ your guitar books back tomorrow. (future)
9. The Spanish _____ the horse to the New World. (past)
10. The museum director _____ some dinosaur bones for us to examine. (future)

Burst

11. Bill grabbed the balloon and _____ it. (past)
12. The dirt-covered detectives _____ through the door. (past)
13. When I dropped it on the floor, the fat tomato _____ open. (past)
14. The cherry trees _____ into bloom all around Washington, D.C. (future)
15. My zebra finches _____ into song whenever a light is turned on. (present)

Eat

16. They _____ candy on the bus. (past)
17. The construction workers _____ their lunch in the truck. (future)
18. We _____ Italian dressing on our tossed salad. (present)
19. I _____ dinner with my family tonight. (future)
20. My friend has an allergic reaction if she _____ chocolate. (present)

Choose

21. Magpies usually _____ thorny sticks for their nests. (present)
22. The hikers _____ a spot under a sprawling oak tree for the picnic. (past)
23. Oliver Smith _____ a plaid tie as his favorite. (past)
24. The club _____ its slogan with a secret vote. (future)
25. Lola _____ these flowers for the hall table. (present)

Wear

26. The players _____ their uniforms for the first time. (past)
27. Alice always _____ the ring her parents gave her. (present)
28. He _____ a penguin outfit to the costume party. (future)
29. The men _____ their hair short. (present)
30. I _____ an orange obi, or belt, with my flowered kimono. (present)

Practice Power

▶ Pretend you are marooned on a deserted island. Write a paragraph explaining the situation you are in, how you got on the island, and what you will do to survive. Use verbs in the present, past, and future tenses in your paragraph.

LESSON 8 Compound Tenses

The compound tenses are the present perfect tense, the past perfect tense, and the future perfect tense.

The present perfect tense shows action completed in present time.

He already *has sung* today.

We *have studied* geometry today.

The present perfect tense is formed by the auxiliary *have* or *has* plus the past participle of the verb.

The past perfect tense shows action completed before some definite time in the past.

He *had sung* before we arrived at the recital.

We *had studied* algebra before we studied geometry.

The past perfect tense is formed by the auxiliary *had* plus the past participle of the verb.

The future perfect tense shows action that will be completed before some specified time in the future.

He *will have sung* the song before you return.

We *shall have studied* geometry before evening.

The future perfect tense is formed by the auxiliaries *shall have* or *will have* plus the past participle of the verb.

VERBS

Exercise 1

Find the verb phrase in each sentence and give its tense.

1. My brother has driven his car about one thousand miles.
2. The prince and the pauper had switched places.
3. By dawn, my father will have reached his secret fishing spot.
4. Have you heard any good jokes lately?
5. I have done my best with the snake-charming act.
6. Had the zookeepers decided on a name for the baby panda?
7. Carrie has spilled perfume all over her dresser.
8. Rick and Paul have made a beautiful wreath for the front door.
9. Where have the cowhands taken that noisy herd of longhorns?
10. The slick tires had made a strange noise on the pavement.
11. Mr. Andretti and his wife have fed the pigeons the last bread crumbs.
12. Thomas had never made apple cider before.
13. By tomorrow, they will have completed decorations for the party.
14. The carpenter has hit his thumb with the hammer.
15. The dog had wanted the scraps of leftover meat.

Exercise 2

Complete each sentence by supplying the tense indicated in parentheses for the verbs listed.

Talk

1. Carl _____ about the monster movie all day. (present perfect)
2. The bus driver already _____ to us about wearing seat belts. (past perfect)
3. Ms. Wilson _____ to the contest committee by Saturday. (future perfect)
4. Our neighbors _____ to the construction crew about the noise. (present perfect)
5. The newspaper reporter _____ to many witnesses before writing the story. (past perfect)

Eat

6. I was surprised that the acid _____ a hole in my lab coat. (past perfect)
7. Helena _____ three dozen sardines in the contest! (present perfect)
8. Everyone in camp _____ breakfast before sunrise. (future perfect)
9. Who _____ all the peanut brittle? (present perfect)
10. The campers _____ the entire box of raisins by midnight. (future perfect)

Burst

11. Last winter the pipes under the house _____ before the renters moved in. (past perfect)
12. After days of rain, the sun _____ through the clouds. (present perfect)
13. Mysteriously, the soda bottles _____ during the night. (past perfect)
14. The thinnest balloons _____ before they reach the ground. (future perfect)
15. _____ your bicycle tire ever _____ before? (past perfect)

Bring

16. Lila _____ oranges from Florida for me. (present perfect)
17. The substitute mail carrier _____ the mail early. (present perfect)
18. Carol and Jody _____ their raincoats but not their umbrellas. (present perfect)
19. He _____ the film projector before you return. (future perfect)
20. Before I realized it, the dog _____ mud into the house. (past perfect)

Choose

21. The government _____ the rose as the national flower. (present perfect)
22. The boys _____ the chicken soup with rice, but they changed their minds. (past perfect)
23. Everyone _____ geography projects by Friday. (future perfect)
24. _____ they _____ Sancha as the new Safety Squad leader? (present perfect)
25. The worms _____ the juiciest apples in the crate. (past perfect)

Wear

26. That snowman _____ the same hat every day. (present perfect)
27. The coach reported that the cheerleaders _____ their new uniforms to the rally. (past perfect)
28. _____ he _____ that navy suit before graduation? (past perfect)
29. They _____ their graduation gowns before the actual day. (future perfect)
30. I _____ holes in all of my socks. (present perfect)

Exercise 3

Complete each sentence by supplying the tense indicated in parentheses for each verb.

place   **1.** Under his head, she _____ a blue-and-white striped pillow. (past tense)

order   **2.** Doctor Chin _____ him to go to a warm, sunny climate. (past tense)

gain   **3.** By the time she joined Buffalo Bill's Wild West Show, Annie Oakley _____ fame as a sharpshooter. (past perfect tense)

lie   **4.** Grandmother's silver thimble _____ in her sewing basket. (past tense)

finish   **5.** The artists _____ their work with oils. (present perfect tense)

study   **6.** The astronomer _____ the distant planets through a powerful telescope. (present tense)

drift   **7.** The lion cubs _____ to sleep beside their mother. (present perfect tense)

fall   **8.** Snow _____ off and on during the skiing lessons. (past tense)

win   **9.** Our team _____ the debate on which president was the greatest. (past tense)

grow   **10.** Thousands of buttercups _____ around the abandoned log cabin. (present tense)

take   **11.** My brother _____ a test to check his eyesight. (future tense)

appear   **12.** Stars soon _____ in the gray twilight sky. (past tense)

see   **13.** We _____ abstract paintings in the art gallery. (past tense)

bring   **14.** The delivery person _____ the pizza in only thirty minutes. (past tense)

hide   **15.** The armadillo _____ behind the trash can for a while before we noticed it. (past perfect tense)

pack	**16.** Explorers _____ eighty pounds of equipment on each burro. (present tense)
close	**17.** The grocery store _____ at eight o'clock. (present tense)
build	**18.** Wrens _____ a nest under the rusty tractor seat. (present perfect tense)
tell	**19.** I _____ him the unbelievable news by tonight. (future perfect tense)
bake	**20.** Vito _____ a delicious peach pie. (present tense)
increase	**21.** Michael _____ his pitching accuracy through practice. (past tense)
celebrate	**22.** People in Great Britain and Canada _____ Boxing Day on December 26. (present tense)
come	**23.** Shetland ponies _____ from an island off Scotland. (past tense)
give	**24.** Gail, the zoo guide, _____ you directions to the aviary. (future tense)
teach	**25.** Aristotle _____ his pupils a clear method of reasoning. (past tense)

Practice Power

▶ The synopsis of a verb is a short way to practice using a verb in all the tenses. Any nominative case pronoun can be used. Study the example below, and then complete two synopses on your own—one with the verb *land* and the personal pronoun *it,* and the other with the verb *run* and the personal pronoun *they*.

Example:
Synopsis for the Verb *See*

Present Tense	He sees
Past Tense	He saw
Future Tense	He will see
Present Perfect Tense	He has seen
Past Perfect Tense	He had seen
Future Perfect Tense	He will have seen

Agreement of Subject with Verb—*Part I*

VERBS

> **Verbs should agree with their subjects, both in person and in number.**

A verb may be in the first person, the second person, or the third person. The first person refers to the speaker, the second person refers to the one spoken to, and the third person refers to the one spoken about.

In addition, the verb may be singular or plural in number. Singular refers to one; plural refers to more than one.

Note the changes in the verb in the sentences below as the subject changes from singular to plural or from first person to second and third persons. *The verb always agrees with the subject in person and number.* Note that all nouns are in the third person.

	SINGULAR NUMBER	PLURAL NUMBER
FIRST PERSON	I *am* his friend.	We *are* his friends.
SECOND PERSON	You *are* his friend.	You *are* his friends.
THIRD PERSON	She *is* his friend.	They *are* his friends.
FIRST PERSON	I *have* a two-dollar bill.	We *have* a two-dollar bill.
SECOND PERSON	You *have* a two-dollar bill.	You *have* a two-dollar bill.
THIRD PERSON	He *has* a two-dollar bill.	They *have* a two-dollar bill.
FIRST PERSON	I *walk* in the park.	We *walk* in the park.
SECOND PERSON	You *walk* in the park.	You *walk* in the park.
THIRD PERSON	It *walks* in the park.	They *walk* in the park.

Exercise 1

Name the subject and verb or verb phrase in each sentence.
Tell the person and number of each verb or verb phrase.

1. Conifers are the only kind of tree near the top of a mountain.
2. We usually jog all the way home.
3. Your train has left!
4. I have already taken the prescription to the pharmacy.
5. You have taped my finger to the box.
6. Louis flops on the couch with a bag of barbecue-flavored potato chips after football practice.
7. The twins often burst into laughter over their secret switches.
8. I was putting blue and green candles on Mia's birthday cake.
9. The Mediterranean Sea contains a great amount of salt.
10. With every crash of thunder, the dog crawls farther and farther under my bed.
11. They speak softly in the library.
12. Grandmother has always kept a box of peppermints on a high shelf.
13. The trucks have come to clean the streets.
14. Huge caves lie under the earth's surface.
15. These albums contain photographs of early gold miners.

Singular and Plural Subjects

> A singular subject requires a singular form of the verb. A plural subject requires a plural form of the verb.

Notice the change in the form of the verb in each of the following sentences.

SINGULAR NUMBER	PLURAL NUMBER
A picture *hangs* on the wall.	Pictures *hang* on the wall.
She *sleeps* well.	They *sleep* well.
He *walks* to the park.	They *walk* to the park.
She *has* waited.	They *have* waited.

A noun or pronoun in the third-person singular requires a verb that ends in *s* for the present tense.

Exercise 2

Find the subject in each sentence. Tell whether it is singular or plural. Then choose the correct verb.

1. My grandfather (sells, sell) antique furniture.
2. The logs on the truck (needs, need) a canvas cover.
3. The scouts (seems, seem) eager to leave for the mountains.
4. The starter (flags, flag) the cars to line up.
5. Loudness (is, are) measured in units called decibels.
6. Seven Indian elephants (was, were) walking to the tent.
7. Those chairs (has, have) been repainted every summer.
8. The magician (show, shows) us a new trick at every performance.
9. Hail (has, have) ruined the corn crop this year.
10. The rolling hills (was, were) covered with purple and yellow wildflowers.
11. Do the avocados (looks, look) ripe enough for guacamole?
12. The sunset (has, have) beautiful shades of red and orange!
13. We (finds, find) quite a few fossils in rocky areas.
14. Arizona's state flower (is, are) the saguaro.
15. Ms. Winston's miniature muffins (has, have) been sold.

Exercise 3

Rewrite each sentence and change the italicized nouns from the plural to the singular. Then change the verb to agree with the new subject.

1. The *pictures* of sunflowers hang on the wall.
2. The *chalkboards* were full of sentences by students.
3. Have the *plates* been washed?
4. When left alone, the *puppies* climb up on the sofa.
5. Marge's front *teeth* are loose.
6. The *cookies* are cool enough to eat.
7. The *guards* direct traffic during rush hour.
8. There go the *trucks* to the fire!

Now change the italicized nouns from the singular to the plural. Then change the verb to agree with the new subject.

9. The *messenger* brings us the daily report.
10. The new *book* about outer space is on display in the library.
11. The *train* shakes the windows in our house.
12. The silly *rooster* crows at sunset.
13. Does the *squirrel* bite?
14. Has the *wharf* been repaired?
15. My *sister-in-law* swims a mile every day.

Practice Power

▶ Write a paragraph explaining how you come to school. Then rewrite the paragraph explaining how you come to school with a group of classmates. Remember to have your verbs agree with your subjects.

Correct Use of Subject and Verb Agreement

LESSON 10

There Is and *There Are*

> ***There is*** or ***there was*** should be used when the subject, which follows the verb, is singular. ***There are*** or ***there were*** is used when the subject is plural.

There (is, are) three windows in this room.

Here is the correct form: There *are* three windows in this room.

The subject *windows* is plural in number. To find the subject, omit the word *there* and rearrange the sentence: Three windows are in this room.

When a sentence begins with *there*, look for the subject after the verb.

Doesn't and *Don't*

> If the subject of the sentence is in the third person, ***doesn't*** is the correct form in the singular. ***Don't*** is the correct form in the plural.
>
> In the first and the second persons, the correct form is ***don't***, whether the subject is singular or plural.

	SINGULAR NUMBER	PLURAL NUMBER
FIRST PERSON	I *don't* have a pet.	We *don't* have a pet.
SECOND PERSON	You *don't* have a pet.	You *don't* have a pet.
THIRD PERSON	He *doesn't* have a pet.	They *don't* have a pet.

VERBS

You as the Subject

> Use the forms *you are* and *you were* whether the subject is singular or plural. Never use *is* or *was* when the subject is in the second person.

(Was, Were) you at the game today?

Here is the correct form: *Were* you at the game today?

The subject *you* is in the second person.

Exercise 1

Find the subject in each sentence. Then choose the correct verb.

1. There (is, are) more than one billion people in China.
2. There (was, were) four robins eating.
3. There (is, are) many beautiful parks there.
4. There (were, was) seven wonders in the ancient world.
5. There (was, were) five kinds of flowers in this arrangement.
6. There (is, are) a group of baseball players warming up.
7. There (was, were) no key for this unusual box.
8. There (is, are) numerous groves of olive trees in Portugal.
9. There (was, were) a sudden knock at the door.
10. There (is, are) a thousand grams in a kilogram.
11. There (was, were) several ripe peaches in the basket.
12. There (is, are) a box of saltwater taffy on the table.
13. There (is, are) thirty days in April.
14. There (was, were) ten gulls standing on the sandbar.
15. There (is, are) a beautiful rainbow in the sky.

Exercise 2

Complete each sentence with _doesn't_ or _don't_.

1. Leprechauns _____ really exist.
2. Why _____ Mr. MacGregor wear his tartan kilt?
3. Leta _____ want to leave Hawaii.
4. _____ Mrs. Rivera live northeast of the airport?
5. This _____ solve any of our problems.
6. They _____ know how to change a flat tire.
7. _____ a stalactite hang down from a cave ceiling?
8. If Kenny _____ watch out, he'll trip and fall.
9. Why _____ any of these letters have zip codes?
10. If you _____ want these photographs of old cars, let me have them.

Exercise 3

Choose the correct form of the verb in each sentence.

1. (Is, Are) you looking for a four-leaf clover?
2. (Was, Were) you angry about the price of a hamburger?
3. (Was, Were) you frightened when the tree fell near your house during the storm?
4. You (are, is) welcome!
5. You (wasn't, weren't) there!
6. (Were, Was) you listening to the radio?
7. (Is, Are) you collecting rocks?
8. Where (was, were) you during vacation?
9. You (is, are) wrong about that.
10. You (are, is) late again!

Practice Power

▶ Pretend you are a TV news reporter in an age of dragons, knights, and princesses. Describe the action as a reporter would. Use the nouns listed below as subjects in your sentences, and use strong action verbs in the present tense. Underline the subject and verb in each sentence.

dragons	cave	forest	knights
castle	princess	fire	horses

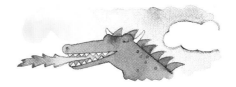

LESSON 11

Agreement of Subject with Verb—*Part II*

Compound Subjects Connected by *And*

> Compound subjects connected by *and* usually require a plural verb.

Janice and Marie (is, are) good friends.

Here is the correct form: Janice and Marie *are* good friends.

The subjects *Janice* and *Marie* are connected by *and*.

Special Pronouns

> The distributive pronouns *each, either,* and *neither* and the indefinite pronouns *anyone, no one, anybody, nobody, everyone, everybody, someone,* and *somebody* are always singular and require singular verbs.

Everybody (was, were) pleased to see the whale.

Here is the correct form: Everybody *was* pleased to see the whale.

The subject *everybody* is singular.

Special Nouns

> Such nouns as *deer, sheep, fish, swine, trout, salmon, cod, cattle, moose,* and *corps* and certain proper nouns, such as *Portuguese, Chinese, Swiss,* and *Iroquois*, have the same form in the singular and the plural.

This trout (is, are) twelve inches long.

Here is the correct form: This trout *is* twelve inches long.

The subject *trout* is singular.

Many trout (is, are) caught in that stream.

Here is the correct form: Many trout *are* caught in that stream.

The subject *trout* is plural.

The sense of the sentence lets you know whether the subject is singular or plural.

Exercise 1

Find the compound subject in each sentence. Then choose the correct verb.

1. King Arthur and Sir Galahad (was, were) friends.
2. The cat and her kitten (lie, lies) in the sun.
3. She and I (was, were) worried about the puppy.
4. Mr. Williams and his puppet (performs, perform) at the Red Globe Theater.
5. (Was, Were) your mother and father in the audience?
6. The parrot and the man (sings, sing) in tune with the radio!
7. The lake and the river (was, were) covered with thin ice.
8. Hal and his staff (paints, paint) colorful designs on T-shirts.
9. Our stereo and television (are, is) both broken.
10. Tennis and golf (is, are) summer sports.

Exercise 2

Complete each sentence with the correct form of the present tense of the verb at the left.

know   **1.** No one _____ for certain why whales sing.

contain   **2.** Either of these books _____ information on Dutch holidays.

enjoy   **3.** I hope everybody _____ my sassafras tea.

agree   **4.** Neither of the students _____ with your theory.

like   **5.** Nobody _____ to get lost in a swamp full of snakes!

Exercise 3

Find the subject in each sentence. Tell whether it is singular or plural. Then choose the correct verb.

1. There (is, are) several sheep grazing on the hillside.
2. This sheep (is, are) the only one that hasn't been sheared.
3. A salmon (swim, swims) in the tank.
4. Salmon (are, is) found in the Columbia River.
5. Portuguese (is, are) a musical language.
6. The Portuguese (were, was) great explorers.

Putting It All Together

In a group of three, examine and cross-examine a historical figure. Choose one member of the group to play the character and take the stand. The other members should choose the roles of prosecutor and defense attorney.

The prosecutor and defense attorney should ask questions of the character, and the character should answer in complete sentences. Each member of the group should make a final statement, including singular and plural verbs in past, present, and at least two compound tenses.

Chapter Challenge

Read this paragraph carefully and answer the questions.

¹Icebergs contain more than half the world's fresh water. ²Scientists may have created a plan for the future that involves towing icebergs from the Antarctic to hot desert countries. ³The fresh water could irrigate the dry, thirsty land. ⁴Imagine it is the year 2050. ⁵The plan for the future works this way. ⁶First, scientists choose a very large iceberg—at least five miles long and two miles wide. ⁷The iceberg itself actually becomes the ship. ⁸The crew members for the "ship" live on board the iceberg, which is driven by an engine. ⁹After the "ship" crosses the ocean, it is put into a giant plastic bag. ¹⁰The iceberg slowly melts, and water is piped into the fields to irrigate the land. ¹¹Scientists have estimated that one iceberg alone holds a supply of trillions of gallons of water. ¹²That is a big ice cube!

1. In sentence 1, is the verb singular or plural?

2. Name the verb phrase in sentence 2.

3. In sentence 3, name the receiver of the transitive verb *could irrigate*.

4. In sentence 5, is the verb *works* singular or plural in number? Why?

5. Name the verb in sentence 6. Give the past and past participle of this verb.

6. Name the linking verb and subjective complement in sentence 7.

7. In sentence 8, what person, number, and tense is the verb *live?*

8. In sentence 9, is the verb *crosses* transitive or intransitive?

9. In sentence 10, is the verb *melts* transitive or intransitive?

10. In sentence 11, which verb is present perfect tense?

11. In sentence 11, what person, number, and tense is the verb *holds?*

12. Name the linking verb in sentence 12. Does it link the subject with a noun, a pronoun, or an adjective?

ADVERBS

CHAPTER

13

394

LESSON 1

Kinds of Adverbs

An adverb is a word that modifies a verb, an adjective, or another adverb.

The cowhand jumped on the horse quickly.

In this sentence, the adverb *quickly* modifies the verb *jumped*.

The bronco was quite wild.

In this sentence, the adverb *quite* modifies the adjective *wild*.

The cowhand rode the bucking bronco very skillfully.

In this sentence, *very* modifies *skillfully*, another adverb. *Skillfully* modifies the verb *rode*. *Very* is an adverb of degree. It tells how much or how little.

ADVERBS

Adverbs of Time

Adverbs of time answer the question *when* or *how often.*

The fountain is *now* sparkling.   I have seen him *often.*

Adverbs of time usually modify verbs. The following are adverbs of time.

again	before	finally	late	seldom
already	early	first	now	soon
always	ever	immediately	often	usually

About the Photograph

This girl's team is winning today. The players are running fast, hitting the ball hard, and throwing accurately. Which adverbs would you use to describe a sport you enjoy?

Exercise 1

Complete each sentence with an adverb of time.

1. Professor Kent wants to start experiments with the robots _____ .
2. I hope the power will _____ be restored.
3. Have you _____ seen such a huge gorilla?
4. Ellie answered the phone _____ .
5. We have _____ heard that it is bad luck to spill the salt.
6. Tour buses _____ stop at the oldest house on Shadow Street.
7. _____ , you preheat the oven.
8. Edward got up _____ on his twelfth birthday.
9. Tom Sawyer was _____ able to get someone else to do his work.
10. Earth _____ rotates around the sun.
11. We _____ play that old videotape.
12. Tarantula bites are not _____ dangerous to people.
13. I liked that book so much I read it _____ .
14. We were _____ for the movie so we ate a box of popcorn before it began.
15. I have never seen so many tulips _____ .

Adverbs of Place

Adverbs of place answer the question *where*.

> Put your tuba *here*.   The giraffes roamed *far*.

Adverbs of place usually modify verbs. The following are adverbs of place.

above	below	forth	in	there
away	down	forward	inside	up
back	far	here	out	within

Exercise 2

Complete each sentence with an adverb of place.

1. The balloons floated _____ .
2. A whistling from the corner caused me to look _____ .
3. _____ are all those missing socks!
4. When the tide moves _____ , the beach is under water.
5. Jake stayed _____ because of the storm.
6. Wait _____ with the flashlight.
7. Claudia left her uncle's straw hat _____ .
8. I opened the package, but there was nothing _____ .
9. An army of black ants marched _____ .
10. One lone hawk circled _____ .
11. The skier lost her balance and fell _____ .
12. I cannot go _____ this weekend.
13. When the doors opened, the shoppers rushed _____ .
14. When the fireworks began, we jumped _____ .
15. A boomerang always comes _____ to you.

Adverbs of Manner

> **Adverbs of manner answer the question *how* or *in what manner.***

      Our band plays *well.*   The car stopped *quickly.*

Adverbs of manner usually modify verbs. The following are adverbs of manner.

bravely	eagerly	hard	resolutely	steadily
carefully	easily	honestly	slowly	swiftly
cheerfully	fast	neatly	smoothly	truly
clearly	gracefully	rapidly	softly	well

Exercise 3

Complete each sentence with an adverb of manner.

1. The frog's tongue flicked _____ at the gnats.
2. Icicles hanging from the roof melted _____ .
3. An architect has looked _____ at the house plans.
4. A hare can _____ outrun a tortoise.
5. You'll have to enter the cave _____ .
6. He contributed _____ to the collection for the needy families.
7. You can count on A. J. to brush the horses' coats _____ .
8. Swans glided _____ along the banks of the Test River.
9. The famous scientist Albert Einstein did not do _____ in school when he was young.
10. Canaries sing _____ .
11. Falcons are trained to return _____ to their handlers.
12. Andrea tore open the surprise package _____ .
13. We could _____ see the comet in the sky.
14. The signatures on the Declaration of Independence were written _____ .
15. The juggler tossed the oranges _____ .

Practice Power

▶ Look at the photograph on page 394. Write six sentences that describe it. Use adverbs in your sentences that tell when, where, and how about the picture.

LESSON 2

More Kinds of Adverbs

Adverbs of Degree

Adverbs of degree answer the question *how much* or *how little.*

Julia has *almost* finished the long novel.
(modifies a verb)

Steve drank the cold water *too* quickly.
(modifies an adverb)

Carol's handwriting is *scarcely* readable.
(modifies an adjective)

Adverbs of degree modify verbs, adjectives, or other adverbs.

almost	greatly	merely	quite	sufficiently
barely	hardly	much	rather	too
fully	little	partly	scarcely	very

Exercise 1

Complete each sentence with an adverb of degree.

1. A dragonfly _____ landed on my fishing pole.
2. Kathryn, approach the fawn _____ slowly.
3. This coffee is _____ hot to drink.
4. It was _____ warm enough to go out without a jacket.
5. The goats had _____ finished one stack of hay when they began on the other.
6. Stamps with errors are _____ rare.
7. I don't _____ understand the atom model.
8. The electric eel is a _____ long and skinny fish.
9. Jon has rehearsed _____ for the trombone solo.
10. Maria had _____ eaten her hamburger.

Adverbs of Affirmation and Negation

> **Adverbs of affirmation or negation tell whether a statement is true or false.**

Alice will *not* go.   *Yes,* Neil is here.

Adverbs of affirmation are *yes, indeed,* and *undoubtedly.*

Adverbs of negation are *no, not,* and *never.*

Exercise 2

Find the adverbs in each sentence. Tell whether each shows affirmation or negation.

1. Yes, I have finished reading the sports page.
2. We do not know the answers to any of those trivia questions.
3. Shelby's advice to rub the plant leaves with milk was indeed strange.
4. Undoubtedly, baked potatoes have fewer calories than french fries.
5. Van's father never allowed him to use the electric saw without wearing safety glasses.
6. Mark Twain was indeed an American novelist.
7. We'll never know how that grand piano got through the door!
8. Yes, a speleologist is a scientist who studies caves.
9. The peanut butter cookies are not ready yet.
10. No, I did not see the sand dollar.

Exercise 3

Find the adverbs in each sentence. Tell whether each is an adverb of time, place, manner, degree, affirmation, or negation.

1. Scarlett tied the bow on her lace dress very neatly.
2. Yes, the sea is exceedingly rough, Meg.
3. There are too many hot peppers in these chimichangas!
4. Here are the dog biscuits Blue has been stashing away.
5. The astronauts float around weightlessly in space.
6. Do turtles walk slowly because their shells are heavy?
7. Two volunteers stepped forward for the magic trick.
8. The Senate sometimes hears rather long speeches.
9. Above, we could see the banner announcing a street fair.
10. There was barely enough birthday cake for everyone.
11. The audience immediately sat down when the music began.
12. Hearing the clock chime, I looked up.
13. We always keep a supply of cherry preserves in the pantry.
14. Pansies are quite hardy and grow well in cool temperatures.
15. I promise to count the bags of bagels very carefully.
16. The crowd laughed heartily at the clown's antics.
17. We did not know that the tire was flat.
18. Blue whales are the largest animals that have ever lived.
19. I almost knocked the ant farm over.
20. News travels fast!
21. We quickly wrote a menu for our hot-dog stand.
22. He secured the loose objects on deck and climbed below.
23. Mrs. Kellog complains that she seldom sees a blue jay at her bird feeder.
24. They were fully prepared for a sensational air show.
25. Searching for her photograph, Kelly flipped through the magazine rapidly.

Practice Power

▶ **Next to each verb in the list below is an adverb that modifies it. Write at least one synonym for each adverb. Write a sentence with the verb and the new adverb.**

	VERBS	ADVERBS
1.	answer	immediately
2.	gallop	briskly
3.	sing	merrily
4.	speak	honestly
5.	drive	cautiously
6.	act	courageously
7.	move	quietly
8.	run	swiftly
9.	shout	loudly
10.	trot	slowly
11.	steer	skillfully
12.	leap	gracefully

LESSON 3 — Adverbs That Compare

Many adverbs can be compared. Like adjectives, they have three degrees of comparison: positive, comparative, and superlative.

Regular Comparison

Some adverbs form the comparative degree by adding *-er* to the positive and form the superlative degree by adding *-est* to the positive.

POSITIVE	COMPARATIVE	SUPERLATIVE
high	higher	highest
fast	faster	fastest
hard	harder	hardest
late	later	latest
soon	sooner	soonest
early	earlier	earliest

Adverbs ending in *-ly* generally form the comparative degree by adding *more* or *less* to the positive and form the superlative degree by adding *most* or *least* to the positive.

POSITIVE	COMPARATIVE	SUPERLATIVE
swiftly	more swiftly	most swiftly
	less swiftly	least swiftly
bravely	more bravely	most bravely
	less bravely	least bravely
gracefully	more gracefully	most gracefully
	less gracefully	least gracefully

ADVERBS

Irregular Comparison

Some adverbs are compared irregularly. It is necessary to learn the comparative and the superlative degrees.

POSITIVE	COMPARATIVE	SUPERLATIVE
badly	worse	worst
far	farther	farthest
late	later	latest, last
little	less	least
much	more	most
well	better	best

Most adverbs indicating time and place (*here, now, then, when, where, again, always, down, above*) and adverbs expressing completeness (*eternally, universally, never, forever, continually, entirely*) cannot be compared.

Exercise 1

Find the adverbs in these sentences. For those adverbs that can be compared, tell the degree of comparison: positive, comparative, or superlative.

1. We searched everywhere for the missing car keys.
2. The winner must stay on the bronco the longest.
3. During the thunderstorm, Jorge acted more bravely than the rest of us.
4. The dog barked furiously at the passing cars.
5. Andy dove most courageously from the high diving board into the pool.
6. With the sudden gust of wind, the kite soared higher into the sky.
7. Our fire died sooner than we had expected.
8. That detective gathered clues the least patiently of all.
9. Read the poem in French slowly, Carole.
10. The carpenters need to work faster to meet their deadline.
11. This burro walks more steadily than a horse across rocks.
12. I always comb my hair this way.
13. At its mouth, the Amazon flows more swiftly than the Mississippi.
14. The workers are entirely finished with the roof.
15. Henri arrived latest.

Exercise 2

One degree of the adverb is given in the chart below.
Write out the complete comparison of each adverb.

POSITIVE	COMPARATIVE	SUPERLATIVE
1. quietly	_____	_____
2. _____	more slowly	_____
3. _____	_____	nearest
4. early	_____	_____
5. _____	_____	most sincerely
6. _____	less harshly	_____
7. sharply	_____	_____
8. _____	_____	most happily
9. _____	less accurately	_____
10. anxiously	_____	_____
11. _____	_____	most probably
12. _____	less kindly	_____
13. well	_____	_____
14. _____	_____	least firmly
15. sorrowfully	_____	_____
16. _____	_____	soonest
17. _____	more willingly	_____
18. late	_____	

Practice Power

▶ From Exercise 2, choose two adverbs in the positive
degree, two in the comparative, and two in the
superlative. Write sentences using each adverb correctly.

Using Adverbs Correctly

Adverbs and Adjectives

> An adjective describes a noun or pronoun.
> An adverb modifies a verb, an adjective, or
> an adverb.

Adverbs are often confused with adjectives that follow and
complete verbs. Study the following examples.

> The gymnast stood on the beam (unsteady, unsteadily).
> The gymnast on the beam looked (unsteady, unsteadily).

The correct form for the first sentence is *unsteadily:* The
gymnast stood on the beam *unsteadily. Unsteadily* modifies
the verb *stood* and tells how.

The correct form for the second sentence is *unsteady:* The
gymnast on the beam looked *unsteady. Unsteady* follows the
linking verb *looked* and describes the subject *gymnast.*

To tell whether you use an adverb or adjective, try this: If some
form of the verb *be* can be used in place of the verb in the
sentence, the verb is a linking verb, and an adjective should
follow it.

> This peach tastes good. (=This peach is good.)

The adjective form *good* correctly follows a linking verb.

> These peaches grow well in Georgia.

Well is an adverb. It tells how the peaches grow. If a form of
the verb *be* is used in place of the verb *grow,* the sentence
does not make sense.

406

Exercise 1

Choose the correct word to complete each sentence.
Tell whether it is an adjective or an adverb.

1. Those red roses smell (sweet, sweetly) but have thorns.
2. The day grew (cool, coolly) as clouds hid the sun.
3. Nightingales sing (soft, softly) under the emperor's window.
4. Few people use a spinning wheel (good, well).
5. After sitting in the sun, Leo felt (warm, warmly).
6. Has he explained the directions (good, well)?
7. Your report on ethnic foods was (good, well).
8. The bobcat growled (fierce, fiercely) at an intruding dog.
9. Lamb's wool feels (soft, softly).
10. Without a rider, the bicycle bounced (aimless, aimlessly) down the hill.
11. Reel in the fish (careful, carefully)!
12. George Washington was (honest, honestly) in answering his father's question.
13. She answered the phone (cheerful, cheerfully).
14. Carmen paddled the boat against the current (smooth, smoothly).
15. Mr. Barlow's apple fritters always taste (good, well).
16. How (good, well) Huong imitates that famous singer!
17. Your voice sounds (different, differently) over the phone.
18. After their parents fed them, the baby robins chirped (merry, merrily).
19. We closed the office door (quiet, quietly) behind us.
20. The twelve o'clock whistle blew (sharp, sharply).
21. A kudzu vine will grow (quick, quickly).
22. These lemon drops really do taste (sour, sourly).
23. Cows chew their cud (slow, slowly).
24. Your mattress should be (firm, firmly) if you have a bad back.
25. I'll sleep (good, well) after picking strawberries all day.

Their and *There*

> **_Their_ is an adjective and shows possession or ownership.**

The explorers lost *their* compass!

> **_There_ is an adverb that means "in that place."**

The Eiffel Tower is over *there*.

> **_There_ is sometimes used as an introductory word, usually before a form of the verb _be_.**

There are many fascinating things to see in Europe.

Exercise 2

Complete each sentence with *their* or *there*.

1. The Beatles became famous in the 1960s, and _____ songs are still popular.
2. Flying squirrels can glide through the air because _____ are skin flaps between _____ front and hind legs.
3. The settlers named _____ new home Cranberry Lake.
4. _____ were three hundred fans standing in line for the rock concert!
5. _____ is a watering hole nearby, and the zebras usually gather _____ .
6. _____ brother is at summer camp.
7. The electricians did _____ best work.
8. _____ are one hundred zeros in a googol.
9. The calico cat sat _____ to clean its paws.
10. Hockey players carried _____ skates into the arena.
11. People who live in deserts often cover _____ heads and faces.
12. Marie and Pierre Curie did experiments in _____ laboratory.

13. Adam, leave the lawn mower _____ .

14. It was _____ first attempt at carving whistles for _____ grandchildren.

15. _____ was much excitement about the first snow of the season.

16. _____ prizes were movie passes.

17. We can't use the gym because the cheerleaders are practicing _____ .

18. I've already looked _____ .

19. _____ bus is coming.

20. _____ was a spider _____ !

Two, Too, and *To*

> ***Two*** **is a numeral adjective and refers to the number 2.**

There are *two* liters of water in that pitcher.

> ***Too*** **is an adverb and has the same meaning as** ***also, more than enough,*** **or** ***besides.***

Todd can make omelets—and pancakes, *too.*
This portion of food is *too* much for me.

> ***To*** **is a preposition and usually indicates motion toward some place or some person.**

The entire school went *to* the gym for an assembly.

Exercise 3

Complete each sentence with *two, too,* or *to.*

1. You may come, _____ .
2. The movement of rivers carries silt _____ the sea.
3. _____ students went _____ the science workshop.
4. At _____ o'clock in Chicago, it is three o'clock in New York.
5. My parents talk about the days when movie admission was _____ dollars.
6. Rocky sent a basketball _____ his nephew.
7. Matt, _____ , likes this kind of watch.
8. We need _____ typewriters sent _____ the repair shop.
9. There are _____ sailors in that sloop.
10. It is _____ cold in Antarctica for many animals to survive.
11. Mom put the peanuts _____ far back on the shelf.
12. Which scientists are going _____ the rain forest?
13. We read the letters aloud _____ each other.
14. Nomads are people who move from place _____ place.
15. A tiger is _____ ferocious to have as a pet.

Practice Power

▶ Try writing tongue twisters. First write a sentence that includes *two, too,* and *to.* Then write a sentence that correctly uses both *there* and *their.*

LESSON 5 — Using More Adjectives and Adverbs Correctly

Negative Adjectives and Adverbs

> **If a sentence has one negative adverb such as _not_, avoid using another negative word, such as _no_ or _never_.**

> I haven't (no, any) money.
> No one (never, ever) goes there.

Here are the correct forms:

> I haven't *any* money.
> No one *ever* goes there.

The first sentence already has a negative word: *haven't*, the contraction for *have not*. The second sentence also has a negative word: *No one*. Another negative should not be used in either sentence.

Exercise 1

Choose the correct word to complete each sentence.

  1. We found (no, any) shells on this beach.
  2. Marietta hasn't (any, no) time to start a new hobby.
  3. She didn't spend (no, any) time oiling the bike chain.
  4. There hasn't been (no, any) rain for over a month.
  5. Haven't you (ever, never) missed a day of school?
  6. A two-year-old has (any, no) use for an encyclopedia.
  7. I (never, ever) make the same mistake twice!
  8. You have (no, any) excuse for letting the chickens loose.
  9. Weren't you (never, ever) here before?
 10. The detectives could not find (no, any) clues.

Words Used as Adjectives and Adverbs

There are words that can be used either as adjectives or adverbs. Check to see how the word is used in a sentence. If it modifies a noun, it is an adjective. If it modifies a verb and tells how, where, or when, it is an adverb.

> That girl is a *fast* baker.   (adjective—describes *baker*)
> That girl bakes *fast*.   (adverb—answers *how*)

Exercise 2

Tell whether each word in italics is an adjective or an adverb.

1. A *high* fence protects the old mansion.
2. The swarm of bees flew *high* into the air.
3. The geese are walking in one long, *straight* line.
4. Hit that golf ball *straight*.
5. On the first day of band rehearsal, Jody awoke *early*.
6. An *early* frost will damage any late corn crops.
7. Diamonds are the *hardest* substance.
8. Believe it or not, Franco works *hardest!*
9. The wheels of the bicycle went *round* and *round*.
10. Missie uses an empty *round* can to cut the biscuit dough.
11. The old portrait resembles his grandmother *very* closely.
12. President Washington ate in this *very* tavern!
13. Two dollars is the *best* price for this used book.
14. Some people work *best* in the early hours of the morning.
15. I think Yolanda Allen is the *best* candidate for mayor.

Putting It All Together

Choose a topic from Exercise 2 and write stage directions for a short skit about that topic. Include adverbs when describing how a character should act, and use adjectives when describing objects in the skit.

Chapter Challenge

Read this paragraph carefully and then answer the questions.

¹Two pioneers of the western United States were Lewis and Clark, explorers of the Louisiana Territory. ²Asked by President Jefferson, these men organized a party and bravely undertook a difficult mission. ³Their extremely challenging trip through unknown land lasted more than two years. ⁴Very slowly and patiently they pushed up the Missouri River to its source. ⁵Each day they traveled farther into the wild. ⁶Their progress was often slow, but with the aid of their guide Sacagawea, a Shoshone woman, they crossed the mighty Rockies. ⁷They descended the Columbia River and finally sighted the Pacific Ocean. ⁸Courageously, the explorers continued until they reached their goal.

1. In sentence 2, name the adverb and tell what kind it is.

2. In sentence 3, which adverb of degree modifies *challenging?*

3. In sentence 3, what part of speech does the adverb of degree modify?

4. Find two adverbs of manner in sentence 4.

5. In sentence 4, find an adverb that modifies another adverb.

6. Give the comparative and superlative degrees of the two adverbs of manner in sentence 4.

7. Name an adverb of place in sentence 5.

8. Write the positive and superlative degrees of the adverb in sentence 5.

9. In sentence 6, what kind of adverb is *often?*

10. In sentence 7, name the adverb of time.

11. Can the adverb in sentence 7 be compared?

12. Give the comparative and superlative degrees of the adverb of manner in sentence 8.

PREPOSITIONS, CONJUNCTIONS, INTERJECTIONS

LESSON 1 | Prepositions

A preposition is a word placed before a noun or a pronoun. The preposition shows the relation of the noun or pronoun to some other word.

In each of these sentences, the preposition shows the relation between a noun or pronoun and some other word in the sentence.

> The kite moved *from* the ground.

From shows the relation between *moved* and *ground*.

> A friend *of* my brother helped me fly the kite.

Of shows the relation between *friend* and *brother*.

> The kite looked *like* a colorful cloud soaring through the sky.

Like shows the relation between *looked* and *cloud*.

The word *preposition* means "placed before." The noun or pronoun that follows the preposition is called its object.

PREPOSITIONS, CONJUNCTIONS, INTERJECTIONS

About the Photograph

How do you like to listen to music? Through headphones? Out loud? Where do you listen? Sitting on a couch? In your bedroom? In the backyard? On your porch?

The most commonly used prepositions are

about	around	by	in	through
above	at	down	near	to
across	before	during	of	toward
after	behind	except	off	under
against	beside	for	on	up
among	between	from	over	with

Exercise 1

Complete each sentence with an appropriate preposition from the list above. Note that some sentences may have more than one possible answer.

1. Quite a few diseases are carried _____ insects.
2. On the track team, I learned how to jump _____ the hurdle.
3. She was leaning _____ an old wooden fence.
4. We watched stars fall _____ the summer sky.
5. The red-haired baby toddled _____ me.
6. He spread peanut butter _____ the bread and topped it _____ bananas.
7. Gaining speed, the bowling ball bounced _____ the stairs.
8. Read the directions _____ the bottom of the box.
9. Aunt Edna had to sit _____ the mischievous twins.
10. Louie jumped _____ the trampoline.
11. _____ the show we went out for ice cream.
12. Come and sit _____ me.
13. We had to go _____ customs at the airport when we arrived in London.
14. The story _____ George Washington Carver's peanut studies is interesting.

Prepositional Phrases

> A preposition and the noun or pronoun that follows it are separate words, but they do the work of a single modifier. This group of related words is called a phrase. Since it is introduced by a preposition, it is called a prepositional phrase.

Washington, D.C., lies *on the Potomac River.*

In the sentence above, *on the Potomac River* is the prepositional phrase. It is introduced by the preposition *on.* The proper noun *Potomac River* is the object of the preposition. The entire phrase modifies the verb *lies.*

Exercise 2

Write a prepositional phrase for each preposition listed below. Then name the object of each preposition. Follow the example.

PREPOSITION	PHRASE	OBJECT
Example: through	through the fields	fields

1. with
2. for
3. down
4. across
5. in
6. between
7. of
8. around
9. during
10. about
11. on
12. at
13. near
14. above
15. over

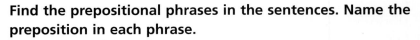

Exercise 3

Find the prepositional phrases in the sentences. Name the preposition in each phrase.

1. The pear trees were white with blossoms.
2. Robin Hood lived in Sherwood Forest.
3. The field, with its rows of pineapples, was well kept.
4. Angry waves crashed over the dunes.
5. Books were once written on long rolls of parchment.
6. Tarzan clung to the vine above the thrashing reptiles.
7. There are no vitamins or minerals in sugar.
8. We heard the sound of trumpets.
9. *Treasure Island* was written by Robert Louis Stevenson.
10. The orphan had been living among wolves since infancy.

Exercise 4

Complete each sentence with a prepositional phrase.

1. The hikers placed the log _____ .
2. When it began to hail, the picnickers ran _____ .
3. We left our dog _____ .
4. I must have put too much sugar _____ .
5. That photograph _____ is very old.
6. The biggest mosquito I ever saw just flew _____ !
7. Our class is saving money _____ .
8. In the fairy tale, the witches cast a spell _____ .
9. One cricket after another jumped _____ .
10. The silly cow just tried to jump _____ .

Practice Power

▶ Use prepositional phrases to write a poem like the one below. Think of an interesting topic.

A shadow
Slyly
Skipped
    across my window
    under my chair
    around my walls
Should I try to catch it?

Using Prepositions Correctly

Some sets of prepositions can be confusing. Each preposition may have a slightly different meaning and suggest a different idea. Carefully study the troublesome prepositions in this lesson. Learn how to use each one correctly.

At and *To*

At shows presence in.

To shows motion toward.

Toby and Tanya were *at* the party. (presence in)

Toby and Tanya went *to* the store. (motion toward)

Between and *Among*

Use *between* to speak of two persons or objects.

Use *among* to speak of more than two.

The king divided his fortune *between* the two princesses.

The king divided his fortune *among* his four children.

Beside and *Besides*

Beside means "at the side of" or "next to."

Besides means "in addition to."

Lisa walked *beside* the shark exhibit. (next to)

Besides Lisa, Carla was also there. (in addition to)

In and *Into*

> Use *in* to show location within.
>
> Use *into* to show motion toward a place or change of position.

There are five puppies *in* the basket. (location within)

Five students ambled *into* the room. (motion toward a place)

Exercise 1

Choose the correct preposition, *at* or *to*, to complete each sentence.

1. Vinnie is going (at, to) dinner.
2. About a hundred onlookers were (to, at) the farm auction.
3. Zack's pet stegosaurus comes (to, at) him when he whistles.
4. Yes, we were (to, at) the parade.
5. Helen couldn't come (at, to) the party because she was sick.
6. Were you (to, at) the last festival meeting?
7. Pedro sauntered (at, to) the gate.
8. The children are feeding apples (at, to) the horses.
9. Ricardo is (to, at) Robin's house working on the solar energy project.
10. Linda is not (at, to) home right now.

Exercise 2

Choose the correct preposition, *among* or *between*,
to complete each sentence.

1. A tall sunflower stood (among, between) the twins.
2. The king walked (between, among) the people.
3. A music stand stood (between, among) the duo.
4. Watch for a helicopter (between, among) the clouds.
5. There is a pact (among, between) the two countries.
6. Jo's picture was (between, among) the two windows.
7. (Between, Among) the four students, there was a secret.
8. Many chestnuts are (among, between) the fallen leaves.
9. Skip a line (between, among) answers.
10. (Between, Among) the three train cars, the first was the most crowded with passengers.

Exercise 3

Choose the correct preposition, *beside* or *besides*,
to complete each sentence.

1. Who is that (beside, besides) the railroad tracks?
2. Have you anything to drink (beside, besides) milk?
3. Sit here (beside, besides) me during our train ride.
4. A shark suddenly appeared (besides, beside) the boat.
5. Gwen has five dogs (beside, besides) this one!
6. (Beside, Besides) french fries, we also had onion rings.
7. (Beside, Besides) the plate sat a glass of lemonade.
8. (Beside, Besides) birds, did you know that some kinds of butterflies also migrate?

Exercise 4

Choose the correct preposition, *in* or *into*, to complete each sentence.

1. The boy brought the potatoes (in, into) the kitchen for his mother.
2. A cuckoo prefers to move (into, in) another bird's nest, rather than to build its own.
3. I'll put Arnie's books (in, into) my briefcase.
4. The game requires you to drop clothespins (into, in) the bottle.
5. I can throw the paper (in, into) the basket from six feet away.
6. The Inca civilization developed (into, in) South America.
7. She pushed the envelope (into, in) the mailbox.
8. The boy's dog was excited as he ran (in, into) the house.
9. They have been (into, in) the hobby shop for an hour.
10. The storekeeper put the artichokes (in, into) the basket.

Practice Power

▶ Write a pair of sentences for each set of troublesome prepositions discussed in this lesson. Underline the prepositional phrases in your sentences.

LESSON 3 | Words Used as Prepositions and Adverbs

> **A preposition shows the relation between its object and some other word in the sentence.**

> **An adverb tells *how*, *when*, or *where*.**

Some words may be used either as prepositions or as adverbs.

> *Below* the hills lay the beautiful valley. (preposition)
> The captain went *below*. (adverb)

HINT: A preposition is followed by an object—usually a noun.

Exercise 1

Tell whether the italicized word in each sentence is an adverb or a preposition.

1. All explorers left the Himalayas soon *after*
2. I shall see you *after* the dance competition.
3. A couple skated *down* the ice-covered river.
4. The sun went *down*, leaving a dull red sky.
5. Weeds were springing *up* uncontrollably.
6. Sheep climb *up* the mountainside often.
7. Our school flag flies *above* the stadium.
8. What message was written *above*?
9. Ellen's guide dog never has to wait *outside*.
10. The quarterback stood *outside* the huddle.
11. Have you visited this optometrist *before*?
12. Chi barely finished the assignment *before* school.
13. The bottom of a snail's body is a foot to help it get *about*.
14. Anne Frank kept a diary *about* her experiences.
15. Jana wrote a paper *about* the explosion of Mount Vesuvius.

Practice Power

▶ Imagine that you are a world-class mountain climber. Write a paragraph describing your adventures and accomplishments. Use six of the following words in your description. Use three of them as prepositions and three as adverbs.

A. about
B. above
C. after
D. before

E. between
F. down
G. from
H. in

I. off
J. through
K. under
L. up

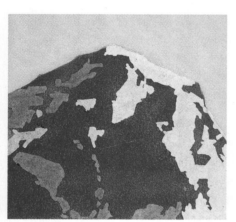
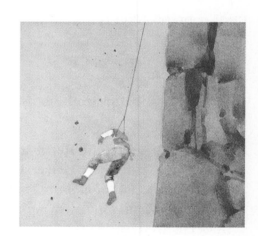

Conjunctions

A conjunction is a word used to connect words, phrases, or clauses in a sentence.

The bicycle *and* the car are in the garage. (connects words)

Phil could not go to the game *nor* to the picnic. (connects phrases)

The sky is blue, *and* the sun is shining. (connects clauses)

Conjunctions that connect words and word groups of equal importance are called *coordinate conjunctions.* The principal coordinate conjunctions are *and, but, yet, or,* and *nor.*

Conjunctions Connecting Words

Coordinate conjunctions connect words that have the same use or function in a sentence. These words may be

- **nouns (subjects, objects, or subjective complements).**
- **verbs (predicates).**
- **adjectives.**
- **adverbs.**

Subjects

Rita *or* Clare will play left field during the game.

Cosmetics *and* ice cream contain seaweed!

Objects

Brass is a mixture of copper *and* zinc.

Have you eaten the ham *or* the cheese?

Subjective Complements

Last Friday evening was bright *but* cool.

Was the painter Leonardo da Vinci *or* Michelangelo?

Verbs (Predicates)

Sara tried *but* failed to stand up on her skis.

A telescope gathers *and* focuses light into a tiny, sharp point.

Adjectives and Adverbs

Bamboo plants make very light *and* strong building material.

Fill out the registration form quickly *but* accurately.

Exercise 1

Find the conjunction in each sentence. Tell what words each connects.

1. Pencils and pens are stored in the desk drawer.

2. The Red Cross sends food and medical supplies to people in need.

3. Goodwin, the magician, needed a black cape and a rabbit.

4. On his tombstone was a long but interesting epitaph.

5. Ms. Ybarra sells pottery and jewelry.

6. Children clapped and laughed at the puppet show.

7. The skillful but careless chess player lost her game.

8. Early peoples made ornaments and weapons of bronze.

9. Luciano finished the third plate of linguini surely but slowly!

10. Would you like lemon or milk in your tea?

11. The students worked quickly and quietly on the quiz questions.

12. Maybe a box of candy will surprise and please Mom.

13. Sailors steer their ships by the direction of the sun, moon, and stars.

14. Athletes walk or run around the larger track.

15. The detective's assignment is dangerous but important.

16. The pond is covered with snow and ice.

17. The Thai food on this menu is tasty but spicy.

18. Water and wind do not exist on the moon.

19. Lucius whistles or sings in the shower.

20. Beth seems excited but nervous about moving to a new neighborhood.

Conjunctions Connecting Phrases

> Coordinate conjunctions connect prepositional phrases. These phrases may be adjectival or adverbial.

Adjectival Phrases

Carvings of ivory *and* of wood are for sale here.

Pineapples from the Philippines *and* from Hawaii are sold throughout the world.

Adverbial Phrases

The stream flowed across the field *and* under the bridge.

The cat ran under the bush *or* up the tree.

Exercise 2

Find the conjunction in each sentence. Tell which phrases each connects.

1. Porcupines ran out of the field and into Mrs. Barrett's truck.
2. Shall I sit with you or with him?
3. Wild ponies on the island play happily on the beach and in the water.
4. There are strawberries in the refrigerator and in the cooler.
5. Silk from China and from Japan is imported to the United States and western Europe.
6. A honeysuckle vine is growing around the porch and across my window.
7. Will you send the package by parcel post or by express mail?
8. Flags of many colors and of many designs fly above the United Nations.
9. Huckleberry's raft swirled down the river and into the bay.
10. The Burmese child wore earrings of gold and of silver.
11. Our principal handed awards to Denise and to Ollie.
12. We searched in the drawers and in the closet for my key.
13. You may play on the porch or in the yard.
14. We'll visit the zoos in New York and in San Diego.
15. A dog with a collar but without a name tag has been found.

Conjunctions Connecting Clauses

Coordinate conjunctions connect independent clauses. An independent clause has a subject and a predicate and expresses a complete thought.

California is on the West Coast, *and* New York is on the East Coast.

Synonyms are words of similar meanings, *but* antonyms are words of opposite meanings.

You may take the package with you, *or* we will deliver it.

Each conjunction in the above sentences connects a pair of independent clauses. Each clause contains a subject and a predicate, and it expresses a complete thought. Notice how the two independent clauses in the first example can each stand as a separate sentence.

California is on the West Coast.

New York is on the East Coast.

Exercise 3

Find the conjunction in each sentence. Tell which clauses each connects.

1. The curtain rose, and the tumblers rolled onto the stage!
2. You may come on the camping trip, but you'll have to carry your own gear.
3. Erase a file from the computer disk, or use a blank disk.
4. The water was icy cold, but many people were swimming.
5. Sam must pass the lifesaving test, or he will have to take the class again.
6. The human skeleton has 206 bones, and the bones come in many shapes.
7. I got up at 6:00 A.M., but I didn't see the sunrise.
8. The band warmed up, and an audience gathered.
9. I thought I wrote a haiku, but it had too many syllables.
10. We must buy the tickets today, or they will be completely sold out.

Exercise 4

Find the coordinate conjunction in each sentence. Tell whether the conjunction connects words, phrases, or clauses.

1. Humpty Dumpty fell off the wall, but no one could put him together again.
2. I tossed the hook into the water, and something big jerked the cork under.
3. Rita laughed and cried at the same time.
4. Neil Armstrong and Edwin Aldrin walked on the moon.
5. His bike was in the attic, but Ed didn't know it.
6. Barb sells newspapers in the morning and in the evening.
7. The planets are divided into two groups—the inner and the outer planets.
8. Chalk or crayons were used in the children's drawings.
9. We were wary but curious in the laboratory.
10. Every country has a flag, and most countries have a national anthem.
11. A doomed egg rolled off the table and onto the brick floor.
12. Shevonne and Jaye are basketball guards.
13. Unicorns might have run through these woods or across this meadow.
14. Halley's comet came into view, but then it quickly disappeared.
15. Will the craft fair be in the auditorium or in the gymnasium?

Practice Power

▶ Write a sentence that contains a coordinate conjunction to connect each pair of words, phrases, or clauses below.

1. muffins/rolls
2. collects/labels
3. quick/easy
4. slowly/confidently
5. from the country/to the city
6. Mark read the map/Teresa drove the van

LESSON 5

Interjections

An interjection is a word that expresses a strong or sudden emotion.

> *Oh!* We are too late to enroll in the swimming class.
> *Sh!* The baby is finally asleep.

The word *interjection* means "thrown in." What emotion do you think is expressed by the word *Oh?* It is not directly connected with any other word in the sentence, but from the idea of the sentence we understand that it expresses disgust or disappointment. The word *Sh* calls for silence.

Interjections may express delight, disgust, pain, agreement, joy, impatience, surprise, sorrow, wonder, and so on. They are not grammatically related to other words in the sentence. An interjection is usually set off from the rest of the sentence by an exclamation point. An entire sentence, however, may be exclamatory. If the sentence is exclamatory, the interjection is followed by a comma, and the exclamation point is put at the end of the sentence. If the interjection expresses a mild feeling, a comma follows it.

> Ah, there she goes again! (entire sentence is exclamatory)
> Well, what should I do? (milder feeling)

Some common interjections are

Ah!	Good!	Hooray!	Oh!
Aha!	Good-bye!	Hush!	Ouch!
Beware!	Hello!	Indeed!	Sh!
Bravo!	Hey!	No!	Well!

O and *Oh*

The interjection *O* is used only before a noun in direct address. It is not directly followed by an exclamation point.

Oh is used to express surprise, sorrow, or joy. It is followed by an exclamation point unless the emotion continues throughout the sentence. If the emotion continues, *oh* is followed by a comma, and the exclamation point is put at the end of the sentence.

> *O Helen!* I like your new bike. (direct address)
>
> *Oh!* What do you think caused the trouble? (emotion does not continue)
>
> *Oh,* how happy I am! (emotion continues—milder feeling)

Exercise 1

Tell what idea or feeling is suggested by the interjection in each sentence.

1. Hooray! We won!
2. Oh! That can't be true.
3. Bravo! You passed the exam.
4. Oh! Have you heard the news?
5. Hey! It's raining again.
6. Ah, what a close call!
7. Well, my homework is finally finished!
8. Ouch! I twisted my ankle.
9. Beware! The curve is dangerous at high speeds.
10. Hello! We're glad you made it!

Putting It All Together

Did you ever watch a cooking or remodeling show on public television? Imagine how funny those shows would be if the hosts kept getting things wrong!

In a small group, develop and present a "how-to" program in which the host keeps making mistakes. Give the host a sidekick who uses pronouns, conjunctions, and interjections to cover up the mistakes of the host.

Chapter Challenge

Read this paragraph carefully and answer the questions that follow.

¹The trails were lined with redwood trees as we headed toward Moccasin Lake. ²Ms. Hally, our guide, told us that these trees were the tallest and largest in the world. ³"Some are so big," she said, "people put holes into them and drive cars through their centers." ⁴"Hooray!" we soon heard her exclaim. ⁵She had just found a soap plant beside a thick clump of bushes. ⁶Slowly and carefully, she pulled it from the ground. ⁷Its white, onionlike root made it look like real soap. ⁸"Sh!" whispered Ms. Hally as we neared the lake. ⁹She pointed to a turtle digging a hole in the mud to lay her eggs, and then we spied a water snake sunning itself on the rocks. ¹⁰What other wonders would Ms. Hally be able to show us before the day would come to an end?

1. In sentence 1, name two prepositional phrases.

2. In sentence 2, the conjunction *and* connects what two words? These two words are what parts of speech?

3. In sentence 3, the conjunction *and* connects *put* and *drive.* These two words are what parts of speech?

4. Name any two interjections in the paragraph. What feeling or emotion does each express?

5. In sentence 5, name two prepositional phrases.

6. In sentence 6, what two words does the coordinate conjunction connect? These two words are what parts of speech?

7. Name a prepositional phrase in sentence 6.

8. In sentence 9, does the coordinate conjunction connect words, phrases, or clauses?

CHAPTER 15 PHRASES, CLAUSES, SENTENCES

434

LESSON 1

Adjectival Phrases

A phrase is a group of words used as a single part of speech.

A prepositional phrase, which may be adjectival or adverbial, consists of a preposition and a noun or pronoun.

> We lay on the deck *of our sailboat* all morning in the bright sunshine. (adjectival phrase)

> *In the afternoon,* we ate the sandwiches we had packed for our day. (adverbial phrase)

Each group of italicized words in these sentences takes the place of a single part of speech. In the first sentence, the phrase *of our sailboat* modifies the noun *deck* and explains what kind of deck it was. The phrase *In the afternoon* in the second sentence does the work of an adverb by answering the question *when*.

> **About the Photograph**

These two girls are playing. These two girls are playing on the bars in the park. Which sentence is more interesting?

PHRASES, CLAUSES, SENTENCES

Chapter 15 **435**

An adjectival phrase is a phrase used as an adjective.

The peak *of the strawberry season* was over.

The phrase *of the strawberry season* tells what peak. *Of the strawberry season* is an adjectival phrase modifying the noun *peak*.

Note how adjectives can be replaced by phrases.

My mom asked the *camp* counselor if she could enroll me and my sister.

My mom asked the counselor *of the camp* if she could enroll me and my sister.

The counselor was a *French* exchange student.

The counselor was an exchange student *from France*.

Exercise 1

Find the adjectival phrase in each sentence. Tell the noun that each phrase modifies.

1. The walls of the castle were colorfully decorated.
2. This is the workshop of a wood-carver.
3. One very strong natural fiber is silk from spiders.
4. The capital of Belgium is Brussels.
5. The workers' standard of living is low.
6. He earned a doctorate from Columbia University.
7. The author of this story is a young Panamanian.
8. The house across the street has always been painted green.
9. We all enjoyed her vivid account of ancient Egyptian customs.
10. The laughter of the amused crowd delighted the apes.
11. Sheena collects seashells from the Pacific.
12. The day after tomorrow will be my birthday.
13. Those joggers in the rear look fatigued.
14. He has told wonderful tales of King Arthur's knights.
15. The old clock above the fireplace slowly struck the hour.

Exercise 2

Change each italicized adjective to an adjectival phrase.

Example: *Courageous* sailors sailed the ship.
         Sailors *with courage* sailed the ship.

1. *Spring* blossoms are a welcome sight!
2. The *river* bank was steep and rocky.
3. We want an *intelligent* dog.
4. Lee trimmed the *garden* hedge carefully.
5. We watched a *cowboy* film.
6. *Musical* sounds could be heard across the lake.
7. More than half the world's fresh water is in *Antarctic* icebergs!
8. *Dirt* roads wind between the squash fields.
9. Many salmon are found in *Alaskan* waters.
10. This summer we are going to start a *bug* zoo.

Exercise 3

Complete each sentence with an adjectival phrase.

1. The postcard _____ took four weeks to arrive.
2. The first game _____ was played in this stadium.
3. Batteries _____ can be expensive.
4. A bowl _____ was placed in front of the cat.
5. We need two people to help carry this basket _____ .
6. Many fans collect souvenirs _____ .
7. That girl _____ is my cousin.
8. We took photographs _____ .
9. Rugs _____ will be displayed.
10. A troop of kangaroos followed the path _____ .
11. The center _____ is hot.
12. Aunt Jeanette keeps a vase _____ in the hall.

Practice Power

▶ **Use the following as adjectival phrases in sentences.**

1. with curly red hair
2. in our path
3. behind the orange sunglasses
4. of different sizes
5. with green skins
6. of stones and twigs

Adverbial Phrases

An adverbial phrase is a phrase used as an adverb.

My mom gave me a clover leaf *before summer camp.*

The phrase *before summer camp* tells *when* the mother gave the clover leaf. *Before summer camp* is an adverbial phrase modifying the verb *gave.*

In the following examples, adverbs have been replaced by adverbial phrases.

At the assembly, Ben spoke *sincerely.*
At the assembly, Ben spoke *with sincerity.*

Carol waited in the line *patiently.*
Carol waited in the line *with patience.*

The meteor fell *there.*
The meteor fell *into the wheat field.*

Exercise 1

Find the adverbial phrase in each sentence. Tell the verb that each phrase modifies.

1. Pine logs blaze in the old fireplace.
2. On the steps stood a large black dog.
3. One twilight star glowed in the darkening sky.
4. On every corner, balloon vendors gathered.
5. The ice fishers made a hole in the thick ice.
6. Louis Braille was born in 1809.
7. We strolled through the Dutch tulip fields.
8. Early settlers came from many countries.
9. Sam's arrow whistled through the air swiftly.
10. In the desert, the coyotes howl.

Exercise 2

Change the italicized word in each sentence to an adverbial phrase. An example has been done for you.

Example: Orchids bloom *there*.
             Orchids bloom *in the greenhouse*.

  1. The ballet dancers leap *gracefully*.
  2. Our group built the model city *carefully*.
  3. He erased the pencil marks *hastily*.
  4. *Faultlessly*, Keenan recited his poem.
  5. The teacher handed me the test *immediately*.
  6. Those chipmunks will disappear *instantly*.
  7. *Formerly*, the Aztecs used chocolate beans as money.
  8. Rain clouds travel *fast*.
  9. Put your math books away *now*.
 10. The audience listened *attentively* to the French fairy tale.

Exercise 3

**Complete each sentence with an adverbial phrase.
Tell whether each expresses time, place, or manner.**

  1. The dolphins leaped _____ .
  2. We shall leave _____ .
  3. A jogger ran _____ .
  4. The two toddlers swim _____ .
  5. _____ stands a very old barn.
  6. The extinct pterodactyl once glided _____ .
  7. Carved vases were placed _____ .
  8. The art club will meet _____ .
  9. Ride the skateboard _____ .
 10. _____ the sun peeked.
 11. Greyhounds race _____ .
 12. _____ the leaves fell.
 13. Every book fell _____ .
 14. _____ the flag floated.
 15. Jeremy walked _____ .

Exercise 4

Find the phrase or phrases in each sentence. Tell whether it is adjectival or adverbial.

1. My grandfather saw many deer among the hills.
2. The Eskimos from Canada call themselves Inuit.
3. Gary drives the bus with great care.
4. The checker rolled under the rocking chair.
5. The surface of the pond froze during the night.
6. A baby robin with a broken wing fell to the ground.
7. After the spelling bee, Colleen sank into a chair.
8. Mr. Pernelli's building was destroyed in the fire.
9. I wanted to release the monkeys from their cages.
10. The strange color of the sky came from the sunset.
11. The largest signature of the statesmen was written by John Hancock.
12. The migrants saw their destination on the horizon and grew excited.
13. At the signal of the referee, the game began.
14. Dana keeps her cactus garden on a sunny shelf.
15. Usually each line of poetry begins with a capital letter.
16. The air was filled with the fragrance of pine.
17. The mobile of driftwood pieces was very unusual.
18. Cleopatra was a powerful queen of Egypt.
19. Hungry bears waded through the stream.
20. Will Kelly climb to the top of the lighthouse?
21. Enduring hardship, pioneer families settled in the new land.
22. Bumblebees were flying through the open window.
23. Ornaments of paper dangle from the reindeer's antlers.
24. Shadows of planes pass over our house.
25. A long line of covered wagons rolled into the valley.

Exercise 5

Complete each sentence with a phrase. Tell whether each phrase is adjectival or adverbial.

1. _____ flew three squawking chickens.
2. We listened to the noise _____ .
3. _____ all contestants should walk quietly.
4. Long, blue feathers were found _____ .
5. A crate _____ is on our front porch.
6. A large lion prowled _____ .
7. The young knights searched thoroughly _____ .
8. A small, red car rolled _____ .
9. Orange and red leaves danced _____ .
10. The daisies _____ look like tiny stars.
11. I am carving a statue _____ .
12. A giggling child sat _____ .
13. _____ were jugglers, dancers, and singers.
14. The bottoms _____ were covered with mud.
15. Ralph, the dog, always jumps _____ .

Practice Power

▶ **Use the following as adverbial phrases in sentences of your own.**

1. on a T-shirt
2. into the knapsack
3. through the open window
4. onto the horse
5. out of the woods
6. from outer space
7. across the boundaries
8. over the doghouse
9. above the mountains
10. of our lives

The Essential Elements of a Sentence

Subjects and Predicates

The subject names the person, place, or thing about which a statement is made.

To determine the subject of a sentence, place *who* or *what* before the verb to form a question.

> *Annabelle* picked flowers from our garden. (names a person)

"Who picked flowers?" The answer is *Annabelle,* the subject of the sentence.

> The *garden* has many colorful flowers. (names a place)

"What has many colorful flowers?" The answer is *garden,* the subject of the sentence.

> Those *flowers* are very beautiful. (names things)

"What are beautiful?" The answer is *flowers,* the subject of the sentence.

The person, the place, or the thing about which a statement is made is called the simple subject.

The predicate states a fact about the subject.

> The flowers in the garden *bloomed.*

The subject of this sentence is *flowers.* What does this sentence state about the flowers? It states that the flowers *bloomed.* The predicate of this sentence, therefore, is *bloomed.*

The word that states what the subject is or does is called the simple predicate.

A simple predicate may contain more than one word. It may contain an auxiliary verb and a principal verb.

Few low plants *can grow* in a rain forest.

A sentence is a group of words that expresses a complete thought. A sentence contains a subject and a predicate.

COMPLETE THOUGHT	INCOMPLETE THOUGHT
The sky is blue.	Blue as a summer sky
Sally went there.	There in the country
The sun shines.	Shining sun
Go to your room.	There in your room
The scientist designed a telescope.	The designer of the telescope

Exercise 1

Find the simple predicate and then the simple subject in each sentence.

1. Marbles bounced.
2. Multicolored marbles bounced noisily.
3. Marbles of many colors bounced all around the room.
4. The leaves rustled.
5. Dry, amber leaves rustled occasionally.
6. Leaves of a reddish hue rustled in the breeze.
7. Anthony rode the subway into the city.
8. The city has many interesting museums.
9. These museums attract thousands of visitors each year.
10. I will owe you a favor.
11. A blustery wind has disturbed the papers.
12. The last plums in the orchard are ripe.
13. A cold glass of water tastes good on a hot day.
14. Frogs jump with their strong hind legs.
15. Strange symbols blinked on the computer screen.
16. The wheelbarrow has a rusty wheel.
17. Greece was home to the first Olympics.
18. Long, yellow strips of flypaper hang from the ceiling.
19. White blocks of ice drifted nearer and nearer.
20. The quartet sang a song about a bicycle for eight.
21. A red stagecoach full of passengers creaked down the road.
22. An excited horse pranced in time to the music.
23. My family visited the Parthenon in Athens, Greece.
24. Greece is home to many temples and statues.
25. The ancient temple appears particularly beautiful at dusk.

Exercise 2

Tell if each group of words expresses a complete or an incomplete thought.

1. The height of the towering trees.
2. Two attempts at winning the election.
3. Cathryn wrote clues for the scavenger hunt.
4. Tinkling noises of small bronze bells.
5. I spotted a figure moving through the empty house!
6. Can you see the sun peeking through the trees?
7. About the worst day in my diary.
8. A distinguished gentleman with a bowler hat and a cane.
9. On an unusual day with no wind.
10. The water of the Dead Sea is salty enough to keep bathers afloat on its surface.
11. Rose-colored castle turrets rose above the trees.
12. Straight up into the sky!
13. The Himalayas are the highest mountains in the world.
14. Five ballet dancers, already best friends.
15. One hundred centimeters equals one meter.
16. Bamboo serves many purposes for the people of Asia.
17. To the sky without thinking twice.
18. On the next transit bus!
19. Listen to the sound of the birds in the trees.
20. A flock of sparrows rose from the flowering thicket.

Exercise 3

Each group of words below does not express a complete thought. Add words or phrases to each to make a complete sentence.

1. Reeked of the skunk's scent
2. A laughing hyena
3. The pieces of the puzzle
4. A museum with exhibits
5. Clapped to the music
6. Will grow in desert regions
7. In a sailboat
8. Miles and miles of flooded plains
9. Stretching their branches skyward
10. Over a wooden bridge
11. Bright orange tents in rows
12. Amid the rolling waves
13. A shiny new penny
14. The telltale sign
15. Had scattered confetti everywhere

Practice Power

▶ Read this short paragraph. Rewrite it so that each sentence expresses a complete thought. You can combine ideas into one sentence.

George saved money to buy a trampoline. He had fun jumping up and down on it. He invited all the kids. On his block to take turns on it. The kids loved it. An exciting activity. Now a person can jump high. As high as a kangaroo!

Working with Subjects and Predicates

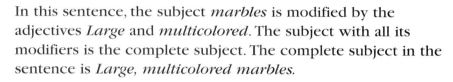

The subject with all its modifiers is called the complete subject.

> Marbles rolled across the pavement.

In this sentence, *marbles* answers the question *what rolled?* *Marbles* is the simple subject.

> Large, multicolored marbles rolled across the pavement.

In this sentence, the subject *marbles* is modified by the adjectives *Large* and *multicolored*. The subject with all its modifiers is the complete subject. The complete subject in the sentence is *Large, multicolored marbles*.

Study the following examples. The simple subjects are underlined. The complete subjects are italicized.

> *The <u>athletes</u> on our team* exercise.
> *The long <u>bridge</u>* is outside New Orleans.

The predicate with all its modifiers and complements is called the complete predicate.

The word that tells something about the subject is the simple predicate. The simple predicate may contain an auxiliary verb.

> Summer has arrived!

In this sentence, the simple predicate is *has arrived*. It contains the auxiliary verb *has*.

The simple predicate may be modified by an adverb or an adverbial phrase. It may also have a direct object or complement to complete its meaning.

Look at the following sentences. The simple predicates are underlined. The complete predicates are italicized.

The caterpillar *moved gracefully.* (adverb)

Tad *hid in the tree house.* (adverbial phrase)

The birds *ate worms.* (direct object)

In the sentences below, each simple subject and each simple predicate is underlined. Each complete subject is separated from the complete predicate by a vertical line.

The boys | love the tree house.

The tree house | was built by the father for his son's birthday.

Exercise 1

In each sentence, separate the complete subject from the complete predicate by a vertical line. Then underline the simple subject and the simple predicate.

1. A pink ribbon fluttered in the breeze.

2. Broken shells cover the beach.

3. The letter was signed by the mayor of Philadelphia.

4. The Manx cat has no tail.

5. The rusty key fit perfectly into the lock.

6. A snail's pace is actually about three hundredths of a mile an hour!

7. The sky darkened suddenly.

8. The chair fell with a crash.

9. Georgina joined the cocker spaniel owners' club.

10. Servers in the restaurant were dressed as pilgrims.

11. This puzzle has two missing pieces.

12. Tall trees swayed in the warm, tropical breeze.

13. The right side of the brain controls the left side of the body.

14. Dragonflies always appear in the warm, summer weather.

15. Jorge waxed the fiberglass surfboard eagerly.

16. A panel of students will test new games for the toy manufacturers.

17. Ms. Carlyle writes musical scores with a computer.

18. The cover of the magazine showed a photograph of the newborn quintuplets.

19. You need to bring two pencils to the exam.

20. A large dragonfly whirled around the flowers.

Practice Power

▶ Add words to the simple subject and simple predicate in each sentence. Then draw a vertical line to separate the complete subject from the complete predicate.

Example: The bus driver drove.

The cautious bus driver | drove carefully down the icy road.

1. The flowers grew.   3. Thunder banged.

2. Parrots squawked.   4. The child fell.

Compound Subjects and Predicates

> **A compound subject consists of more than one noun or pronoun.**

> **A compound predicate consists of more than one verb.**

Aldrin and *Armstrong* walked on the moon. (compound subject)

The astronauts *trained* and *planned* for their landing. (compound predicate)

In the first sentence, *walked* has two subjects, *Aldrin* and *Armstrong*. In the second sentence, *astronauts* is the subject of two verbs, *trained* and *planned*.

> **A sentence may have a compound subject, a compound predicate, or a compound subject and a compound predicate.**

Jean and *Mike* enjoy poetry. (compound subject)

Jean *reads* and *writes* poetry. (compound predicate)

Jean and *Mike* read and write poetry. (compound subject and compound predicate)

Exercise 1

Find the compound elements in each sentence.

1. Rick set up the football and kicked a field goal for the team.
2. Gina and Gary told us a story, "How the Duck Got Its Bill."
3. The holidays came and went.
4. Football and baseball are my favorite sports.
5. Minneapolis and St. Paul are called the Twin Cities.
6. The wolf pups jumped and barked.
7. The photographer shoots and develops her own prints.
8. Oranges or lemons make refreshing summer drinks.
9. Francis and Rosie are twin calves.
10. Dandelions and clover have overrun the herb garden.
11. In the Ice Age, people lived and hunted together.
12. Mosquitoes and bees come with the warm weather.
13. I read and reread *Romeo and Juliet,* a tragedy by William Shakespeare.
14. Sarah cracked the eggs and beat them with a fork.
15. My uncle composes his own music and performs it, too.

Exercise 2

Complete each with a compound predicate to form a sentence.

1. The fireworks
2. My aunt and uncle
3. The trained seal
4. At the seventy-fifth floor, the window washers
5. For exercise, my friends and I

Complete each with a compound subject to form a sentence.

6. pedaled and pushed the bicycle uphill
7. climbed to the top of the tower
8. will go to the street fair tomorrow
9. need oxygen and water
10. can tell time

Practice Power

▶ Write five sentences about some things you and your friends like to do. Use compound subjects and predicates.

Natural and Inverted Order in Sentences

> **A sentence is in the natural order when the predicate verb follows the subject.**

NATURAL ORDER   A fresh, cool breeze swept through the house.

In this sentence, the predicate verb is *swept.* You can find the subject by asking the question *who or what swept?* The answer is *A fresh, cool breeze* swept. The subject *breeze,* and all its modifiers, comes before the predicate verb. Therefore, this sentence is in the natural order.

> Who went with him?

The subject *Who* comes before the predicate verb *went.* This sentence is also in the natural order.

> **A sentence is in the inverted order when the predicate verb or an auxiliary verb comes before the subject.**

INVERTED ORDER   Through the house swept a fresh, cool breeze.

In this sentence, the verb *swept* and the adverbial phrase *Through the house* come before the subject *breeze* with its modifiers. This sentence is in the inverted order.

> Did you go with him?

In this sentence, the word *Did* in the verb phrase *Did go* comes before the subject *you.* This sentence is also in the inverted order.

Exercise 1

Change each sentence from the inverted order to the natural order. In some cases, you may need to change the end punctuation of the sentence.

1. After the picnic came the thunderstorm.

2. In what state is Seattle located?

3. Did the audience applaud the performance?

4. Under the porch was a scared rabbit.

5. Beside the lake stands a beautiful cottage.

Exercise 2

Change each sentence from the natural order to the inverted order.

1. Loaves of bread were on the counter.

2. Trinkets from around the world were in the glass cabinet.

3. The child rode on her bicycle through the garden.

4. On the mountain a black bear appeared.

5. Through the open gate a Shetland pony trotted.

Exercise 3

Tell if each sentence is in the natural order or the inverted order.

1. Onto the yellow primrose climbed a ladybug.
2. Coach Bremer planned a new line of defense.
3. Around the tiger's tail, the zoologists tied a small bell.
4. Noah Webster published the first American dictionary.
5. In the Torrid Zone, the climate is extremely hot.
6. Laurie will stop at the secondhand bookstore.
7. Under which tree did you find the four-leaf clover?
8. Delicately carved statues line the sides of the fountain.
9. In 1513, Ponce de León reached Florida.
10. Up the giraffe's neck crawled the green inchworm.
11. The missing ticket lay in the top drawer.
12. Eric dragged the camping equipment up the long hill.
13. Through the ocean, currents race.
14. In an orchestra, there are more strings than any other type of instrument.
15. The cheetah is the fastest animal on land.

Practice Power

▶ Make up three questions using information from social studies or science. Write your answers, first with a sentence in the natural order, and then with a sentence in the inverted order.

Example:
Where does the baby kangaroo hide?
The baby kangaroo hides in its mother's pouch.
In its mother's pouch hides the baby kangaroo.

LESSON 7

Sentences Grouped According to Use

A declarative sentence is a sentence that states a fact.

Niagara Falls is on the border between the United States and Canada.

An interrogative sentence is a sentence that asks a question.

Have you ever visited Niagara Falls?

An imperative sentence is a sentence that expresses a command.

Look at this old painting of Niagara Falls.

In an imperative sentence, often the subject is not expressed. It is understood to be *you.*

An exclamatory sentence is a sentence that expresses strong or sudden emotion.

How magnificent is Niagara Falls!

Exercise 1

Tell whether each sentence is declarative, interrogative, imperative, or exclamatory.

1. The peacock stared at its tail in the mirror.
2. Why did the chicken peck at you?
3. What a long snake that is!
4. Look at the peacock's magnificent colors!
5. Was the rain dance successful?
6. Little League players wear safety helmets.
7. Are we having spinach noodles for lunch?
8. Take the cat for a walk.
9. Southern Europe has mild winters.
10. The Hebrew word *shalom* means "hello" and "good-bye."
11. How many eggs does a sea turtle lay?
12. Avoid that dangerous road, Jerri.
13. Oh, how I love a warm cup of tea!
14. Who broke the teapot?
15. That was my mother's new teapot!

Practice Power

▶ Write a paragraph about things you are thankful for. Use at least one each of the four sentence types: declarative, interrogative, imperative, exclamatory.

Sentences Grouped According to Form

Sentences are divided according to form. Many sentences are simple or compound.

Simple Sentences

A simple sentence contains a subject and a predicate. Either or both may be compound. A simple sentence expresses one complete thought.

The bicycle had a flat tire.

This sentence contains a subject, *bicycle,* and a predicate, *had.* Neither the subject nor the predicate is compound.

The elephant raised its trunk and lifted one foot.

This simple sentence contains a subject, *elephant,* and a compound predicate, *raised* and *lifted.*

The cymbal and the triangle are simple instruments.

This sentence contains a compound subject, *cymbal* and *triangle*, and a simple predicate, *are.*

The wheels and the gears on the fantastic machine whirled and hummed.

This sentence contains a compound subject, *wheels* and *gears*, and a compound predicate, *whirled* and *hummed.*

Exercise 1

Find the subject and the predicate in these sentences.

1. The panda and its cub clutched bamboo leaves in their paws.
2. A quart of snow will not become a quart of water.
3. Elena and Wyatt designed and built a birdhouse for us.
4. Mares and their foals ran through the field.
5. White tables and chairs were under the yellow tents.
6. Licorice is made from the root of a plant.
7. Gymnasts run and somersault on a narrow beam.
8. Tony and I took photographs at the soapbox derby.
9. The *Iliad* tells the story of the war between the Greeks and the people of Troy.
10. Stephanie, your pencil fell and broke.

Compound Sentences

> **A compound sentence contains two or more independent clauses.**

> My dad prepared the mast, and I cleaned the deck for our family's sail on the lake.

In this sentence, there are two complete thoughts. The first is *My dad prepared the mast.* The second complete thought is *I cleaned the deck.* Each thought could be used as a separate simple sentence. These complete thoughts are called independent clauses.

An independent clause contains a subject and a predicate and expresses a complete thought. Any part of an independent clause may be compound.

Independent clauses usually are connected by a coordinate conjunction. The commonly used coordinate conjunctions are *and, but, or, nor,* and *yet.* When the clauses of a compound sentence have no connecting word, the connection is then indicated by a semicolon.

> We often sail on Lake Michigan, but we never fish there. There are five Great Lakes; the largest is Lake Superior.

Exercise 2

Find the subject and the predicate in each independent clause of these compound sentences.

1. Brian jiggled the weeds with a stick, and fireflies appeared.
2. I like stories of adventure, but Marian prefers biographies.
3. He has not come, nor has he sent an excuse.
4. Wildflowers were abundant, and we decorated the house with them.
5. The sky turned black, and we hurried for shelter.
6. Leonardo da Vinci was a man of many talents, but we remember him most as an artist.
7. The cage was open; the animal had escaped!
8. The little boy whistled, and the dog followed.
9. Charlemagne was a wise king, and during his reign his territories flourished.
10. Those mountains contained valuable timber, and the settlers found many uses for it.
11. The Phoenicians made purple dye, and their traders carried the dye to the ports of the Mediterranean.
12. He opened the box, and a letter fell into his hands.
13. Tulips grow in many parts of the world, but we associate them most with Holland.
14. Tourists arrived at the wharf, and the guide was waiting there.
15. I take violin lessons, and my sister takes karate lessons.

Practice Power

▶ **Combine the following simple sentences by adding an appropriate conjunction:** *and, but, or, nor, yet.*

1. Suddenly the sky turned very dark. We could hear thunder in the distance.
2. Karl could go to the movies today. He could go to the movies tomorrow.
3. Lori tried to recall what she was supposed to get from the grocery store. She couldn't remember.
4. Paul doesn't like spinach. He doesn't like lima beans.

Punctuation of Compound Sentences

The clauses of a compound sentence connected by the simple conjunctions *and, but, nor, yet,* and *or* are usually separated by a comma.

> Fog and rain made driving difficult, but the flood made it impossible.

If the clauses are short and closely related, the comma may be omitted.

> The whistle blew and work began immediately.

Sometimes the clauses of a compound sentence have no connecting word. The connection is then indicated by the use of a semicolon.

> These are our duties; they are serious responsibilities.

Exercise 1

Add the correct punctuation to each of these compound sentences.

1. The dance-skating competition ended and the happy fans cheered the winners
2. Joseph would play but he didn't finish his homework
3. King Arthur had many knights Galahad was the bravest
4. Betty is busy but she will help you
5. The yellow dress was pretty but Juanita didn't buy it
6. Bowling is a very old sport the ancient Egyptians played it
7. Run quickly or you will miss the bus
8. The box held many old coins but they were unfamiliar to the collector
9. No two snowflakes are alike but each has six sides
10. Madeline washed her father's car her sister waxed it.

Exercise 2

Combine each pair of simple sentences to form a compound sentence.

1. Canada is north of the United States. Mexico is south.
2. Millions of people put objects in their eyes daily. They wear contact lenses.
3. The first algebra problem was difficult. We solved the others rather easily.
4. You can fish from the boat. You can fish from the pier.
5. The hamsters wanted to escape. They had not found a way.
6. Ottawa is the capital of Canada. Toronto is Canada's largest city.
7. Isaac wanted a cloudless day. He waited for a long time.
8. The boat is immense. Bridges must rise to let it pass.
9. Solar energy is being used. It is still rather costly.
10. Mr. Ashton designs cars. His wife builds them.
11. Animals with backbones are vertebrates. Animals without backbones are invertebrates.
12. TV was available in the 1930s. Not much was broadcast then.
13. The anchor is stored in the stern. We drop it when we reach our destination.
14. Many New World monkeys have grasping tails. Old World monkeys do not have this kind of tail.
15. Hockey is a winter sport. Baseball is a summer sport.
16. The student government plans fun activities for the school. A carnival will be held in May.
17. My parents are attending a wedding on Saturday night. My sister will baby-sit.
18. Computers may be entertaining. They are also a tool for learning.
19. The boys wear blue pants as part of their school uniform. Girls may wear a blue skirt or pants.
20. Summer is usually sunny and warm. Mosquitoes and other bugs also enjoy the warm weather.

Exercise 3

Tell whether these sentences are simple or compound.
Explain why.

1. Along the river's edge lay alligators and turtles.
2. At the computer camp, we spent the morning doing nature activities, and we spent the afternoon working on the computer.
3. He stared up at the New York skyscraper for a long time, and he wondered about climbing it.
4. Marty cut oranges, cherries, and peaches for the fruit salad.
5. The Danube River flows into the Black Sea.
6. Nickels, pennies, and dimes rolled all over the sidewalk.
7. Do you have the correct time?
8. I heard the bamboo flute only once, but its music haunted me for years.
9. The far north is the home of the reindeer.
10. What did Mom say to you, and did she sound angry?
11. Tiny strawberry plants peeked out of the terra-cotta jar.
12. Singapore has one of the world's busiest ports.
13. London is the largest city in England; about seven million people live there.
14. Encyclopedias, dictionaries, and atlases are in the reference section.
15. Penguins have wings, but they can't fly.

Putting It All Together

Form a group of five students. Have each member of the group write five examples of one of the following kinds of sentence parts: adjectival phrases, adverbial phrases, simple and compound subjects, simple and compound predicates, and independent clauses.

After each member of the group has finished, construct a story using all the sentence parts. You can add other sentence parts so that the story makes sense, or challenge yourselves to use only the phrases and clauses you've already invented. When you're done, read your story to the class.

Chapter Challenge

Read this paragraph carefully and answer the questions.

¹In the future, what will our cars be like? ²Probably, our cars will listen and will speak to us! ³For example, you will turn on the engine, lights, windshield wipers, defroster, heater, or radio with your voice. ⁴Cars of the future will be more convenient, and they will be safer. ⁵Automatic sensors will control the steering and the brakes. ⁶This automatic system will sense the nearby cars and guide your car through traffic. ⁷You will be able to drive faster, but there will be fewer accidents. ⁸Cars down the road will certainly be a breeze to drive!

1. Is sentence 1 in the natural or inverted order?

2. Find an interrogative sentence and an exclamatory sentence.

3. What is the compound element in sentence 2? What word helps you find it?

4. In sentence 4, is the prepositional phrase adjectival or adverbial?

5. Find one compound sentence in the paragraph.

6. Find a coordinate conjunction in sentence 4 that connects two independent clauses.

7. In sentence 5, name the simple subject and the simple predicate.

8. In sentence 6, name the adverbial phrase.

9. What are the two clauses in sentence 7?

10. Find the complete subject in sentence 8.

LESSON
1

The Period

The purpose of punctuation and capitalization is to make the meaning of what you write clear. In speaking, the tone and inflection of your voice allow the listener to understand your thoughts. In writing, it is the use of punctuation marks and capital letters that help the reader to understand your thoughts.

If what you write is to be easily understood by your readers, you should learn how to use the marks of punctuation correctly. The rules taught in this chapter are the ones you will need to make your writing clear.

Use a period

- at the end of a declarative or an imperative sentence.

    Matt posed for the picture.

    Smile for the picture, Matt.

- after an abbreviation or an initial.

    Sept.   L. M. Montgomery   Mr. Matthew Cuthbert

About the Photograph

The punctuation signals for starting and stopping help us communicate meaning in our writing. Do you think this boy is exclaiming, "Look at this!" or asking, "What's on my head?"

PUNCTUATION/
CAPITALIZATION

Study the following abbreviations.

B.C.	before Christ
A.D.	*anno Domini* (in the year of the Lord)
P.S.	postscript
N.B.	*nota bene* (note well)
U.S.A.	United States of America; United States Army
U.S.N.	United States Navy
Gen.	General
Dr.	Doctor
M.D.	Doctor of Medicine
Lt.	Lieutenant
D.D.S.	Doctor of Dental Surgery
gal.	gallon
qt.	quart
pt.	pint
l	liter*
g	gram*
m	meter*
Blvd.	Boulevard
E.	East
W.	West
C.O.D.	collect on delivery
Mt.	Mount, Mountain

*The symbols used in the metric system are *not* followed by periods.

Here is a list of the two-letter postal abbreviations for each state, the District of Columbia, and other territories of the United States. Both letters in each abbreviation are capitalized, and periods are not used.

AL	Alabama	OK	Oklahoma
AK	Alaska	OR	Oregon
AZ	Arizona	PA	Pennsylvania
AR	Arkansas	RI	Rhode Island
CA	California	SC	South Carolina
CO	Colorado	SD	South Dakota
CT	Connecticut	TN	Tennessee
DE	Delaware	TX	Texas
DC	District of Columbia	UT	Utah
FL	Florida	VT	Vermont
GA	Georgia	VA	Virginia
HI	Hawaii	WA	Washington
ID	Idaho	WV	West Virginia
IL	Illinois	WI	Wisconsin
IN	Indiana	WY	Wyoming
IA	Iowa		
KS	Kansas	GU	Guam
KY	Kentucky	PR	Puerto Rico
LA	Louisiana	VI	Virgin Islands
ME	Maine		
MD	Maryland		
MA	Massachusetts		
MI	Michigan		
MN	Minnesota		
MS	Mississippi		
MO	Missouri		
MT	Montana		
NE	Nebraska		
NV	Nevada		
NH	New Hampshire		
NJ	New Jersey		
NM	New Mexico		
NY	New York		
NC	North Carolina		
ND	North Dakota		
OH	Ohio		

Exercise 1

Add periods where they are needed.

1. Inez would like to learn to dance someday
2. Mark Twain's real name was Samuel L Clemens
3. Mr and Mrs John A Kenneff are in charge of the sale
4. "Seven o'clock, Oct 31—Come and see who's who at Helen's house," stated the invitation
5. Doctors use the letters M D after their names
6. Crossing Mt Holly, we saw mysterious lights
7. Mrs Frisby, a field mouse, is a character in a book by Robert C O'Brien
8. Listen to the sounds of the traffic
9. "Take Rose Blvd and turn left" was written on the note
10. When Maria marries, she will change her title from Ms to Mrs
11. At the top of the list, the name Lt Jorge T Garcia appeared
12. Una did not know what *qt* and *pt* in the cookbook meant

Exercise 2

Give the postal abbreviations for each of these states or territories of the United States.

1. Puerto Rico	5. South Dakota	9. Guam
2. Georgia	6. Illinois	10. Oregon
3. New Jersey	7. Delaware	11. Pennsylvania
4. Texas	8. Virgin Islands	12. Hawaii

Give the state for each postal abbreviation.

13. MA	16. UT	19. KS
14. SC	17. WA	20. AZ
15. NH	18. WY	21. OH

Practice Power

▶ Write one sentence to illustrate each of the two rules for the use of a period. Then draw an envelope, and write an address and return address on it using postal abbreviations.

The Comma

Use a comma

- to separate words or groups of words in a series.

    This map shows countries, cities, rivers, seas, lakes, and mountains.

    Brenda likes going to plays, to movies, and to concerts.

- to set off parts of dates, addresses, and geographic names.

    Armstrong and Aldrin landed on the moon on July 20, 1969.

- to set off *yes* and *no* when they introduce sentences.

    Yes, I plan to study the solar system in science class.

    No, my sister has not returned from the mall.

- to set off words of direct address.

    Marco, have you seen the latest Batman movie?

- after the salutation in a social letter and after the complimentary close in all letters.

    Dear James,   Sincerely yours,   Yours truly,

- to set off an appositive that is not part of the name or that is not restrictive.

    The heart, a vital organ in the body, needs exercise.

    Richard the Lion-Hearted was the king of England for only one year. (In this sentence, *the Lion-Hearted* is restrictive, and so commas are not needed.)

- to set off short direct quotations.

  If the quotation is at the end of the sentence, use a comma before the words of the speaker.

  The teacher asked, "Have you completed your research work on Japan?"

  If the quotation is at the beginning of the sentence, use a comma after the quotation unless a question mark or an exclamation point is required.

  "Tokyo is an important city in Japan," remarked the teacher.

  "Who rules Japan?" asked the teacher.

  If the quotation is divided, two commas are needed.

  "Richard," said the teacher, "locate Japan on the map."

- to separate the clauses of a compound sentence connected by the conjunctions *and, but, or, nor,* and *yet.*

  The English settlers remained along the coast, but the French moved farther inland.

  If the clauses are short and closely connected, the comma may be omitted.

  Go to the stand and buy a newspaper.

  The bus jerked and my backpack slid off the seat.

Exercise 1

Give the rule that applies to the use of the comma in each sentence.

1. Nina played volleyball, tennis, and soccer yesterday.

2. The teacher warned her class, "You should never fly off the handle."

3. *Robinson Crusoe,* a novel by Daniel Defoe, was based on the real-life story of a shipwrecked sailor.

4. Come here, Spot!

5. Yes, I heard the owl call in the night.

6. A famous toy duck of the eighteenth century ate, drank, quacked, and walked.

7. It was too stormy to hunt, and so Tuk stayed inside.

8. My parents were married on March 18, 1965.

9. The limerick, a five-line poem, is often funny.

10. "The lettuce for the salad," said Mother, "is in the bin."

11. There is a circus museum in Baraboo, Wisconsin.

12. No, the fish aren't biting.

13. Contestants in the log-rolling contest balance on a floating log, and the winner is the one who stays on the longest.

14. A special dish of the South is gumbo, a thick soup.

15. The genie's address is 1705 Wishful Avenue, Brass Lamp, Land of Imagination.

16. "Enjoy yourself at the ball," said the fairy godmother, "but be back by midnight."

17. Umbrellas, birdcages, and tennis balls filled the hall.

18. Contact lenses were invented in 1887, but they were made of glass and were not worn by many people.

19. "Pita is a flat bread of the Middle East," explained Yul.

20. "Wake up, girls!" shouted Gail.

Exercise 2

Add commas and periods where they are needed in these sentences.

1. We flew over St Louis Missouri

2. Benjamin Franklin said "A penny saved is a penny earned"

3. No I don't want to throw those magazines away

4. Yellow green and blue stripes covered the hot-air balloon

5. We're going to ride the Ferris wheel the roller coaster and the bumper cars

6. Here is the answer Bruce

7. Beetles crickets and ants are featured in the insect zoo

8. The ripe melons were picked and the workers carried them to the truck

9. Water from the cracked goldfish bowl had leaked onto the floor and Reba mopped it up before her parents got home

10. Charles P Tobias my great-great-uncle flew across India in a hot-air balloon

11. Yes our English papers are due today

12. Your cartoons are great Julie

13. The lion is a strong wild and ferocious cat

14. Icicles were forming on his eyebrows on his mustache and on his beard

15. "Please explain how the satellite works "requested Ann

16. Bruno went up the stairs but Thomas took the elevator

17. A baseball player on third base sang "There's no place like home "

18. Mr Carter shook the tree and the plastic ball fell out

19. The address on the envelope was 933 E Mayflower Blvd Davenport IA

20. No Christine I didn't watch TV last night

21. Thick fog swirled across the lawn and I couldn't see my hand in front of my face

25. The Declaration of Independence was signed on July 4 1776

23. Dr Erg's unusual invention the robot cat is shaking hands with a rat

24. Abraham Lincoln was born near Hodgenville Kentucky

22. Buy cinnamon cloves and allspice for the pumpkin pies

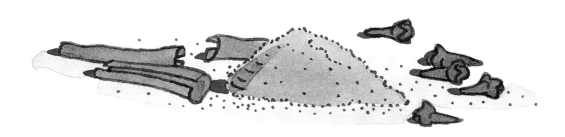

Practice Power

▶ Write one sentence to illustrate each of the eight rules for the use of a comma. Write a few sentences that also include abbreviations.

Exclamation Points and Question Marks

LESSON 3

The Exclamation Point

Use an exclamation point

- at the end of an exclamatory sentence.

  Here comes the parade!

- after an exclamatory word or phrase.

  Hurrah! The work is finished.
  Oh my! My pencil broke.

The Question Mark

Use a question mark at the end of every interrogative sentence.

  Is their flight on time?
  Where can you find elephant seals?

Exercise 1

Add exclamation points where needed, and give the rule that applies.

1. What a noisy pet shop this is
2. Halt Who goes there?
3. How blue your eyes are
4. How unusual that lizard is
5. Ready, set, go
6. O Matt Don't step on that flower
7. Wow Look at that ice-cream sundae
8. Listen
9. Hurry The bacon is burning
10. What a nice surprise this is

474

Exercise 2

Add the correct mark of punctuation to end each sentence: an exclamation point, a question mark, or a period.

1. Do you know how the badger got its name
2. We will make spinach lasagna
3. How tired I was after cleaning the boat
4. How many pretzels have you eaten
5. At the age of fourteen, some boys in the Middle Ages began training for knighthood
6. From whom did the United States purchase the Louisiana Territory
7. What a silly joke I heard
8. What does a milliner make
9. Many sheep are raised in Ireland
10. Can you name the largest insect in the world
11. What a convincing argument Tanya made for a bigger allowance
12. Where is the girls' softball team playing
13. How time flies
14. The geranium is a hardy plant
15. Look out the window at the snow

Practice Power

▶ As a contest winner, you may spend fifteen minutes in the store of your choice selecting anything you would like. There will be no charge for any item! Write a short paragraph naming some of the things you would choose. Include an interrogative and an exclamatory sentence.

LESSON 4

The Semicolon

Use a semicolon to separate the clauses of a compound sentence when they are not separated by *and, but, or, nor,* or *yet.*

Al played the violin; Eileen played the piano.

Exercise 1

Add semicolons where they are needed in these compound sentences.

1. Vanessa cooked the spaghetti Michael made the sauce.
2. They followed every direction the experiment succeeded.
3. Angel Falls in Venezuela is the highest waterfall in the world it is about twenty times higher than Niagara Falls.
4. The sand was firm and not too wet it was perfect for building sand castles.
5. Jean is a talented guitarist she also writes her own songs.
6. The freezing rain made roads slippery motorists drove cautiously.
7. The traffic signals are not working the storm must have affected them.
8. It would take much cheese to make a twelve-foot pizza it would also take many people to eat it.
9. Harry cut the wood he then built a fire.
10. New Guinea is the home for many birds of paradise these birds have magnificently colored feathers.

Practice Power

▶ **Below are simple sentences. Make each into a compound sentence by adding an independent clause and correctly using a semicolon.**

Example: The old jalopy was sitting at the side of the road.

The old jalopy was sitting at the side of the road; it had run out of gas.

1. Asparagus is my favorite vegetable.
2. Alice goes to ballet class on Tuesday after school.
3. We ordered fish soup at the Chinese restaurant.
4. At the carnival, many people tried to knock over the stack of bottles with a ball.
5. Wendy brought a camera to the parade.
6. The path on the right leads to the lake.
7. The dark clouds gathered quickly.
8. The elephant went down the street on roller skates.
9. This summer my dad has promised to teach me how to mow the lawn.
10. Fred likes ketchup on his french fries.
11. My family and relatives play in a huge softball game every year.
12. Sarah enjoys sewing in her spare time.
13. Bill is nervous about entering high school in the fall.
14. Our dog, Hank, never tires from fetching his ball.
15. The Statue of Liberty stands on Liberty Island in New York Harbor.

The Colon

Use a colon

- after the salutation of a business letter.

  Dear Ms. Lee: Dear Sir or Madam:

- before a list of items.

  We ordered the following articles: charts, books, paper, pens, and rulers.

Exercise 1

Give the rule that applies to the use of the colon in these items.

1. Dear Mrs. McKenna:
2. The dragon listed these items on the menu: fried leaves, rock candy, plates of armor.
3. Dear Mr. Clarke:
4. Dear Sir:
5. Provide the following: one bag of marshmallows, one box of graham crackers, ten chocolate bars.
6. Arrange these names in alphabetical order: Mary, Marci, Leo, Larry, Henry.
7. For our camping trip, bring the following items: toothpaste, flashlight, sleeping bag, T-shirts, shorts.
8. To Whom It May Concern:
9. The recipe for these cookies requires the following: brown sugar, flour, vanilla extract, chocolate chips, eggs, milk.
10. Ryan entered these items into the computer: names, addresses, phone numbers, ages.

Exercise 2

Add colons where they are needed in the following items.

1. We glued these together to make the nut ring pecans, peanuts, almonds, hickory nuts.
2. Dear Dr. Ray
3. Ryan wants to use these colors in his computer program turquoise, cyan, lavender, magenta.
4. The following teams will receive new uniforms this year baseball, volleyball, football, track.
5. The florist will use these flowers in the arrangement roses, pansies, carnations.
6. To my fellow co-workers Many thanks for the retirement gift.
7. The teacher told the class they would need these supplies for the school year pencils, crayons, glue, paper.
8. My mom wants to buy these items for our new house coffee table, couch, dresser, coatrack.
9. Dear Mrs. Cunningham
10. The family brought these items for their vacation bicycles, board games, snack food.

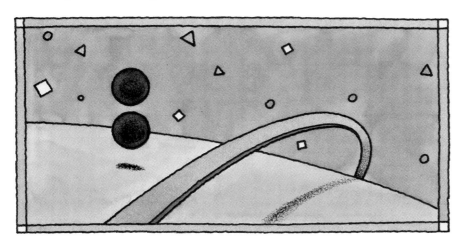

Practice Power

▶ Write a short paragraph about a trip to a zoo. Make use of at least one semicolon and one colon to show that you understand how to use these marks of punctuation.

LESSON 6 Quotation Marks

Use quotation marks

- before and after every quotation and every part of a divided quotation.

> The teacher said, "The field day will be held next Friday."
>
> "Luke," questioned his friend, "have you ever seen a flying squirrel?"

- to enclose titles of short stories, poems, songs, newspaper and magazine articles, TV shows, and radio programs.

> I read Mona Gardner's short story "The Dinner Party," in which a snake is an unwelcome visitor at a dinner.
>
> Ogden Nash wrote the humorous poem "The Hippopotamus."

Titles of books, magazines, newspapers, movies, and works of art are usually printed in italics. In typing or handwriting, italics are indicated by underlining.

> *Wilderness Journey* is an exciting adventure story.
> <u>Wilderness Journey</u> is an exciting adventure story.

Exercise 1

Explain the use of the quotation marks and underlining in these sentences.

1. "My new neighbors," said Sally, "have three dogs, two cats, and a pet chameleon named Arnold."
2. "Let's go for a dip," said one potato chip to the other.
3. "Look at the colors on that chameleon!" exclaimed Sally.
4. I've just finished "I, Hungry Hannah Cassandra Glen . . . ," a clever short story.
5. An old proverb says, "Well begun is half done."

6. "Bob," he asked, "where did you put my tie?"
7. Who wrote the book <u>The Wizard in the Tree</u>?
8. "Who has my copy of <u>The New York Times</u>?" asked Dad.
9. "When I was a baby," explained John Henry, "I had a hammer instead of a rattle."
10. "The Pit and the Pendulum" is a classic short story.

Exercise 2

Add quotation marks and underlining where needed in these sentences.

1. Jackie, he called, why don't you answer?
2. On Friday afternoon, said the class president, we'll have a popcorn party.
3. Going out tonight? one candle asked the other.
4. Indeed, replied Rosa, that story is very interesting.
5. Be prepared is the motto of the Boy Scouts of America.
6. Please pass the hot sauce, said Gary.
7. I thought, remarked Tex, you were going to get TV Guide.
8. His hearing is fine, declared the doctor.
9. Browning retold the old tale   The Pied Piper of Hamelin.
10. I enjoyed the biography Emma and I, the story of a girl and her seeing eye dog.

Practice Power

▶ **Change each direct quotation into a divided quotation.**

1. "Please leave by the rear door," announced the usher.
2. "Henry, where are you?" shouted the upset parents.
3. "What is in your hand?" Agnes asked suspiciously.
4. "Don't move an inch," warned Todd.
5. "The trees are full of hungry vultures," said Brent.

The Apostrophe

Use an apostrophe

- to show possession.

    John's uncle has a butterfly collection.

- with *s* to show the plural of letters.

    a's   *d*'s   *i*'s

- to show the omission of a letter, letters, or numbers.

    I'll   class of '90   o'clock

Study these contractions and note the letter or letters that have been omitted to form each contraction.

they're—they are	he'll—he will
let's—let us	don't—do not
there's—there is	we've—we have
mustn't—must not	aren't—are not

Exercise 1

Add apostrophes where needed in these sentences.

1. I'll take this tomato soup next door to Mrs. Garza.
2. Men's straw hats are on sale here.
3. Wasn't Thomas Edison's most famous invention the electric lightbulb?
4. She'll help you put on the horse costume.
5. My grandfather is a member of the class of '44.
6. You mustn't make wishes carelessly; they might come true.
7. Five-foot-tall cartoon characters decorate the children's wing of the hospital.
8. The class of '60 donated this megaphone to the school.
9. Ed's *g*'s look like *q*'s.
10. In one unusual contest, a contestant's task is to ride down a long hill on a coal shovel.
11. They've not yet returned.
12. Aren't the Jataka tales from India?
13. Chang's brother taught us to write our names in Chinese.
14. It's so hot outside you could fry an egg on the sidewalk!
15. The train pulled out of the station promptly at five o'clock.

Practice Power

▶ Write a sentence for each of the eight contractions listed on page 482.

The Hyphen

Use a hyphen

- to divide a word at the end of a line whenever one or more syllables are carried to the next line.

  Many unusual facts can be found in an encyclopedia, whether of one volume or of many volumes.

  The dictionary shows how a word is correctly divided into syllables. Check the entry for the word in a dictionary when you have to divide a word at the end of a line.

- in compound numbers from twenty-one to ninety-nine.

  The ball cost ninety-five cents.

- to separate the parts of some compound words.

  brother-in-law   bright-eyed   self-respect

Exercise 1

Locate each of the following words in your dictionary. Use hyphens to show where the words could be divided at the end of a line.

Example: disorganize   dis-or-ga-nize

1. forgetful
2. lavender
3. parrot
4. affection
5. ingredient
6. hedgehog
7. unemployed
8. trustworthy
9. stepladder
10. catastrophe

11. embarrass
12. locomotive
13. needle
14. carousel
15. mosaic
16. sausage
17. dandelion
18. reverence
19. preparation
20. enlargement

Exercise 2

Add hyphens where needed in these sentences.

1. I can't believe my brother is twenty five years old.
2. That's a well known card trick.
3. The thirty one days of January often seem like a hundred.
4. Those guitar picks are seventy five cents each.
5. The cream colored pony was the one I wanted.
6. The baby seems good natured.
7. Farmer McGraw owns sixty five acres of prime farmland.
8. Just twenty four hours and vacation will start.
9. Her mother in law owns the grocery down the street.
10. Purple forget me nots are embroidered across the quilt.

Practice Power

▶ **Add the correct punctuation to these sentences. Use commas, semicolons, colons, periods, exclamation points, quotation marks, apostrophes, and hyphens.**

1. Help me gather pinecones said Gilberts dad
2. The ladder just fell Ill need help to get down
3. Sue Ling enjoyed the unusual words in the poem Jabberwocky
4. Josefina signed this parchment on March 15 1818
5. Ms Iarusso are there enough peppermint sticks
6. Graham turned the yard light off and the skunks trotted toward his trash can
7. Our orchestra needs these instruments a harp a clarinet a tuba and a comb kazoo
8. All Summer in a Day by Ray Bradbury is a short story set in an imaginary world but its lesson applies to the real world
9. Lukes friends called Come to lunch
10. Otters are very social animals and family members often hunt and play together
11. Are you going to your sister in laws cottage
12. Theyll learn how to use a hammer saw drill and planes
13. How hot the biscuits are
14. The scolded dog dashed around the corner down the alley and into the shed
15. Weve promised to return before eight oclock

Capital Letters

Capitalize

- the first word in a sentence.

  Scuba equipment is used by divers everywhere.

- the first word of every line of most poetry.

  The day is coming to an end,
  The moon is coming 'round the bend,
  The stars are peeking out at me.
  I wonder what their bright eyes see?

- the first word of a direct quotation.

  The astronaut said, "Get off at the next planet."

- proper nouns and adjectives.

  The names of particular persons or groups of persons, religious denominations, political parties, institutions, buildings, cities, states, countries, streets, months of the year, days of the week, and holidays are proper nouns.

  Christopher, Presbyterian, Catholic, Democratic party, Beloit College, Independence Hall, Baltimore, Maryland, Egypt, Main Street, July, Thursday, Labor Day, Thanksgiving

- titles of honor and respect when preceding the name.

  Princess Caroline   Judge Quinn

- *north, south, east,* and *west* when they refer to sections of the country.

  My sister and her husband live in the South.

- all names referring to a deity, the Bible or parts of the Bible, and other sacred books.

    In my church, we read the New Testament every Sunday.
    The Koran is the sacred book of the Muslims.

- the principal words in the titles of books, plays, poems, and pictures.

    You'll enjoy the poem "Some Fishy Nonsense."

- the pronoun *I* and the interjection *O.*

    Tomorrow, I will begin planting flowers.
    O Karen, how will we solve the mystery?

- abbreviations when capitals would be used if the words were written in full.

    Dr.   Rev.   U.S.A.

Do not capitalize

- the seasons of the year.

    winter   summer

- the articles, conjunctions, or prepositions in titles, unless one of these is the first word.

    We have just read *The Prince and the Pauper.*

- the names of studies, unless they are derived from proper nouns.

    geography   history   English

- the words *high school, college,* and *university,* unless they are parts of the names of particular institutions.

    Kevin goes to college in Detroit.
    Kevin goes to the University of Detroit.

Exercise 1

Give the rules that apply to the use of capital letters in each sentence.

1. The class recited Christina Rossetti's poem "Who Has Seen the Wind?"
2. Listen, my children, and you shall hear
   Of the midnight ride of Paul Revere . . .
3. On Wednesday, I'll begin working in the cafeteria.
4. The West was a land of opportunity for the pioneers.
5. Curious Ursula asked, "Why is the sky blue?"
6. Tomorrow both King Paul and Queen Paula will attend the royal ball.

Exercise 2

Use capital letters where they are needed in these sentences.

1. a scandinavian student is visiting our friends, the wiesners.
2. florida is one of the states in the south.
3. i want to borrow *the pushcart war,* a book by jean merrill.
4. the insects are moving to locust avenue.
5. we'll lead the new year's parade with a chinese dragon.
6. the dentist, dr. tarcov, took a look at the alligator's teeth.
7. twelve jesters twirl in front of king richard.
8. theresa will live on meeting street during august.
9. peter piper picked a peck of pickled peppers.
10. the smithsonian institution is in washington, d.c.

Putting It All Together

Playwright William Shakespeare used line breaks, punctuation, and capitalization as acting cues in his plays. Modern punctuation does the same.

Copy a passage from a story or poem you admire. Then read it aloud, using punctuation as a performance guide. If you wish, mark up your copy to provide yourself with additional performance notes. Capitalize words that deserve extra emphasis, and add underlines, exclamation points, or other marks to help yourself remember how to perform the passage.

Chapter Challenge

Below is part of a story about the meeting between two legendary characters—Pecos Bill and Paul Bunyan. Pecos Bill wanted the land for the grazing of his cattle; Paul Bunyan wanted the mountain for its trees. Pecos Bill thought Paul Bunyan wanted the land, and Paul Bunyan thought Pecos Bill wanted the trees.

Read about the battle that occurred. Then rewrite the selection on a separate sheet of paper, adding the correct marks of punctuation and capitalizing words correctly. Some punctuation is already given.

with the hundred men watching, the fight started. paul bunyan picked up his axe and hit at pecos bill so hard that he cut a huge gash in the earth people call it the grand canyon of the colorado river.

then pecos bill swung his red hot iron missed paul bunyan and scorched red the sands of the desert that was the beginning of the painted desert out in arizona.

again paul bunyan tried to hit pecos bill and again he hit the ground instead the scores of strange shaped rocks that are piled up in the garden of the gods in colorado were split by paul bunyans axe in that fearsome fight.

pecos bills iron, instead of cooling off, grew hotter and hotter, until with one swing of his iron he charred the forests of new mexico and arizona these trees, burnt into stone by the heat from pecos bills running iron, are now the famed petrified forest.

neither man could get the better of the other for the first and only time, pecos bill had met his match. . . . it was the first and only time that paul bunyans crew had seen a man that could stand up to him.

finally they paused to get their breath and paul bunyan suggested lets sit down a minute.

all right agreed pecos bill and they sat down on nearby rocks.

—From *Pecos Bill and Lightning* by Leigh Peck

Model Diagrams

Diagrams show the relationships among the words in a sentence. Since there are simple sentences and compound sentences, and because sentences may contain various kinds of modifiers, no one form of diagram will serve for every type of sentence. The diagrams given here are those that will help you most in your work. When asked to diagram a sentence, look here for a sentence of the same kind and see how the diagram is made.

Nouns in Simple Sentences

Nominative Case

Subject: *Molly* will train for the marathon.

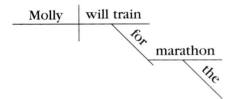

Subjective Complement: A junk is a wooden *sailboat.*

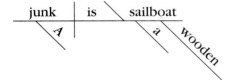

Direct Address: Close the door, *Peter.*

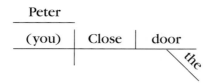

Appositive: Ms. Pucci, an *engineer,* designed a modern bridge.

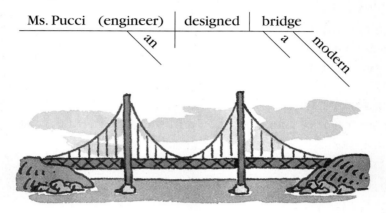

Possessive Case

Sally's mother works at a radio station.

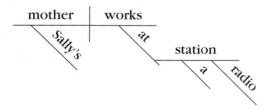

Sarah's mother baked the birthday cake.

I am wearing my *sister's* new shirt.

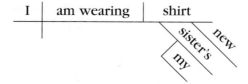

492

Objective Case

Direct Object: The hikers discovered an ancient *cave.*

Object of a Preposition: The spacecraft landed on the *moon.*

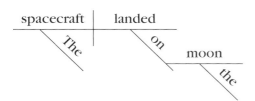

Indirect Object: The geologist showed *Chet* the limestone.

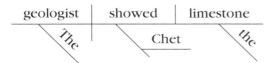

I gave my *dad* a shirt for Father's Day.

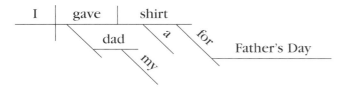

Appositive: We cannot see oxygen, a colorless *gas.*

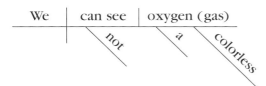

Kinds of Simple Sentences

Declarative Sentence

In the ocean, an aquanaut wears a wet suit.

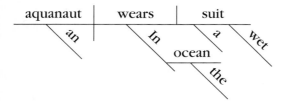

Interrogative Sentence

Have you read *Superfudge?*

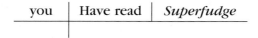

Imperative Sentence

Name two African countries.

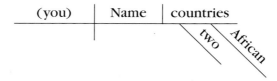

Exclamatory Sentence

How exciting the raft ride was!

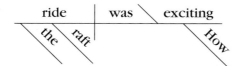

Compound Elements in Simple Sentences

Compound Subject: Laurie and Lynn take their own pictures.

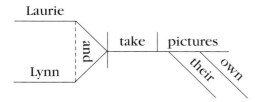

Compound Predicate: Laurie takes and develops her own pictures.

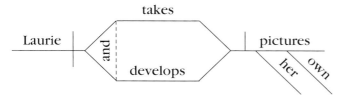

Compound Subject and Compound Predicate: Laurie and Lynn take and develop their own pictures.

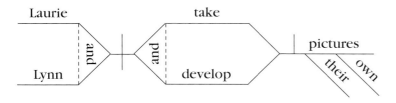

Compound Sentence

Max likes adventure stories, but Marian prefers biographies.

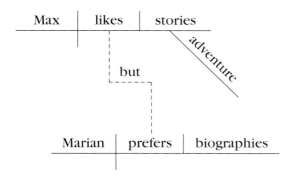

Grammar and Writing Handbook

Grammar

ADJECTIVES

An adjective describes or limits a noun or a pronoun and usually comes before the noun. There are two main kinds of adjectives: descriptive and limiting.

Adjectival Phrases

An adjectival phrase is a phrase used as an adjective.

Jan ordered books *from a catalog.*

Common Adjectives

A common adjective is any adjective not formed from a proper noun.

tall ship
majestic mountains

Comparison of Adjectives

Comparison is the change that adjectives undergo to express different degrees of quality, quantity, or value.

The positive degree shows a quality.

Green Lake is *deep*.

The comparative degree shows a quality in a greater or a lesser degree and is used when speaking of two persons or things.

Green Lake is *deeper* than Fox Lake.

The superlative degree shows a quality in the greatest or the least degree and is used when three or more persons or things are compared.

Green Lake is the *deepest* lake in our state.

Demonstrative Adjectives

The demonstrative adjectives, *this, that, these,* and *those,* point out a definite person, place, or thing. The plural of *this* is *these* and the plural of *that* is *those.*

This and *these* refer to persons or things that are near at hand.

This seat is too close to the movie screen.
These keys in my hand belong to me.

That and *those* refer to persons or things that are farther away.

I would rather sit in *that* seat in the back row.
Those keys on the table belong to my brother.

Descriptive Adjectives

A descriptive adjective describes a noun or a pronoun. The two classes of descriptive adjectives are proper adjectives and common adjectives.

The *Russian* poet spoke about his native country, Russia.
The *timid* cat would not come near us.

Interrogative Adjectives

> An interrogative adjective is used in asking a question. *Which, what,* and *whose* are interrogative adjectives when they modify nouns and ask questions.

Which jacket is yours?
What time is it?
Whose turn is it?

Limiting Adjectives

> A limiting adjective either points out an object or indicates number.

Important kinds of limiting adjectives are

- articles: *the, a, an. The* is the definite article; *a* and *an* are indefinite.
- demonstrative adjectives: *this, that, these, those.*
- numeral adjectives: indicate exact number.

Other limiting adjectives are

- possessive adjectives.
- interrogative adjectives.

Numeral Adjectives

> A numeral adjective may refer to the number of things or to the arrangement of things in numerical order.

six canoes
the *third* bicycle

Possessive Adjectives

A possessive adjective indicates ownership.

Here are the possessive adjectives.

	SINGULAR	PLURAL
FIRST PERSON	my	our
SECOND PERSON	your	your
THIRD PERSON	his, her, its	their

Proper Adjectives

A proper adjective is formed from a proper noun.

When Henri visits France, he eats at *French* restaurants.

ADVERBS

An adverb is a word that modifies a verb, an adjective, or another adverb. Adverbs may indicate time, place, manner, degree, affirmation, or negation.

Adverbs of time answer the question *when* or *how often*.

The chorus *frequently* sings for us.

Adverbs of place answer the question *where*.

Harvey walked *forward* to the edge of the stage.

Adverbs of manner answer the question *how*.

Abraham Lincoln spoke *truthfully*.

Adverbs of degree answer the question *how much* or *how little*. Adverbs of degree modify verbs, adjectives, or other adverbs.

Kim is *almost* finished talking on the phone.
Today is a *very* sunny day.
Hurry! Don't walk *too* slowly.

Adverbs of affirmation or negation tell whether a statement is true or false. Adverbs of affirmation are *yes, indeed,* and *undoubtedly.* Adverbs of negation are *no, not,* and *never.*

> *Yes,* we will go with you.
> Ricky *never* walks alone.

Adverbial Phrases

An adverbial phrase is a phrase used as an adverb.

> The train goes *through the tunnel.*

Comparison of Adverbs

Many adverbs can be compared. Like adjectives, they have three degrees of comparison: positive, comparative, and superlative.

APPOSITIVES

An appositive is a word or group of words that explains a noun and is usually set off by commas. It is said to be in apposition with that noun. A noun in apposition is in the same case as the noun it explains.

> Susan B. Anthony, *a pioneer of women's rights,* was born in Massachusetts.

ARTICLES

The articles are *the, a,* and *an.*

The is a definite article. *The* may be used with either singular or plural nouns.

> *the* door   *the* stairs

A and *an* are indefinite articles. *A* and *an* may be used only with singular nouns.

> *a* car   *an* alligator

The article *an* is used before a vowel sound.

> *an* excellent story

The article *a* is used before a consonant sound.

> *a* beautiful story

CASE

How a noun or pronoun is used in a sentence tells the case.

Nominative Case

A noun in apposition that explains the subject is in the nominative case.

> Marmosets, small *monkeys* of South America, have thick fur.

A noun used in direct address is in the nominative case.

> *Paul,* it's time to practice your saxophone.

A noun or pronoun used as the subject of a verb is in the nominative case.

> The *campfire* glowed in the night.
> *He* smiles when the music box plays.

A noun or pronoun used as a subjective complement is in the nominative case.

> He became the *president* of our club.
> The winner of the spelling contest is *she.*

Objective Case

Appositives that explain nouns in the objective case are in the objective case.

> The team met their new coach, *John Dominguez.*

A noun or pronoun used as the direct object of a verb is in the objective case.

> Bill fixed the *radio.*
> The shopkeeper told *him* to come back tomorrow.

A noun or pronoun used as the indirect object of a verb is in the objective case.

> The bride gave her *bridesmaids* bracelets.
> This hat brings *me* good luck.

A noun or pronoun used as the object of a preposition is in the objective case.

> The bride walked down the *aisle.*
> Let's go with *him.*

Possessive Case

A noun that expresses possession or ownership is in the possessive case.

To form the singular possessive of a noun, add *'s* to the singular form of the noun.

> elephant   elephant's trainer
> witness   witness's testimony

To form the possessive of plural nouns that end in *s,* add the apostrophe only.

> elephants   elephants' parade

To form the possessive of plural nouns that do not end in *s,* add *'s.*

> geese   geese's

Proper names ending in *s* usually form the possessive case by adding *'s.*

> James's tractor

In compound nouns the *'s* is added to the end of the word.

> sister-in-law's apartment

502

CONJUNCTIONS

A conjunction is a word used to connect words, phrases, or clauses in a sentence.

Peter *and* Joe are good friends.
Should we go to the park *or* to the zoo?
Julio would like to go, *but* he has to do his homework first.

Coordinate Conjunctions

Connecting Clauses

Coordinate conjunctions connect independent clauses. An independent clause has a subject and a predicate and expresses a complete thought.

Sophie will toss the salad *and* Rudy will set the table.
The greens are fresh, *but* the tomatoes are overripe.
Would you like cheese *or* would you like black pepper?

Connecting Phrases

Coordinate conjunctions connect prepositional phrases. These phrases may be adjectival or adverbial.

In winter, we enjoy vegetables from Texas *and* from Mexico. (adjectival)

Angela shops at the grocery store *or* at the produce market. (adverbial)

Connecting Words

Coordinate conjunctions connect words that have the same use or function in a sentence. These words may be nouns (subjects, objects, subjective complements), verbs (predicates), adjectives, and adverbs.

Spinach *and* lettuce are tasty in a salad. (subjects)

Do you prefer garlic dressing *or* Italian dressing? (objects)

This salad is fresh *but* tasteless. (subjective complements)

Derrick washed *and* dried the greens. (predicates)

Throw away the brown *and* limp lettuce. (adjectives)

They ate their salads quickly *but* quietly. (adverbs)

DIRECT ADDRESS

A noun used in direct address is in the nominative case.

A noun used in direct address names the person or persons spoken to. It is set off by a comma or commas.

Paul, please show the class your project.
The next project, *class,* will be presented by Kim.

DIRECT OBJECTS

A noun or pronoun used as the direct object is in the objective case.

The receiver of the action of the verb is the direct object.

The direct object of a verb may be determined by placing *whom* or *what* after the verb.

Gary repaired the *door.*

INDIRECT OBJECTS

The object to whom or for whom something is done is called the indirect object.

A noun or pronoun used as the indirect object of a verb is in the objective case.

The prepositions *to* or *for* can usually be placed before the indirect object without changing the meaning of the sentence.

Cecily lent her *brother* five dollars.

INTERJECTIONS

An interjection is a word that expresses a strong or sudden emotion.

Hooray! Now we can all go together.

NOUNS

A noun is a name word. A noun names a person, a place, or a thing. The qualities of a noun are number, gender, and case.

Number shows whether a noun refers to one person or thing (singular number) or more than one (plural number).

Gender is the quality of a noun by which sex is distinguished. There are three genders: masculine, feminine, and neuter.

The case of a noun shows its relation to some other word or words in the sentence. The three cases of nouns are nominative, objective, and possessive.

Abstract Nouns

An abstract noun expresses a quality or condition. It names something that cannot be seen or touched.

patience   idea   freedom

Collective Nouns

A collective noun names a group of persons, animals, or things considered as a unit.

team   herd   majority

Common Nouns

A common noun names one member of a class of persons, places, or things.

friend   island   holiday

Concrete Nouns

A concrete noun names a thing we can see or touch.

Most of the nouns we use are concrete nouns.

librarian   automobile   Fort Hood

Gender of Nouns

> **Gender is a quality of a noun. The gender may be masculine, feminine, or neuter.**

The masculine gender indicates males.

grandfather   brother

The feminine gender indicates females.

Aunt Rosalie   sister

The neuter gender indicates objects.

plates   table

Gender may be distinguished by

- using a different word.

MASCULINE	FEMININE
son	daughter
gander	goose

- using a different ending.

MASCULINE	FEMININE
prince	princess
waiter	waitress

- changing part of the word.

MASCULINE	FEMININE
grandfather	grandmother
landlord	landlady

Proper Nouns

A proper noun names a particular person, place, or thing. Proper nouns may contain several words. The important words in proper nouns are capitalized.

Ben   New York City   Statue of Liberty

PHRASES

A phrase is a group of words used as a single part of speech.

PREDICATES

The predicate states a fact about the subject.

Our team *won.*

Complete Predicates

The complete predicate is the predicate with all its modifiers and complements.

The horses from Kentucky *jump all the hurdles well.*

Compound Predicates

If the predicate of a sentence is made up of more than one verb, it is said to be a compound predicate.

Our team *played* and *won.*

Simple Predicates

> The simple predicate is the word that states what the subject is or does. A simple predicate may contain one word or an auxiliary verb and a principal verb.

Horses *jump.*
The horses *have jumped.*

PREPOSITIONS

> A preposition is a word placed before a noun or a pronoun. The preposition shows the relation of the noun or pronoun to some other word.

We saw a movie *about* a dog.

Prepositional Phrases

> A preposition and the noun or pronoun that follows it are separate words, but they do the work of a single modifier. A prepositional phrase may be adjectival or adverbial.

The books *in the library* appear to be new. (adjectival)
You may place your ballot *into the box.* (adverbial)

PRONOUNS

A pronoun takes the place of a noun.

Distributive Pronouns

A distributive pronoun refers to each person, place, or thing separately. The distributive pronouns are *each, either,* and *neither.* The distributive pronouns are always singular and require singular verbs.

Each of us *is* expected to do his or her best work.

Gender of Pronouns

A pronoun that refers to males is masculine gender. The masculine pronouns are *he* and *him.*

A pronoun that refers to females is feminine gender. The feminine pronouns are *she* and *her.*

A pronoun that refers to an object is neuter gender. The neuter pronoun is *it.*

The pronouns *they* and *them* are used for all three genders in the plural.

Indefinite Pronouns

An indefinite pronoun refers to no specific person, place, or thing.

anybody	everything
many	some

Interrogative Pronouns

> An interrogative pronoun is used in asking a question. The interrogative pronouns are *who, whom, which, what,* and *whose.*

Number

> A singular pronoun takes the place of a singular noun. The singular personal pronouns are *I, me, you, he, she, it, him,* and *her.* These pronouns refer to one person or thing.

> A plural pronoun takes the place of a plural noun. The plural personal pronouns are *we, us, you, they,* and *them.* These pronouns refer to more than one person or thing.

Personal Pronouns

> A personal pronoun shows by its form the speaker (first person), the person spoken to (second person), and the person or thing spoken about (third person).

Personal pronouns of the first person (speaker) are *I, me, we,* and *us.*

The personal pronoun of the second person (person spoken to) is *you.*

Personal pronouns of the third person (person or thing spoken about) are *he, she, it, him, her, they,* and *them.*

Compound Personal Pronouns

> A compound personal pronoun ends in *-self* or *-selves.*

myself	ourselves
himself	themselves

Personal Pronouns in Contractions

> The personal pronouns are used with verbs to form contractions.

The apostrophe (') is used to show where a letter or letters have been left out.

TWO WORDS	CONTRACTION
I will	I'll
we are	we're
it is	it's

Possessive Pronouns

> A possessive pronoun shows possession or ownership by the speaker, the person spoken to, or the person or thing spoken about.

mine	ours
yours	his

SENTENCES

A sentence is a group of words that expresses a complete thought and contains a subject and a predicate. The subject names the person, place, or thing about which a statement is made. The predicate states a fact about the subject.

Reads mystery books (incomplete thought)
Randolph reads mystery books. (complete thought)

Compound Sentences

A compound sentence contains two or more independent clauses.

We often sail on Lake Michigan, but we never stray far from the harbor.

Declarative Sentences

A declarative sentence states a fact.

The river flows through the valley.

Exclamatory Sentences

An exclamatory sentence expresses strong or sudden emotion.

The flowing river is so very beautiful!

Imperative Sentences

An imperative sentence expresses a command.

Tell me where the river flows.

Interrogative Sentences

An interrogative sentence asks a question.

Where does the river flow?

Inverted Order in Sentences

A sentence is in the inverted order when the predicate verb or an auxiliary verb comes before the subject.

Up the mountain climbed Jesse.

Natural Order in Sentences

A sentence is in the natural order when the predicate verb follows the subject.

Jesse climbed the mountain.

Simple Sentences

A simple sentence contains a subject and a predicate. Either the subject or the predicate or both may be compound. A simple sentence expresses one complete thought.

The bicycle has a flat tire.
The bicycle and the truck have flat tires.
The bicycle has a flat tire and needs a new seat.

SUBJECTIVE COMPLEMENTS

A subjective complement completes the meaning of a subject after a linking verb and renames the subject. A subjective complement may be a noun, a pronoun, or an adjective.

Rita is my *neighbor.* (noun)
The winner of the spelling contest is *she.* (pronoun)
These apples are *sweet.* (adjective)

SUBJECTS

The person, place, or thing talked about in a sentence is the subject.

Ask *who* or *what* before the verb to find the subject.
Our *team* won.

Complete Subjects

The complete subject is the subject with all its modifiers.

The sleek horses from Kentucky jump hurdles well.

Compound Subjects

If the subject of a sentence has more than one noun or pronoun, it is said to be a compound subject. Compound subjects connected by *and* usually require a plural verb.

Sari and *Jim* are going to the store.

Simple Subjects

The simple subject is the person, place, or thing about which a statement is made.

Horses jump.

TENSES

The tense of a verb shows the time of the action or being.

Compound Tenses

The present perfect tense shows action completed in present time and is formed by the auxiliary *have* or *has* plus the past participle of the verb.

Billy *has thrown* the ball.

The past perfect tense shows action completed before some definite time in the past and is formed by the auxiliary *had* plus the past participle of the verb.

Billy *had thrown* the ball after time out was called.

The future perfect tense shows action that will be completed before some specified time in the future and is formed by the auxiliaries *shall have* or *will have* plus the past participle of the verb.

By the next inning, Billy *will have thrown* the ball forty-two times.

Simple Tenses

The present tense shows action or being in present time.

I *watch* my little sister.

The past tense shows action or being in past time.

I *watched* my little sister all summer.

The future tense shows action or being in future time. The auxiliary verb *shall* or *will* is used to form the future tense.

I *will watch* my little sister tomorrow.

VERBS

A verb is a word used to express action or being. Without a verb, there can be no sentence. Verbs should agree with their subjects, both in person and in number.

Auxiliary Verbs

Any verb used with the principal verb is called an auxiliary verb.

Here are examples of common auxiliary verbs.

is	did
has	might
should	can

Intransitive Verbs

An intransitive verb has no receiver of its action.

There is no answer to the question *whom* or *what* after an intransitive verb.

The stars *shine* brightly.

Irregular Verbs

An irregular verb does not form its past and its past participle by adding *d* or *ed* to the present.

PRESENT	PAST	PAST PARTICIPLE
hurt	hurt	hurt
swing	swung	swung
write	wrote	written

Linking Verbs

The noun, pronoun, or adjective that follows a linking verb is called a subjective complement.

A linking verb links the subject with a noun, a pronoun, or an adjective.

The verb *be* and its various forms are the most common linking verbs.

The auditorium *is* full.

Number

A verb may be singular or plural in number.

- Singular refers to one.
- Plural refers to more than one.

Person

A verb may be in the first person, the second person, or the third person.

- First person refers to the speaker.
- Second person refers to the one spoken to.
- Third person refers to the one spoken about.

Principal Parts

The principal parts of the verb are the present, the past, and the past participle. The past never takes an auxiliary, or helping, verb. The past participle is always used with an auxiliary, or helping, verb.

Regular Verbs

A regular verb forms its past and its past participle by adding *d* or *ed* to the present.

PRESENT	PAST	PAST PARTICIPLE
use	used	used
play	played	played

Transitive Verbs

A transitive verb expresses an action that passes from a doer to a receiver.

There is an answer to the question *whom* or *what* after a transitive verb. To determine the receiver of the action, ask *whom* or *what* after the verb.

Mr. Bopp *observed* the faint comet.

Verb Phrases

A verb phrase is a group of words that does the work of a single verb. It contains a principal verb and one or more auxiliary, or helping, verbs.

Kelly *will have hiked* twenty miles by the end of the week.

Writing

CAPITALIZATION AND PUNCTUATION

Apostrophes

Use an apostrophe to show possession.

The robin's eggs are blue.
The boys' caps are here.

Use an apostrophe with _s_ to show the plural of letters.

_t_'s

Use an apostrophe to show the omission of a letter, letters, or numbers.

we'll (we will)   Class of '99 (1999)

Capital Letters

Capitalize the first word in a sentence.

Tall trees provide shade.

Capitalize the first word of every line of most poetry.

Capitalize the first word of a direct quotation.

Addie said, "Did you ever see anyone as silly?"

Capitalize proper nouns and adjectives.

Illinois   Kristina   Asian exports

Capitalize titles of honor and respect when preceding the name.

Princess Anne   Judge Quinn

Capitalize *north*, *south*, *east*, and *west* when they refer to sections of the country.

The pioneers settled in the West.

Capitalize all names referring to a deity, the Bible or parts of the Bible, and other sacred books.

God   Allah   the Bible   the Koran

Capitalize the principal words in the titles of books, plays, poems, and paintings.

Number the Stars   *Mona Lisa*

Capitalize the pronoun *I* and the interjection *O*.

When will I have my turn?
O! You startled me.

Capitalize abbreviations when capitals would be used if the words were written in full.

U.S.A. (United States of America)
Rev. Smith (Reverend Smith)

Do not capitalize the seasons of the year.

fall   summer

Do not capitalize the articles, conjunctions, or prepositions in titles unless one of these is the first word.

The Prince and the Pauper

Do not capitalize the names of studies unless they are derived from proper nouns.

arithmetic   history   English

Do not capitalize the words *high school, college,* and *university* unless they are parts of the names of particular institutions.

Kevin goes to college in Detroit.
Kevin goes to the University of Detroit.

Colons

Use a colon after the salutation of a business letter.

Dear Ms. Lee:

Use a colon before a list of items.

Bring the following school supplies: pencils, erasers, pens, paper, and notebook.

Commas

Use a comma to separate words or groups of words in a series.

Meg used red, blue, and purple in her painting.

Use a comma to set off parts of dates, addresses, and geographical names.

They met in Chicago, Illinois, on July 18, 1994.

Use a comma to set off the words *yes* and *no* when they introduce sentences.

Yes, you may go to the shopping mall.

Use a comma to set off words of direct address.

Marilyn, will you read aloud next?

Use a comma after the salutation in a social letter and after the complimentary close in all letters.

Dear Aunt Carrie,   Yours truly,

Use a comma to set off an appositive that is not part of the noun.

The heart, a vital organ in the body, needs exercise.

Use a comma to set off short direct quotations.

"In the future," said Melanie, "I plan to be an astronaut."

Use a comma to separate the clauses of a compound sentence connected by the conjunctions *and, but, or, nor,* and *yet.* If the clauses are short and closely connected, the comma may be omitted.

The girls remembered their lunches, but they forgot their backpacks.
Sound the alarm and seek shelter immediately.

Exclamation Points

Use an exclamation point at the end of an exclamatory sentence or after an exclamatory word or phrase.

Come back here!
Whew! That was a close one!

Hyphens

Use a hyphen to divide a word at the end of a line whenever one or more syllables are carried to the next line.

Many facts can be found on the Inter-
net, if you know where to look.

Use a hyphen in compound numbers and to separate the parts of some compound words.

twenty-one   mother-in-law
ninety-nine   self-respect

Periods

Use a period to mark the end of a declarative or an imperative sentence.

Kara has the lead in the school play.
Speak loudly.

Use a period after many abbreviations.

Dr.   Feb.

Use a period after an initial.

John F. Kennedy

Question Marks

Use a question mark at the end of every interrogative sentence.

When is the last day of school?

Quotation Marks

Use quotation marks before and after every quotation and every part of a divided quotation.

Philip said, "There is going to be an election."
"Philip," Harry asked, "when will the election be held?"

Use quotation marks to enclose titles of short stories, poems, songs, newspaper and magazine articles, television shows, and radio programs.

"The Gift of the Magi" by O. Henry
"The Road Not Taken" by Robert Frost
"The Simpsons" on the Fox Network

Semicolons

Use a semicolon to separate the clauses of a compound sentence when they are not separated by *and, but, or, nor,* or *yet.*

The sand was firm and not too wet; it was perfect for building sand castles.

Index

Steps in THE WRITING PROCESS are set in capitals for easy reference.

Index

how and why tales, 153
journal writing, 67
narrative writing, 123
oral history report, 215
poetry into prose, 93
story, 26-28, 39

Each, 314
Editor's Workshop, 68-69, 94-95,
    124-125, 154-155, 188-189, 216-217,
    242-243
Either, 314
Encyclopedias, 234-236
Ending sentences, 54-57
Entries, in dictionaries, 230
Enunciation, 194, 198
Envelope, addressing, 176-177
Errors, letters reporting, 174
-eth, 90
-ette, 91
Exclamation points, 474-475, 524
Exclamatory sentences, 455-456, 474
    definition of, 455
    diagraming of, 494

Facts, 111-114
Farley, Walter, 101
Feminine gender, 262-264, 507
Fiction books, 219
    card catalog listings for, 223-224
    shelf order for, 220
Figures of speech
    metaphors, 86-89, 94
    similes, 86-89, 94
Forms, filling out, 180-183
Frost, Robert, 202
-ful, 90
Future perfect tense, 377-382
Future tense, 373-376

Gender
    of nouns, 262-264, 504, 507
    of pronouns, 291, 511
geo-, 120-121
Geographic names, use of commas to set
    off, 469, 522
Geographic sections of country, use of
    capital letters for, 486, 521
Grahame, Kenneth, 10-19

Guest, Edgar A., 199
Guide words
    in dictionaries, 229
    in encyclopedias, 234-235
Guinness Book of World Records, 236

Heading
    in business letters, 168
    in social letters, 159
"Hector the Collector" (Silverstein), 196
"Home Sweet Home" (Grahame), 11-19
Homographs, 184-185
Homophones, 150-151
How and why tales, 152-155
    dialogue in, 152
    DRAFTING, 153
    PREWRITING, 152
    PROOFREADING, 155
    PUBLISHING, 155
    REVISING, 154
Hyphen, 484-485, 524

I, 487, 521
-ic, 90
Imperative sentences, 455-456, 513
    definition of, 455
    diagraming of, 494
In/into, 420, 422
Indefinite pronouns, 315-316
    definition of, 315
    and verb agreement, 390, 392
    writing paragraphs with, 316
Independent clauses, 458-459
    combining, 75-77, 503
    definition of, 458
Indirect objects, 279-281, 505
    definition of, 279
    diagraming of, 493
Information Please Almanac, 236
Initials, 465, 524
Inside address, in business letters, 168
Interjections, 431-432, 505
Interrogative adjectives, 336-338, 498
Interrogative pronouns, 311-313, 511
Interrogative sentences, 455-456, 514
    definition of, 455
    diagraming of, 494
Interviewing, 214-217
    guidelines for, 214
Into/in, 420, 422
Intransitive verbs, 366-369

528

Index

Acknowledgments

11–19 "Home Sweet Home" and cover illustration from *The Wind in the Willows* written by Kenneth Grahame, illustrated by Michael Hague, © 1980 by Ariel Books, Inc. Reprinted by permission of Henry Holt and Company, Inc.

93 "Stop-Go" from *I Like Automobiles* by Dorothy W. Baruch. Published by Bertha Klausner International Literary Agency, Inc.

93 "Autumn Woods" from *Crickety Cricket! The Best Loved Poems of James S. Tippett.* Copyright © 1933, copyright renewed © 1973 by Martha K. Tippett. Used by permission of HarperCollins Publishers.

101 Excerpt from *The Black Stallion* by Walter Farley. Illustrated by Keith Ward. Copyright © 1941, 1969 by the author. Published by Random House, Inc.

108 Excerpt from *Sounder* by William H. Armstrong. Illustrated by James Barkley. Copyright © 1969 by William H. Armstrong. Used by permission of HarperCollins Publishers.

135 Excerpts from *Across Five Aprils* by Irene Hunt. Copyright © 1964 by Modern Curriculum Press, Inc., Simon & Schuster Education Group. Used by permission.

140–141 Excerpt from "May I Have Your Autograph?" by Marjorie Sharmat from *Sixteen Short Stories by Outstanding Writers for Young Readers.* Text copyright © 1984 by Marjorie Sharmat. Used by permission of Marjorie Sharmat.

195 "The Man in the Moon." No author listed.

196 "Hector the Collector" (text only) from *Where the Sidewalk Ends* by Shel Silverstein. Copyright © 1974 by Evil Eye Music, Inc. Used by permission of HarperCollins Publishers.

199 "It Couldn't Be Done" from *Collected Verse of Edgar A. Guest* Copyright © 1934. Used with permission of NTC/Contemporary Publishing Company, Chicago.

200 "Velvet Shoes" from *Collected Poems* by Elinor Wylie. Copyright © 1921 by Alfred A. Knopf, Inc. and renewed 1949 by William Rose Benet. Reprinted by permission of the publisher.

201 "Mr. Nobody." No author listed.

202 "Stopping by Woods on a Snowy Evening" from *The Poetry of Robert Frost,* edited by Edward Connery Lathem. Copyright © 1951 by Robert Frost. Copyright 1923, © 1969 by Henry Holt and Company, Inc. Reprinted by permission of Henry Holt and Company, Inc.

203 "The Camel's Complaint" from *The Admiral's Caravan* by Charles Edward Carryl, in the public domain.

204 "Raccoon" from *Laughing Time: Collected Nonsense* by William Jay Smith. Copyright © 1990 by the author. Reprinted by permission.

205 "Wind Song" from *I Feel the Same Way* by Lilian Moore. Copyright © 1967, 1995 Lilian Moore. Reprinted by permission of Marian Reiner for the author.

237 From *The World Almanac and Book of Facts, 1987.* Copyright © 1986 by Newspaper Enterprise Association, Inc. New York.

489 Excerpt from *Pecos Bill and Lightning* by Leigh Peck. Copyright 1940 and © renewed 1968 by Leigh Peck. Reprinted by permission of Clarion Books/Houghton Mifflin Company. All rights reserved.

All attempts possible have been made to contact author and publisher for cited works in this book.

Art & Photography

Cover Nanette Biers, *Boston Harbor.* Used by permission of Nanette Biers/Vicki Morgan Associates.

8-9 Frida Kahlo, *El Camion,* 1929. Schalkwijk/Art Resource, NY. Reproducción autorizada por el Instituto Nacional de Bellas Artes y Literatura, México, D.F. © Estate of Frida Kahlo/Licensed by VAGA, New York, NY.

244-245 Yashima Gakutei, *Bridge Across the Moon.* Janette Ostier Gallery, Paris/Giraudon, Paris/SuperStock.

123 Winslow Homer, *Snap the Whip.* The Metropolitan Museum of Art, Gift of Christian A. Zabriskie, 1950. (50.41)/Photograph © 1992 The Metropolitan Museum of Art.

Photographs: CLEO Photographs, 70, 434. **Jim Cummins/FPG International,** 490. **PhotoDisc, Inc.,** 6(T), 10, 11, 17, 29, 30, 40, 73(B), 84, 87, 92, 96, 98, 110, 117, 126, 142, 154, 156, 179(B), 184, 190, 196, 218, 221, 225(B), 238, 240, 246, 288, 292, 316, 318, 324(B), 328, 339, 345, 348, 367(B), 394, 397, 408, 417, 428, 429, 444, 454, 462, 464, 466, 467, 477(B), 480, 483, 487, 493. **Skjold Photographs,** 414.

Illustrations: Mary Lynn Blasutta, 19(R), 45, 46(R), 51, 71, 73(T), 114, 127, 134, 147, 148, 166, 193, 195(T), 197, 202(T), 204, 208, 265, 293, 299, 313, 314, 329, 354, 356, 361, 365, 367(T), 383, 410, 411. **Susan Blubaugh,** 4(B), 272, 294, 349. **Ted Carr,** 177, 258, 259, 267, 315, 346, 355, 364, 442. **Ralph Creasman,** 82, 202(B), 219, 261, 263(B), 326, 371, 436(B), 455. **David A. Cunningham,** 43, 50, 58, 59, 74, 102, 103, 108, 118, 143, 144, 195(B), 220, 248(B), 334, 368, 376, 384, 420, 421, 424, 440, 441, 445. **Pat Dypold,** 402, 403. **Kerry Gavin,** 3(T), 186, 291, 323. **Jean Cassels Helmer,** 5(T), 7, 48(B), 49, 72, 130, 131, 236, 239, 302, 305(T), 327, 343, 344, 375, 400(B), 409, 436(T), 449, 456, 472(B). **Cynthia Hoffman,** 179(T), 337, 370, 437. **Paul Hoffman,** 200, 262(T), 276, 406, 407. **Mary Jones,** 3(B), 57, 109, 157, 158, 201, 205, 222, 226, 227, 253, 257, 278, 286, 296, 297, 305(B), 309, 336, 351(B), 459, 485. **G. Brian Karas,** 76, 77, 119, 162(B), 198, 209(B), 256, 273, 274, 280, 290, 300, 301, 380, 381, 443, 450(B). **Carl Kock,** 1(T, B), 2, 3(M), 4(T), 19(L, M), 41, 46(T), 47, 48(T), 52, 55, 56, 60, 61, 63, 78, 85, 94, 97, 100, 101, 104, 106, 107, 112, 129, 136, 139, 140, 152, 161, 162(T), 165, 170, 171, 175, 176, 180, 182, 194, 209(T), 224, 225(T), 229(B), 230, 233, 235(B), 248(T), 250, 251, 254, 262(B), 268, 269, 271, 281, 283, 285, 298, 303, 311, 312, 319, 320, 321, 324(T), 330, 331, 332, 333, 341, 342(L), 350, 351(T), 353, 357, 359, 360, 362, 363, 366, 372, 382, 386, 388, 390, 395, 396, 399, 400(T), 412, 416, 418, 427, 431, 432, 435, 438, 447, 448, 450(T), 457, 460, 461, 465, 468, 469, 470, 472(T), 473, 474, 475, 476, 477(T), 478, 479, 482, 484, 486, 492, 494. **Eileen Mueller Neill,** 249, 342(R), 426. **Robert Post,** 80, 99, 111, 398, 439. **Publishers Resource Group,** 68, 178, 229(T), 235(T). **Phil Renaud,** 188, 352. **Slug Signorino,** 89, 192, 206, 207, 307, 358, 369, 378, 379, 422. **William Seabright,** 263(T).